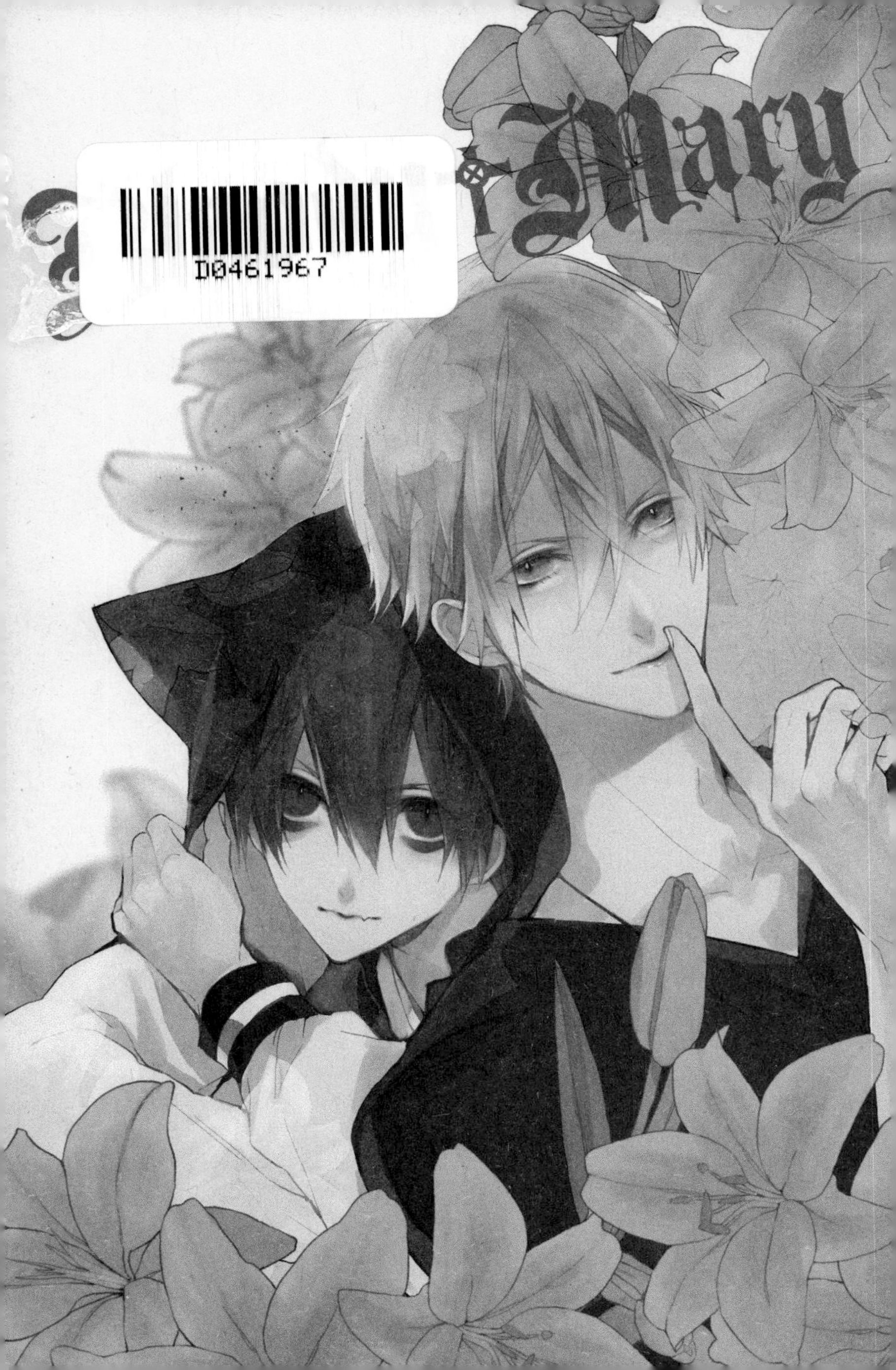
Mary

Bloody✝Mary

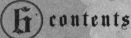 contents

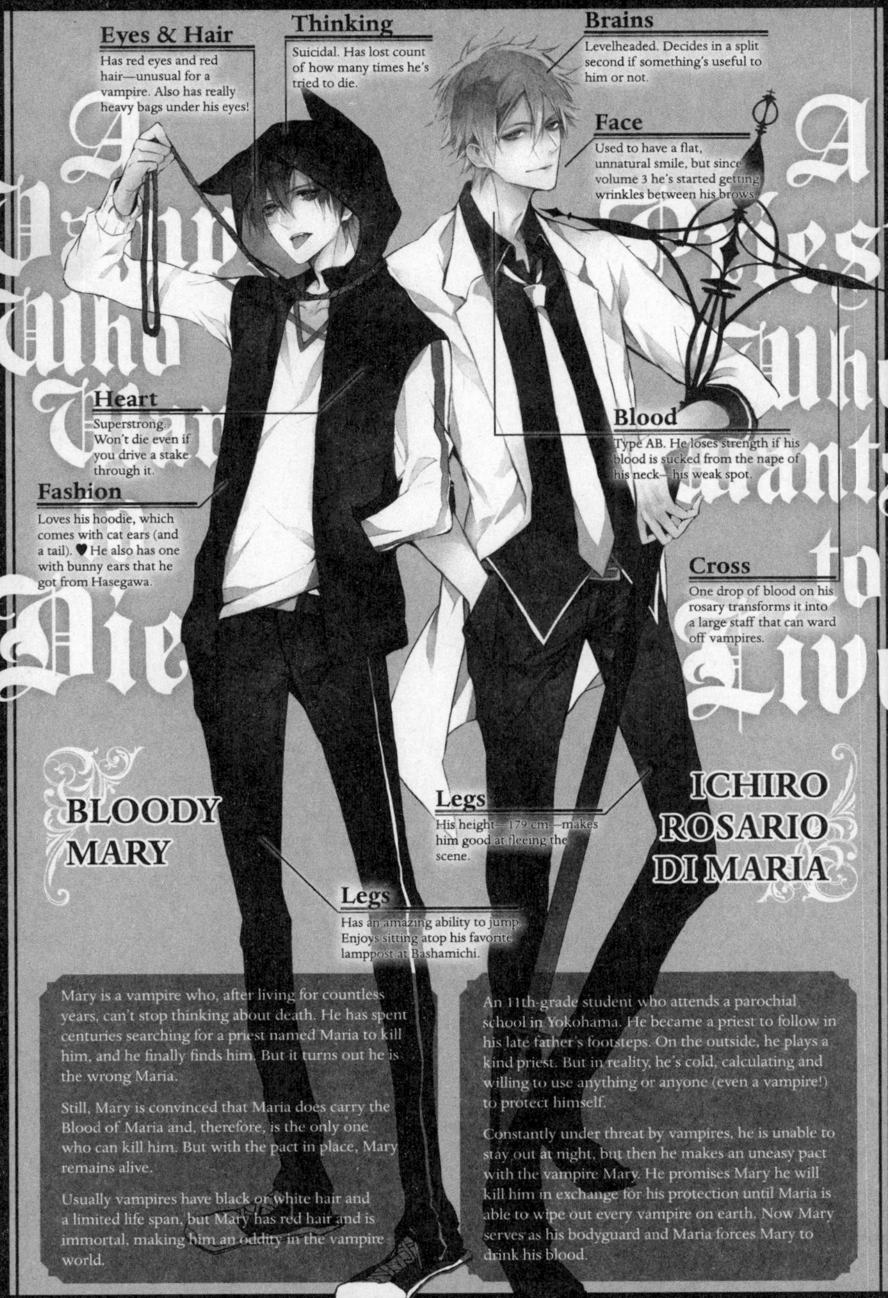
Eyes & Hair
Has red eyes and red hair—unusual for a vampire. Also has really heavy bags under his eyes!
Thinking
Suicidal. Has lost count of how many times he's tried to die.
Brains
Levelheaded. Decides in a split second if something's useful to him or not.
Face
Used to have a flat, unnatural smile, but since volume 3 he's started getting wrinkles between his brows.
Heart
Superstrong. Won't die even if you drive a stake through it.
Blood
Type AB. He loses strength if his blood is sucked from the nape of his neck—his weak spot.
Fashion
Loves his hoodie, which comes with cat ears (and a tail). ♥ He also has one with bunny ears that he got from Hasegawa.
Cross
One drop of blood on his rosary transforms it into a large staff that can ward off vampires.
BLOODY MARY
Legs
His height—179 cm—makes him good at fleeing the scene.
ICHIRO ROSARIO DI MARIA
Legs
Has an amazing ability to jump. Enjoys sitting atop his favorite lamppost at Bashamichi.

Mary is a vampire who, after living for countless years, can't stop thinking about death. He has spent centuries searching for a priest named Maria to kill him, and he finally finds him. But it turns out he is the wrong Maria.

Still, Mary is convinced that Maria does carry the Blood of Maria and, therefore, is the only one who can kill him. But with the pact in place, Mary remains alive.

Usually vampires have black or white hair and a limited life span, but Mary has red hair and is immortal, making him an oddity in the vampire world.

An 11th-grade student who attends a parochial school in Yokohama. He became a priest to follow in his late father's footsteps. On the outside, he plays a kind priest. But in reality, he's cold, calculating and willing to use anything or anyone (even a vampire!) to protect himself.

Constantly under threat by vampires, he is unable to stay out at night, but then he makes an uneasy pact with the vampire Mary. He promises Mary he will kill him in exchange for his protection until Maria is able to wipe out every vampire on earth. Now Mary serves as his bodyguard and Maria forces Mary to drink his blood.

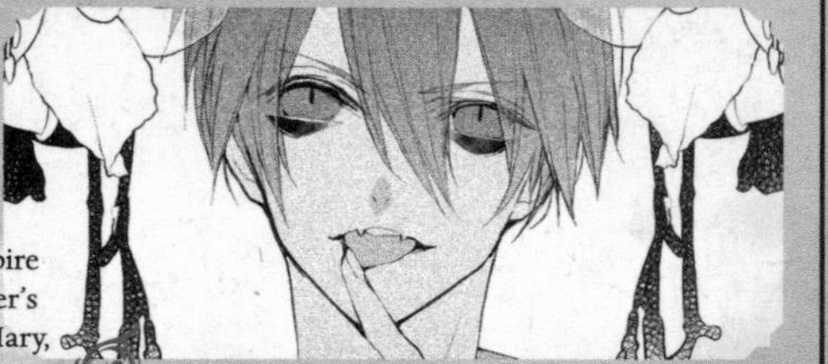

“MARY”

Thought to be an alter ego of Mary (the masochistic one). He’s the red-haired vampire that Maria saw when he witnessed his father’s murder. Unlike the regular (masochistic) Mary, this “Mary” doesn’t wear his hoodie up (thus, no cat ears). He speaks with an attitude, isn’t an idiot and definitely isn’t a masochist!

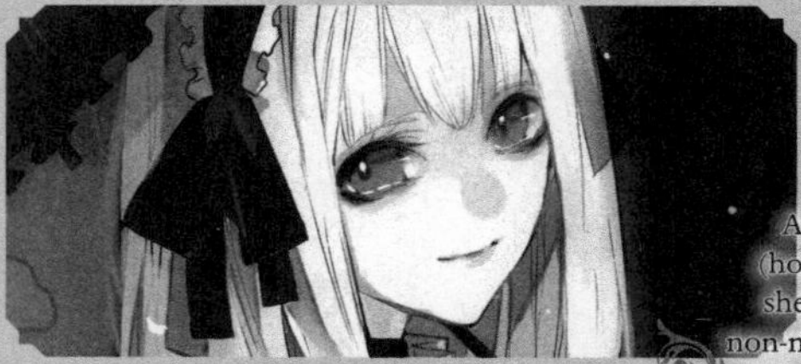

HYDRA

A vampire who takes the form of a little girl (however, her real age is unknown). It appears she has some deep connection to “Mary” (the non-masochistic one) and persistently affixes the “Bloody” part to masochist Mary’s name. She’s considering killing Mary for the sake of “Mary.”

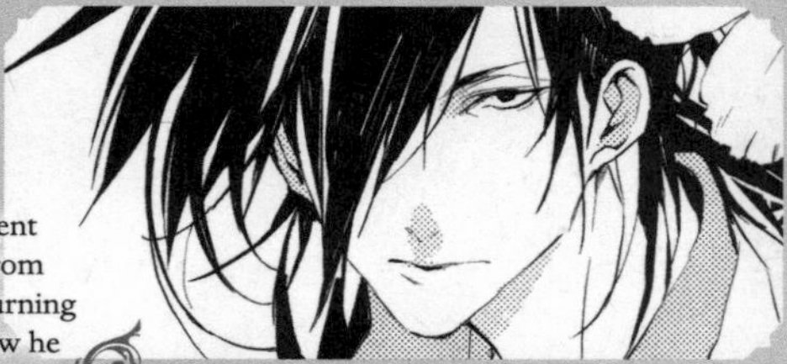

SHINOBU

Maria’s uncle. After his sister’s death, he went to England to learn how to protect Yusei from vampires and the Sakurabas. But upon returning to Japan, Yusei had already been killed. Now he does all he can to protect Maria instead. But recently his job has been comforting Mary, who’s being treated coldly by Maria.

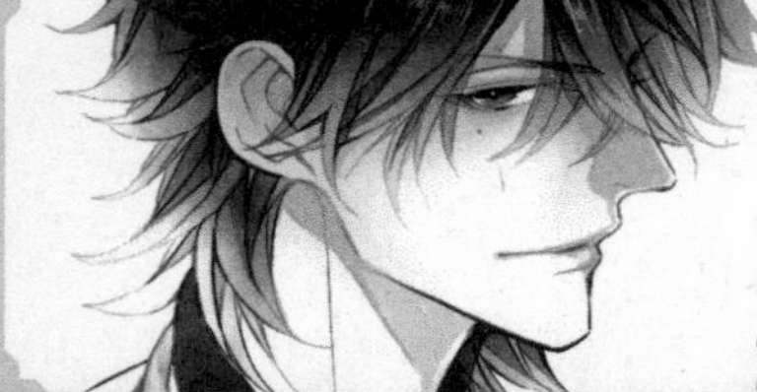

TAKUMI SAKURABA

Like an older brother to Maria. After Yusei died, he looked after Maria, who had been taken in by the Sakurabas. Under the control of Yzak, he betrayed Maria, but now he’s committed to uncovering the dubious actions of Yzak and the Sakuraba family. He’s guided by a strong sense of right and wrong.

Even a masochist could understand it

New facts revealed!

Red-haired Vampires

- Red-haired vampires were once humans.
- To become a vampire, a human must drink the blood of a vampire.
- A vampire's blood is poisonous to a human, so if the body rejects it, the human will die.
- Giving one's blood to a human is regarded as a major taboo by vampires who hold purity in high regard. If discovered, they will be killed by their own kind.
- Because the act puts both human and vampire in danger, it cannot be done unless they love each other deeply.
- Red-haired vampires are not immortal.

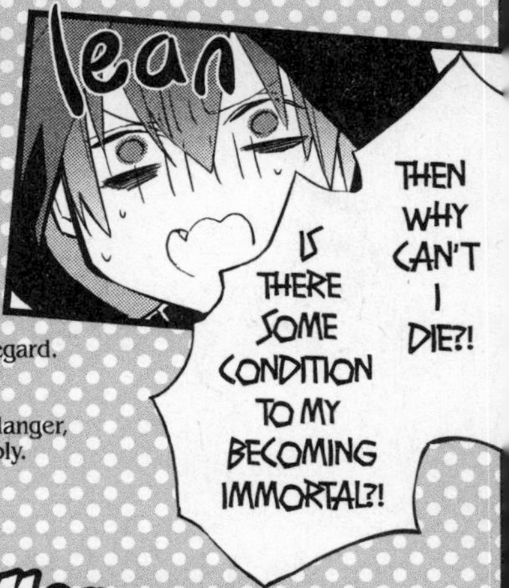
lean
THEN WHY CAN'T I DIE?!
IS THERE SOME CONDITION TO MY BECOMING IMMORTAL?!

Mary and "Mary"

- 400 years ago.
  The two were still human when they were in England.
  But now Mary is a vampire.
  "Mary" is inside of Mary...

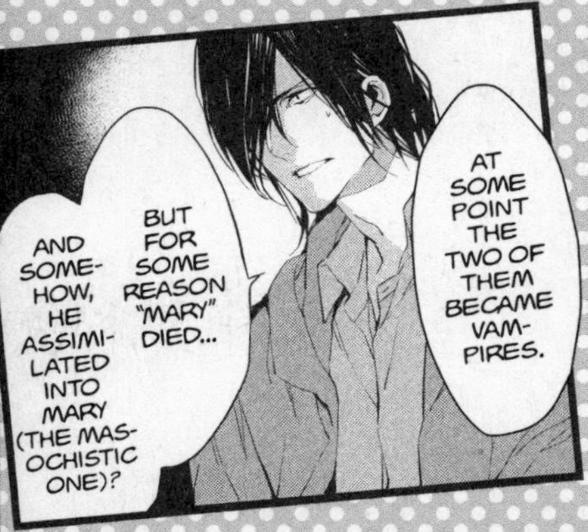
AT SOME POINT THE TWO OF THEM BECAME VAMPIRES.
BUT FOR SOME REASON "MARY" DIED...
AND SOMEHOW, HE ASSIMILATED INTO MARY (THE MASOCHISTIC ONE)?

"Mary" and Hydra

- Hydra was in love with "Mary" when he was human. After that, something happened between the two (details unknown), and now the skeleton of "Mary" resides in an old castle in England where he's been for centuries...

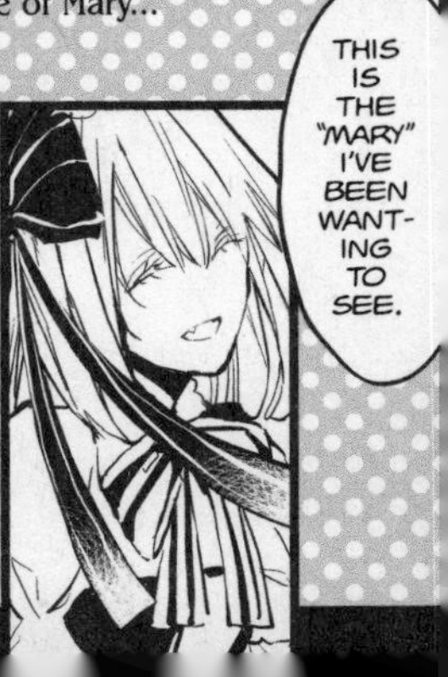
THIS IS THE "MARY" I'VE BEEN WANTING TO SEE.

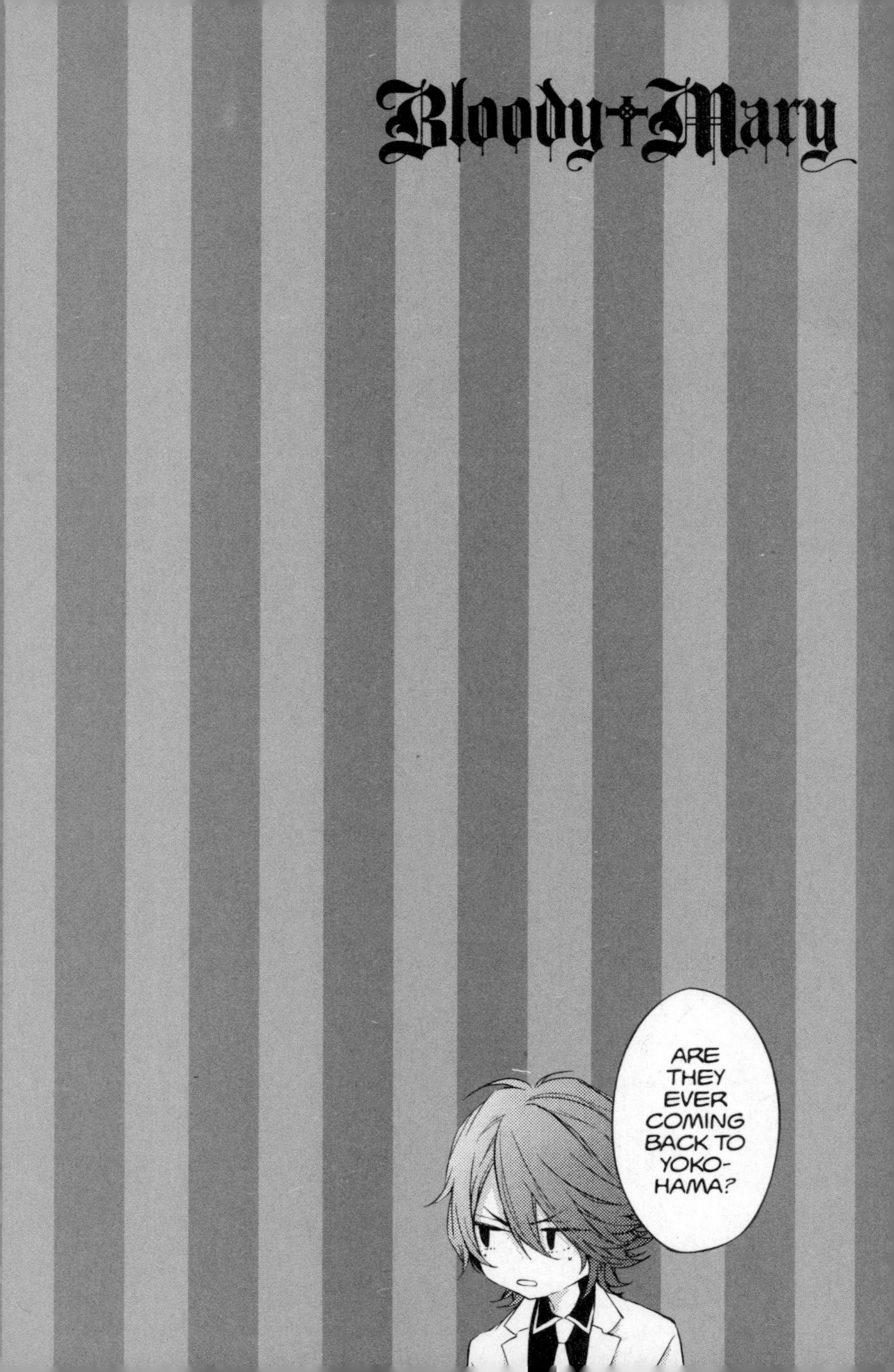
Bloody+Mary
ARE THEY EVER COMING BACK TO YOKO-HAMA?

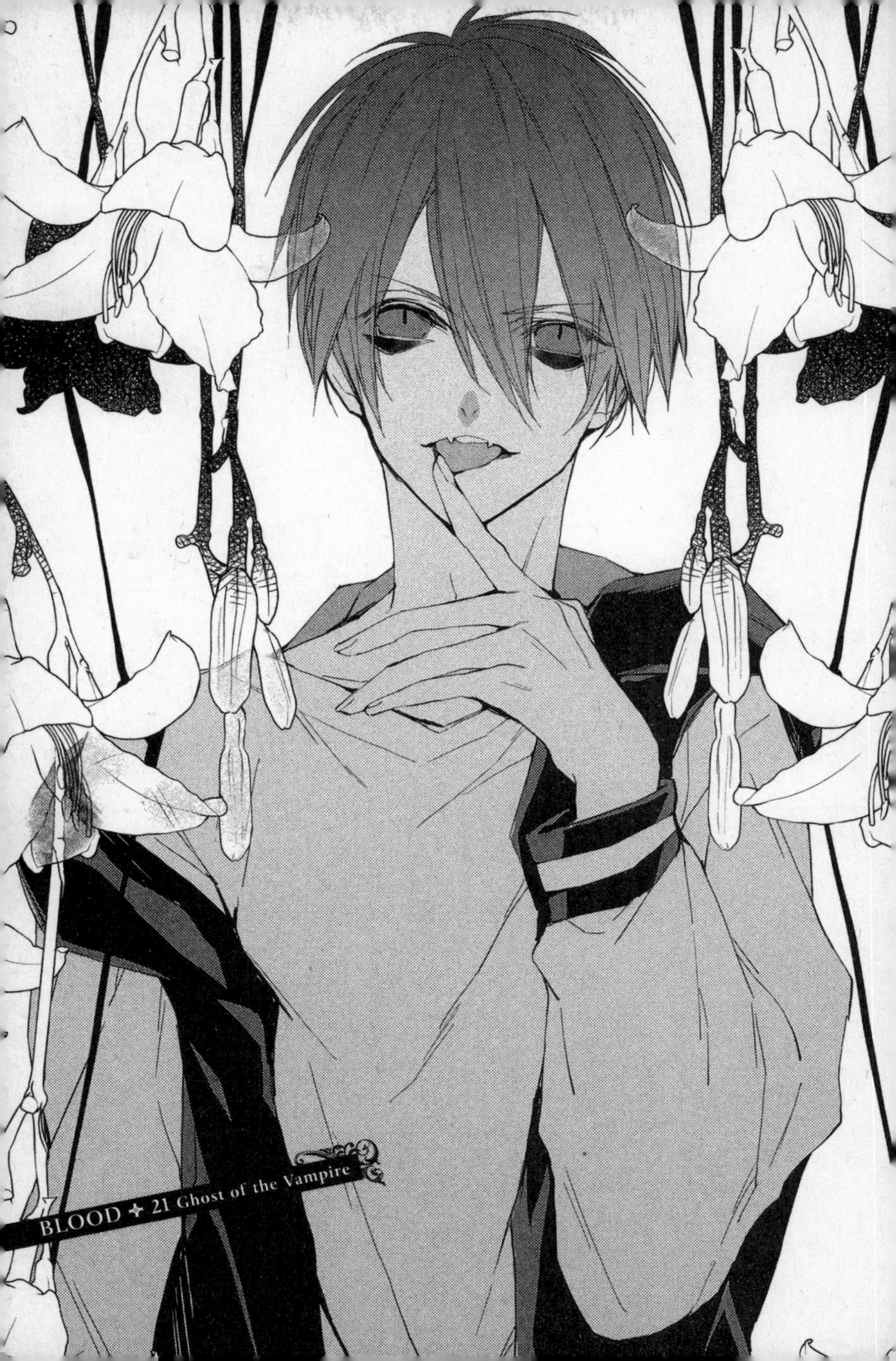
BLOOD ✣ 21 Ghost of the Vampire

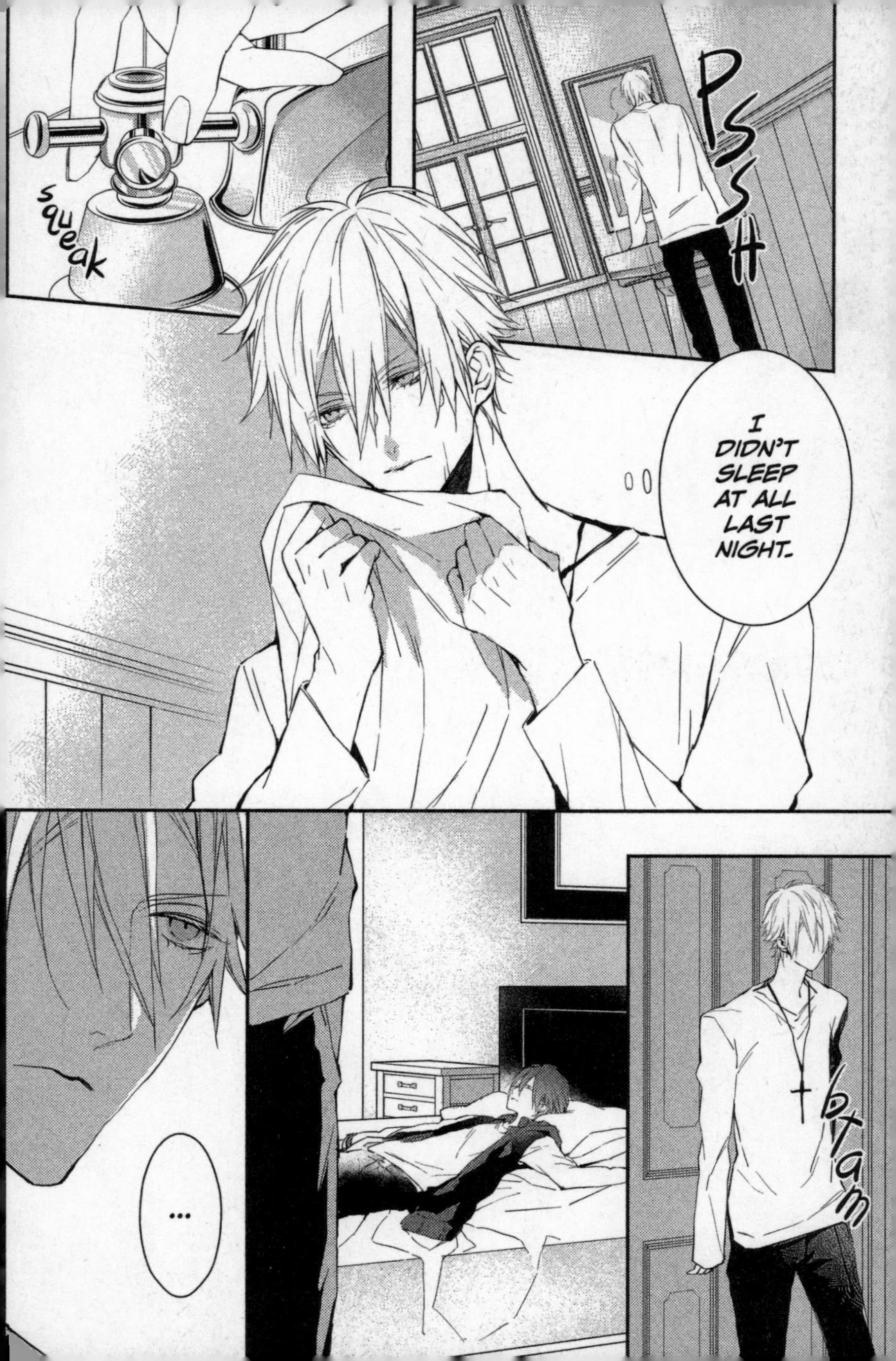
PSSH
squeak
I DIDN'T SLEEP AT ALL LAST NIGHT.
btam
...

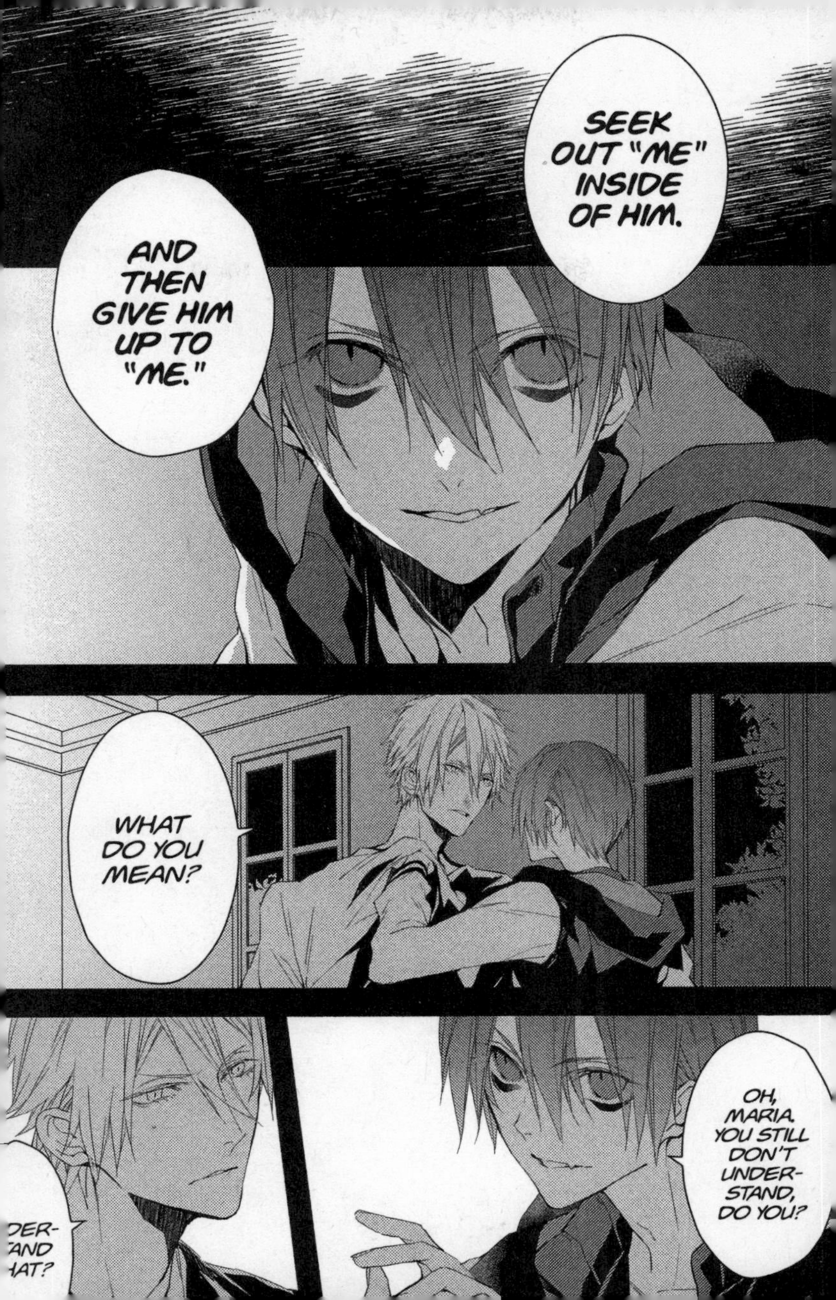
SEEK OUT "ME" INSIDE OF HIM.
AND THEN GIVE HIM UP TO "ME."
WHAT DO YOU MEAN?
OH, MARIA. YOU STILL DON'T UNDER-STAND, DO YOU?

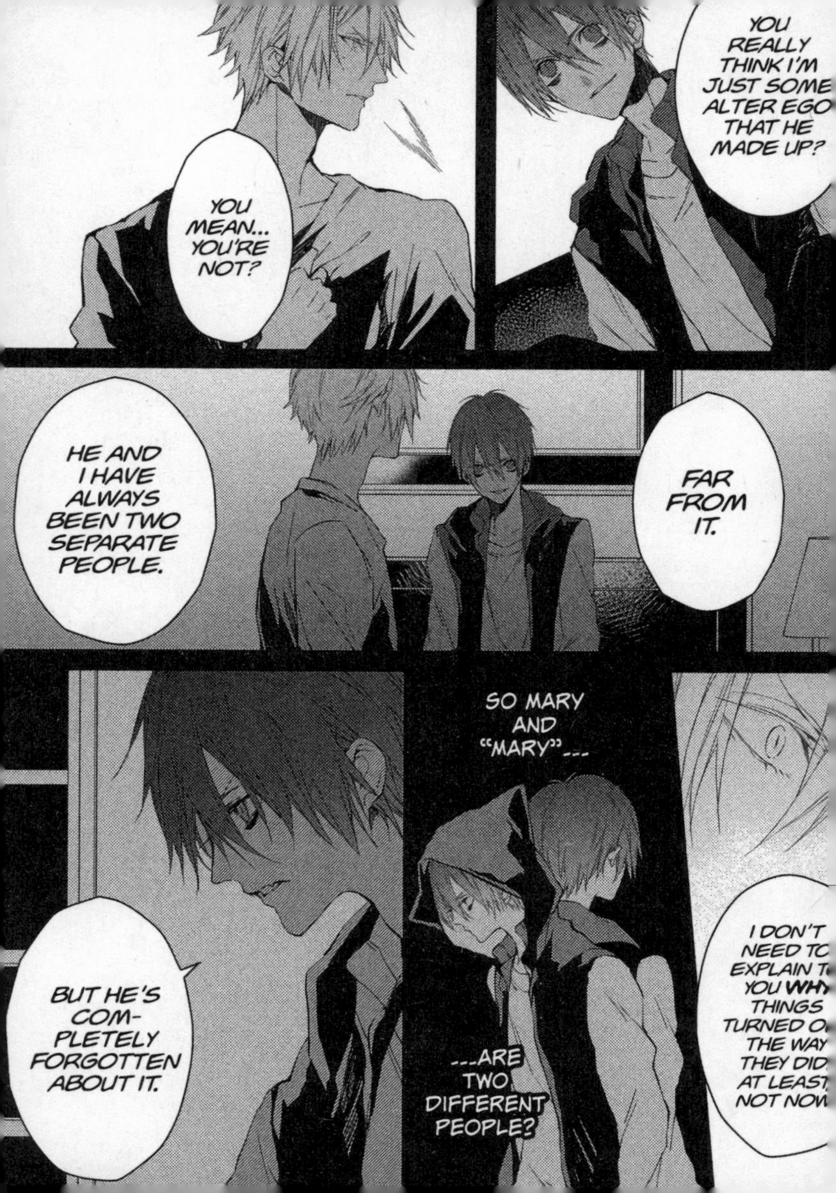
YOU REALLY THINK I'M JUST SOME ALTER EGO THAT HE MADE UP?
YOU MEAN... YOU'RE NOT?
FAR FROM IT.
HE AND I HAVE ALWAYS BEEN TWO SEPARATE PEOPLE.
I DON'T NEED TO EXPLAIN T YOU WHY THINGS TURNED O THE WAY THEY DID AT LEAST NOT NOW
SO MARY AND "MARY"---
---ARE TWO DIFFERENT PEOPLE?
BUT HE'S COM-PLETELY FORGOTTEN ABOUT IT.

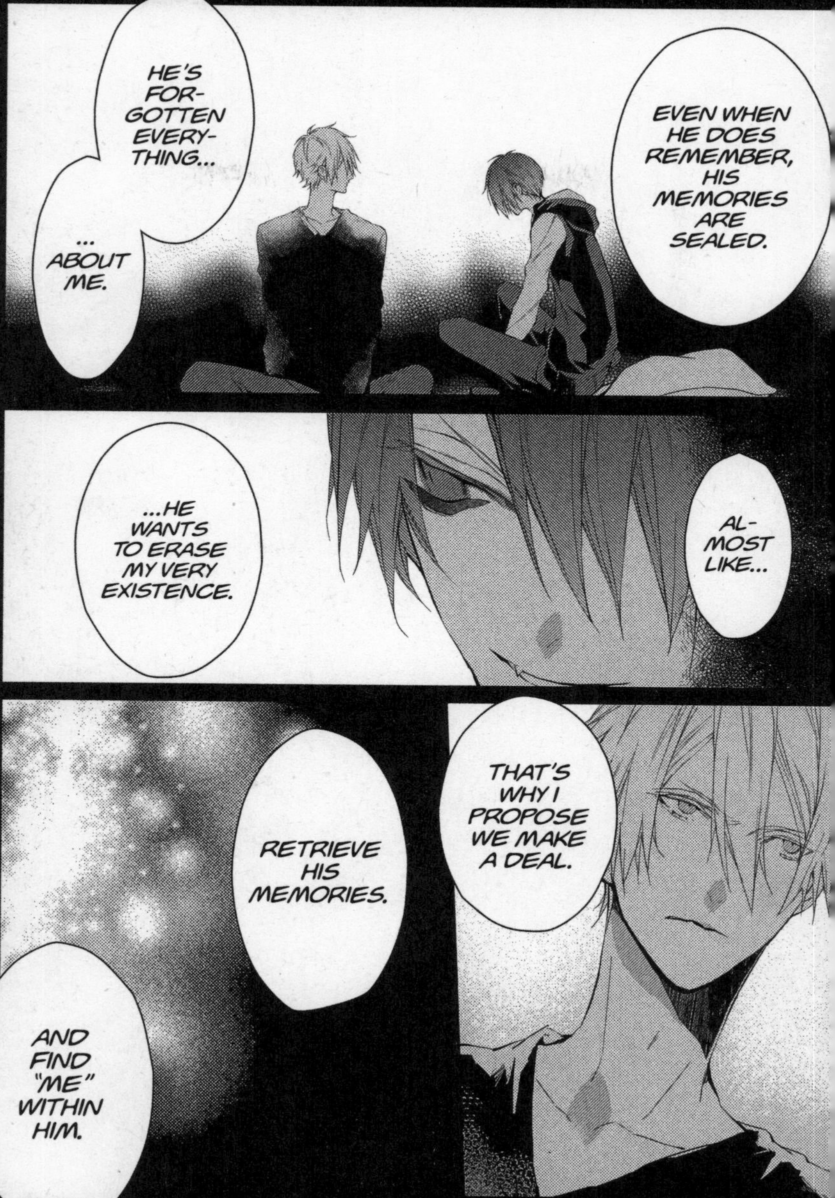
EVEN WHEN HE DOES REMEMBER, HIS MEMORIES ARE SEALED.
HE'S FORGOTTEN EVERYTHING...
...ABOUT ME.
ALMOST LIKE...
...HE WANTS TO ERASE MY VERY EXISTENCE.
THAT'S WHY I PROPOSE WE MAKE A DEAL.
RETRIEVE HIS MEMORIES.
AND FIND "ME" WITHIN HIM.

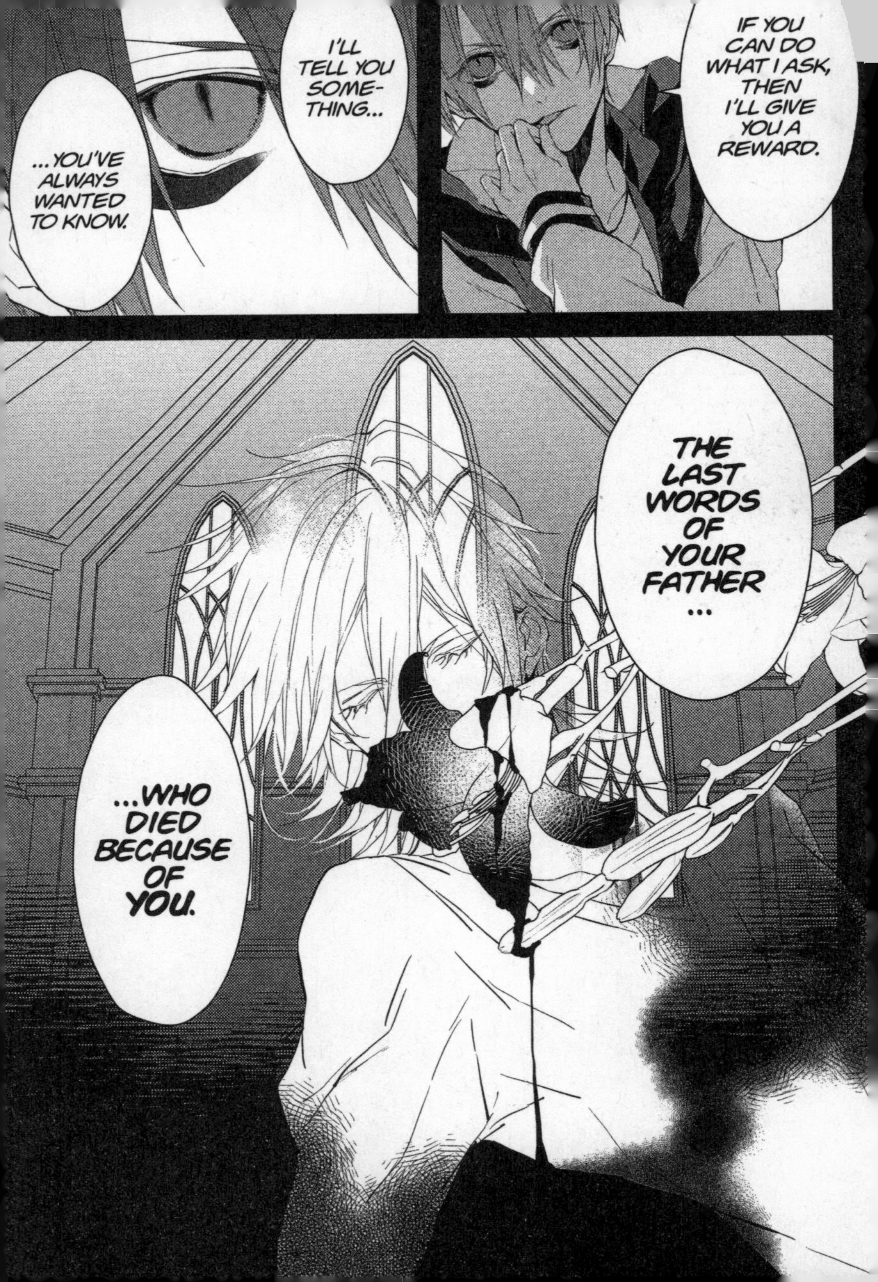
IF YOU CAN DO WHAT I ASK, THEN I'LL GIVE YOU A REWARD.
I'LL TELL YOU SOME-THING...
...YOU'VE ALWAYS WANTED TO KNOW.
THE LAST WORDS OF YOUR FATHER ...
...WHO DIED BECAUSE OF YOU.

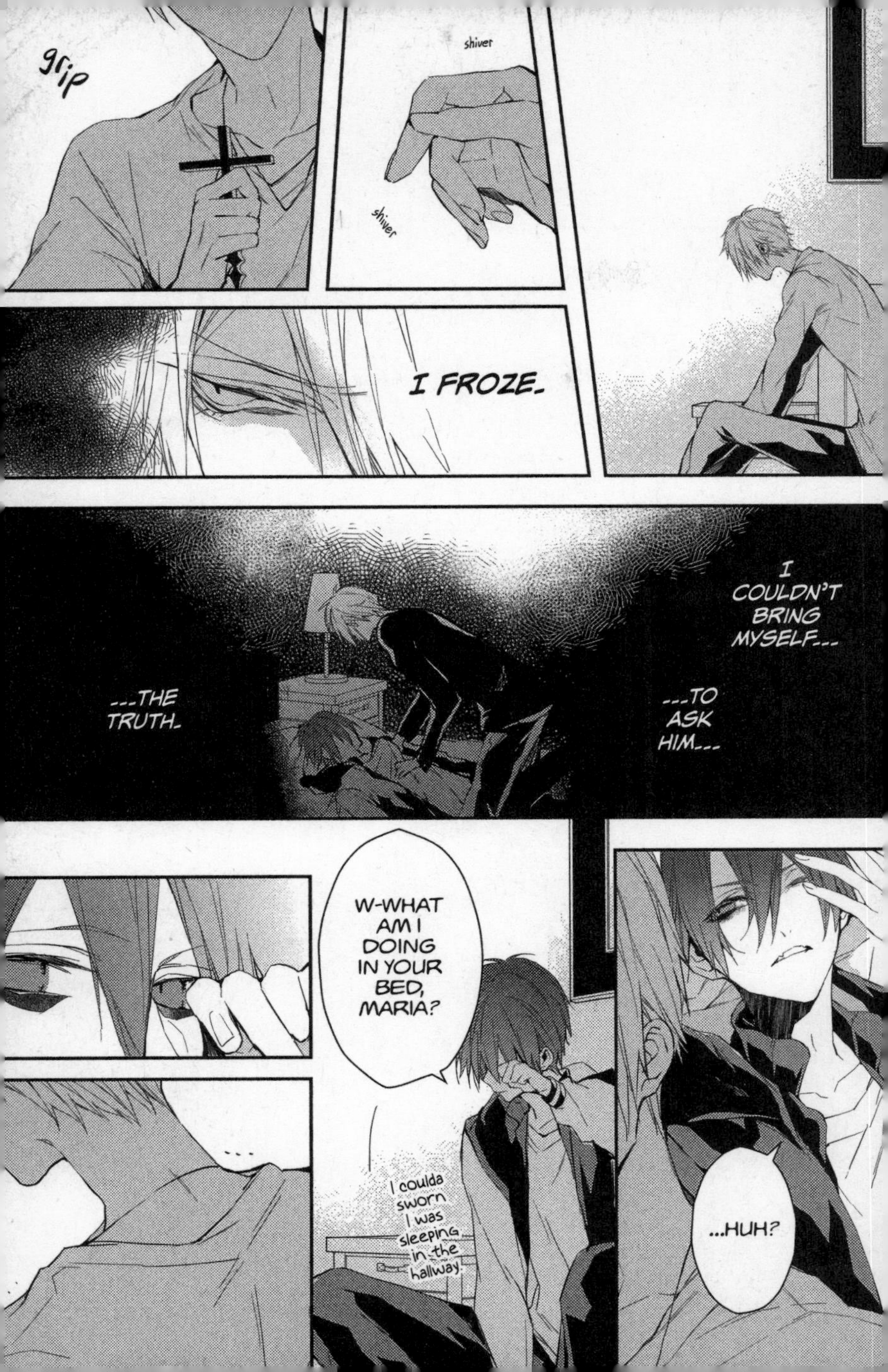
shiver
shiver
grip
I FROZE.
I COULDN'T BRING MYSELF...
...TO ASK HIM...
...THE TRUTH.
...HUH?
W-WHAT AM I DOING IN YOUR BED, MARIA?
I coulda sworn I was sleeping in the hallway.
...

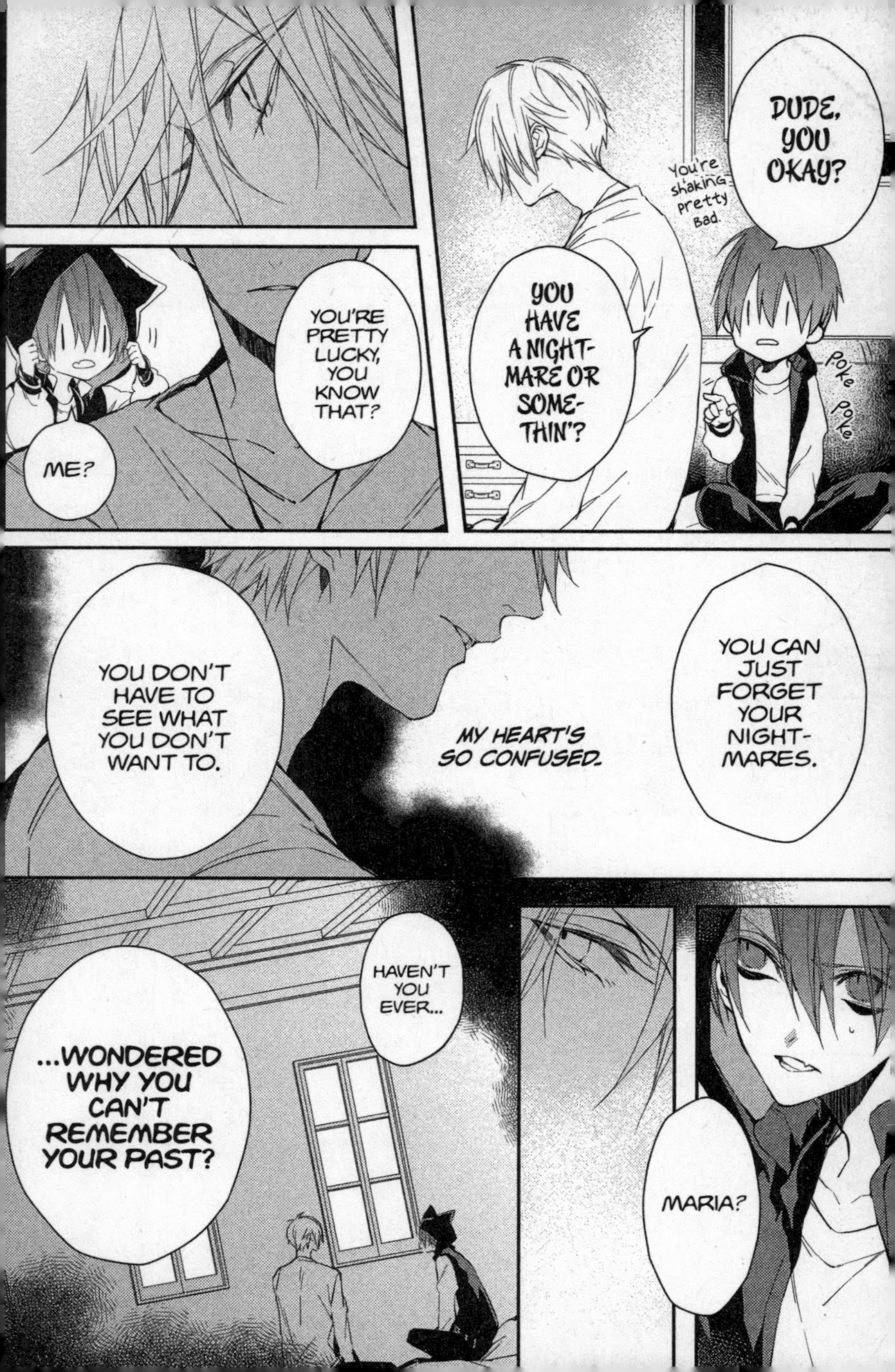
DUDE, YOU OKAY?
You're shaking pretty bad.
YOU HAVE A NIGHT-MARE OR SOME-THIN'?
YOU'RE PRETTY LUCKY, YOU KNOW THAT?
ME?
YOU CAN JUST FORGET YOUR NIGHT-MARES.
MY HEART'S SO CONFUSED.
YOU DON'T HAVE TO SEE WHAT YOU DON'T WANT TO.
MARIA?
HAVEN'T YOU EVER...
...WONDERED WHY YOU CAN'T REMEMBER YOUR PAST?

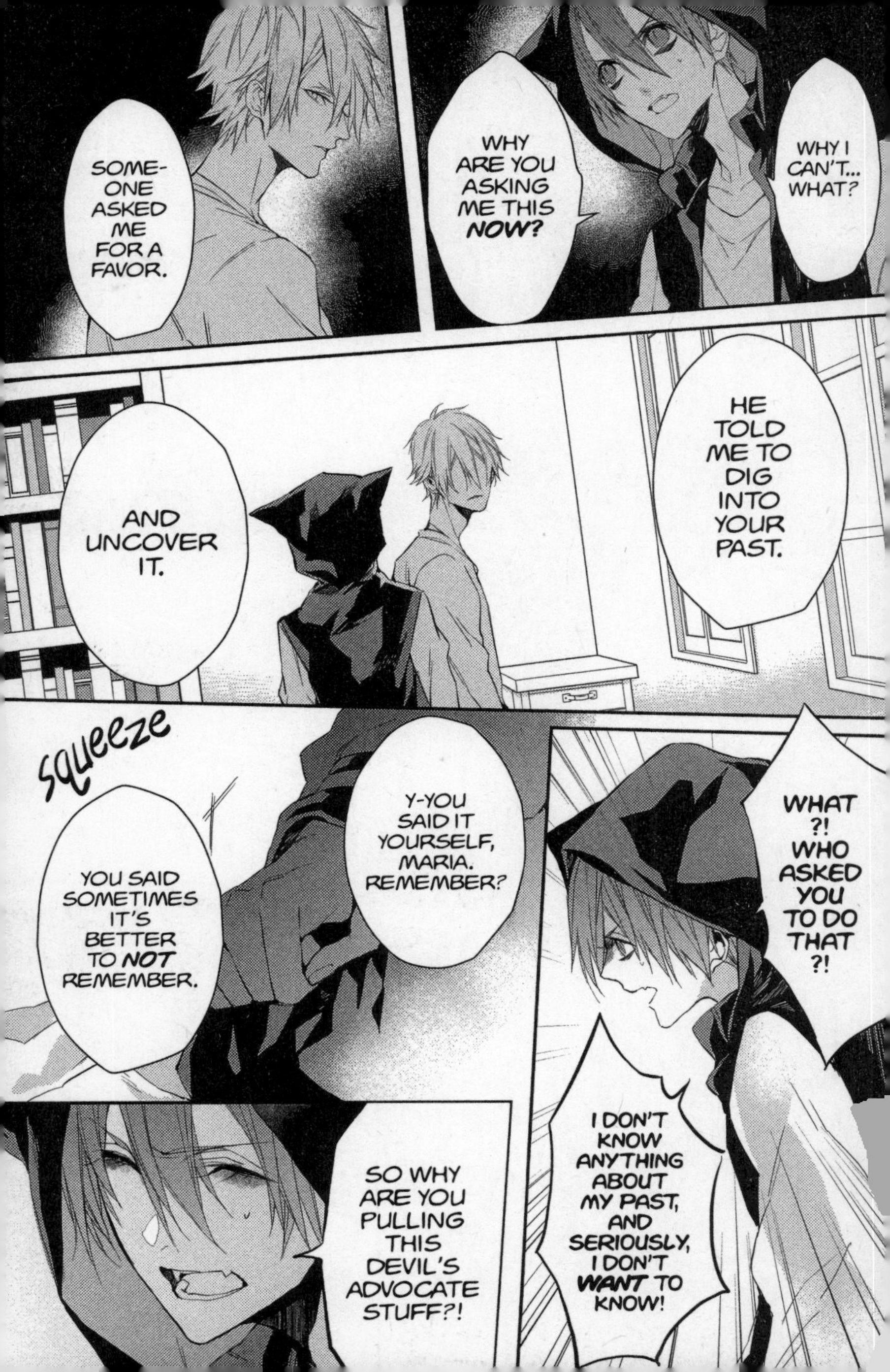
WHY I CAN'T... WHAT?
WHY ARE YOU ASKING ME THIS *NOW?*
SOME-ONE ASKED ME FOR A FAVOR.
HE TOLD ME TO DIG INTO YOUR PAST.
AND UNCOVER IT.
WHAT?! WHO ASKED YOU TO DO THAT?!
I DON'T KNOW ANYTHING ABOUT MY PAST, AND SERIOUSLY, I DON'T *WANT* TO KNOW!
squeeze
Y-YOU SAID IT YOURSELF, MARIA. REMEMBER?
YOU SAID SOMETIMES IT'S BETTER TO *NOT* REMEMBER.
SO WHY ARE YOU PULLING THIS DEVIL'S ADVOCATE STUFF?!

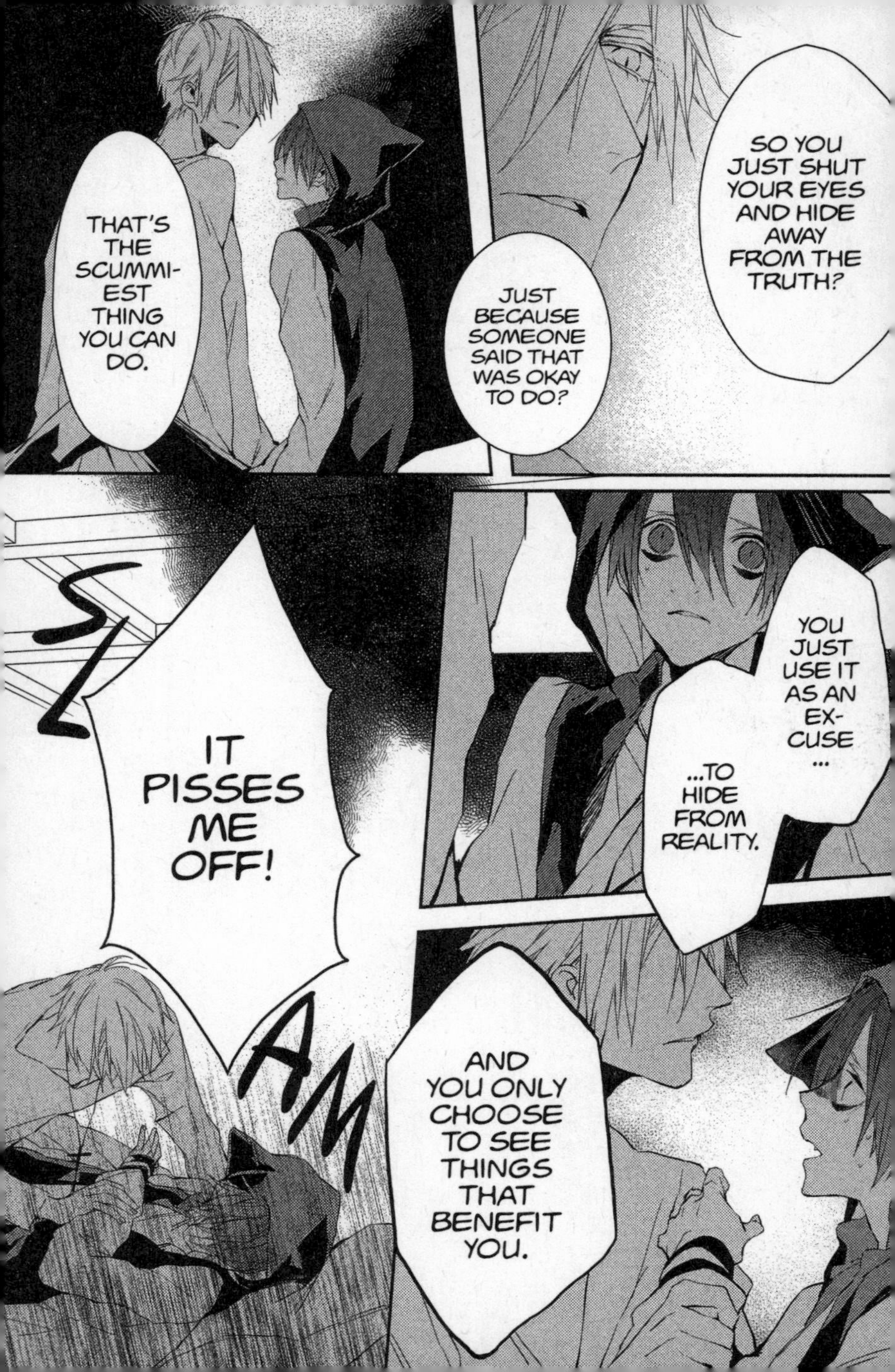
SO YOU JUST SHUT YOUR EYES AND HIDE AWAY FROM THE TRUTH?
JUST BECAUSE SOMEONE SAID THAT WAS OKAY TO DO?
THAT'S THE SCUMMI-EST THING YOU CAN DO.
YOU JUST USE IT AS AN EX-CUSE...
...TO HIDE FROM REALITY.
AND YOU ONLY CHOOSE TO SEE THINGS THAT BENEFIT YOU.
IT PISSES ME OFF!
SLAM

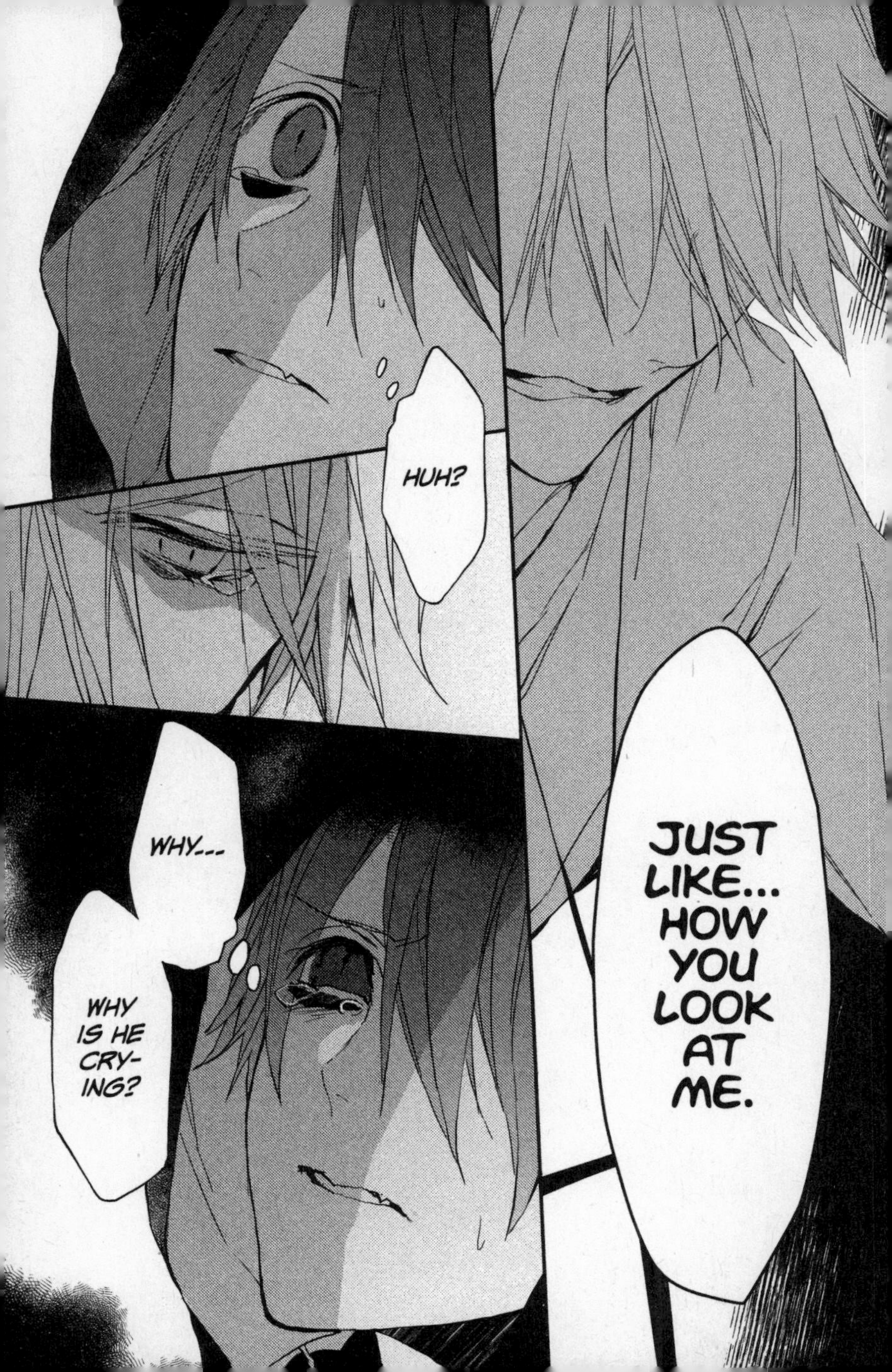
HUH?
JUST LIKE... HOW YOU LOOK AT ME.
WHY---
WHY IS HE CRY-ING?

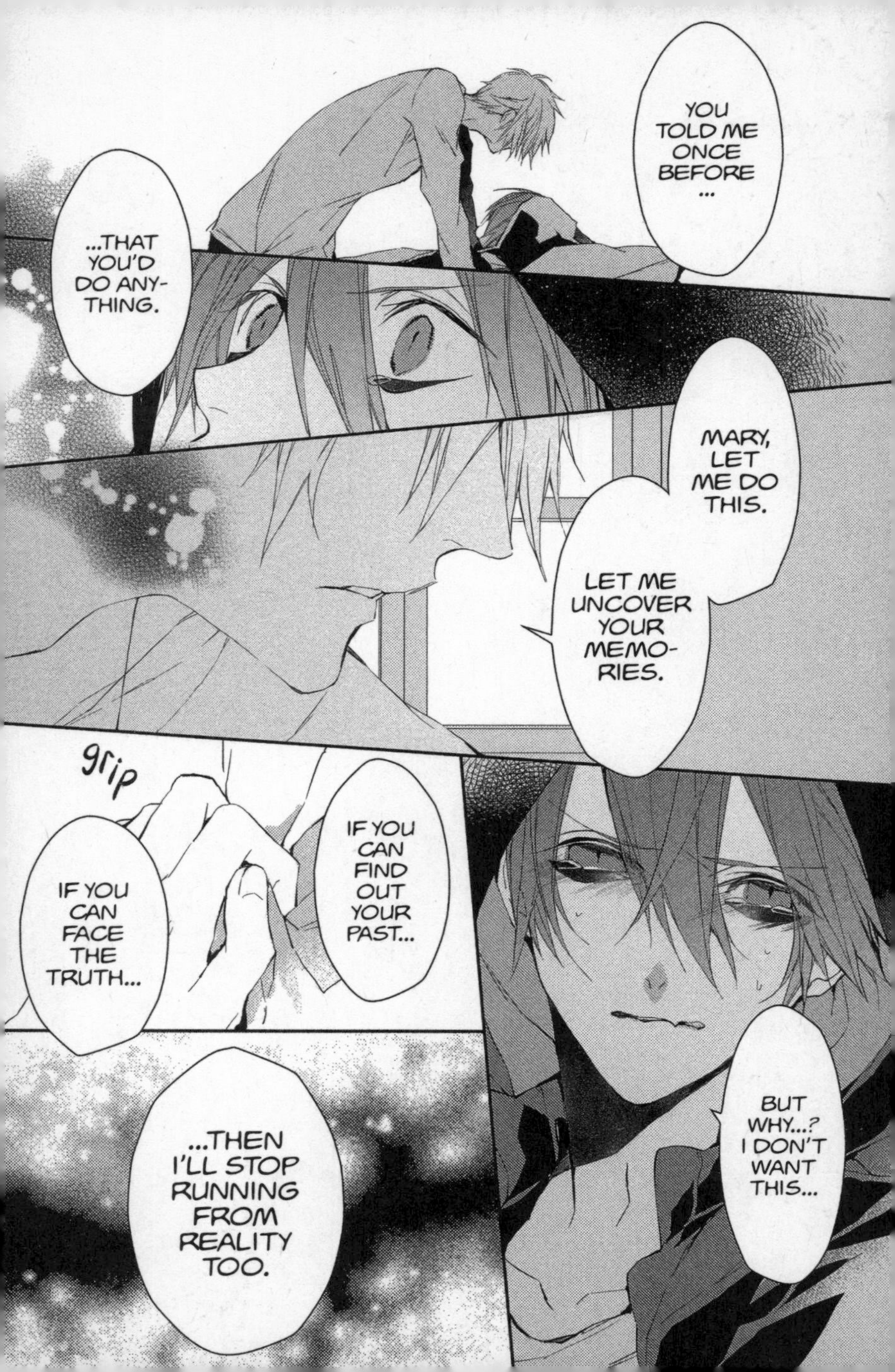
YOU TOLD ME ONCE BEFORE...
...THAT YOU'D DO ANY-THING.
MARY, LET ME DO THIS.
LET ME UNCOVER YOUR MEMO-RIES.
BUT WHY...? I DON'T WANT THIS...
grip
IF YOU CAN FIND OUT YOUR PAST...
IF YOU CAN FACE THE TRUTH...
...THEN I'LL STOP RUNNING FROM REALITY TOO.

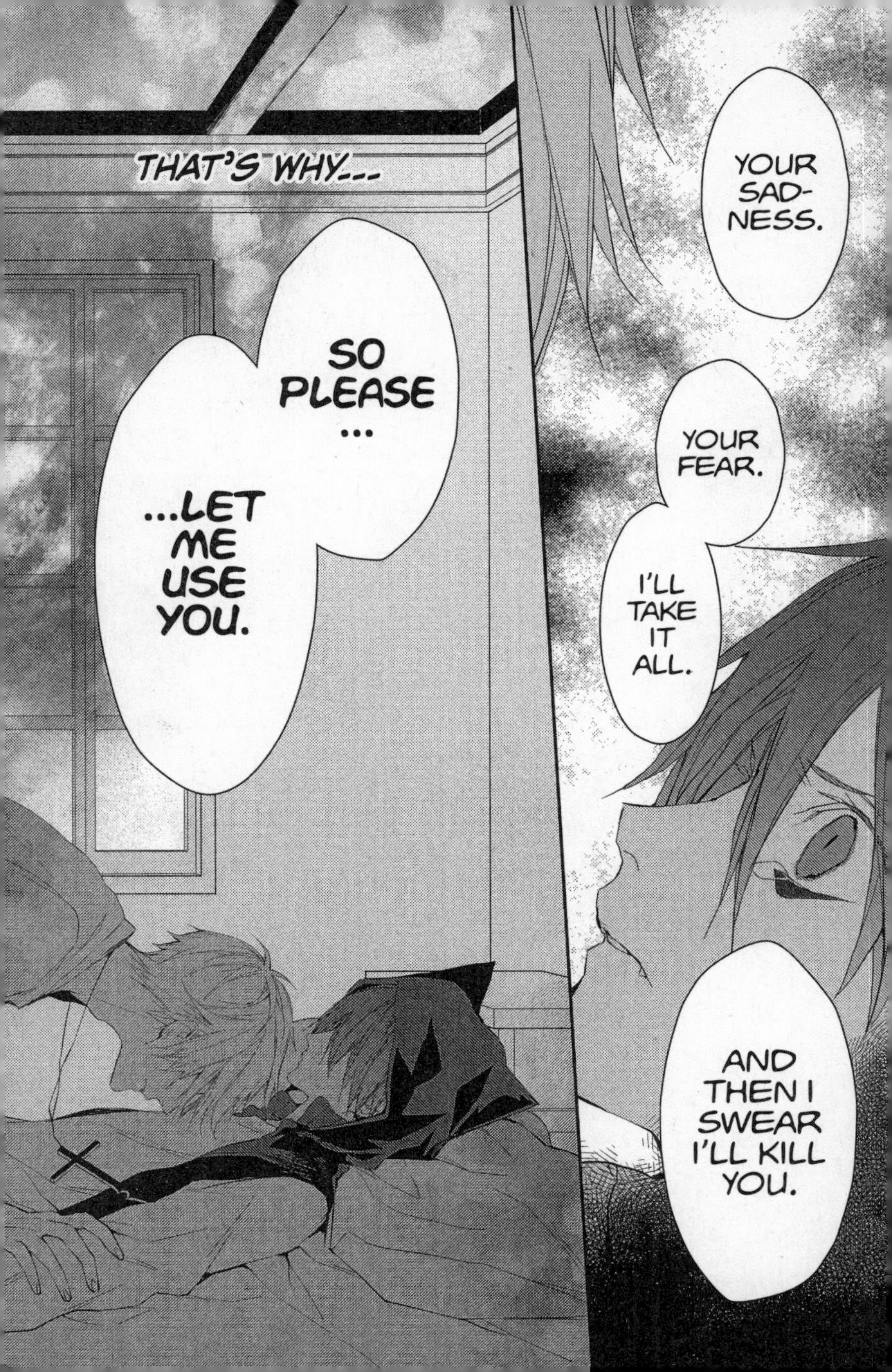
YOUR SADNESS.
YOUR FEAR.
I'LL TAKE IT ALL.
AND THEN I SWEAR I'LL KILL YOU.
THAT'S WHY...
SO PLEASE...
...LET ME USE YOU.

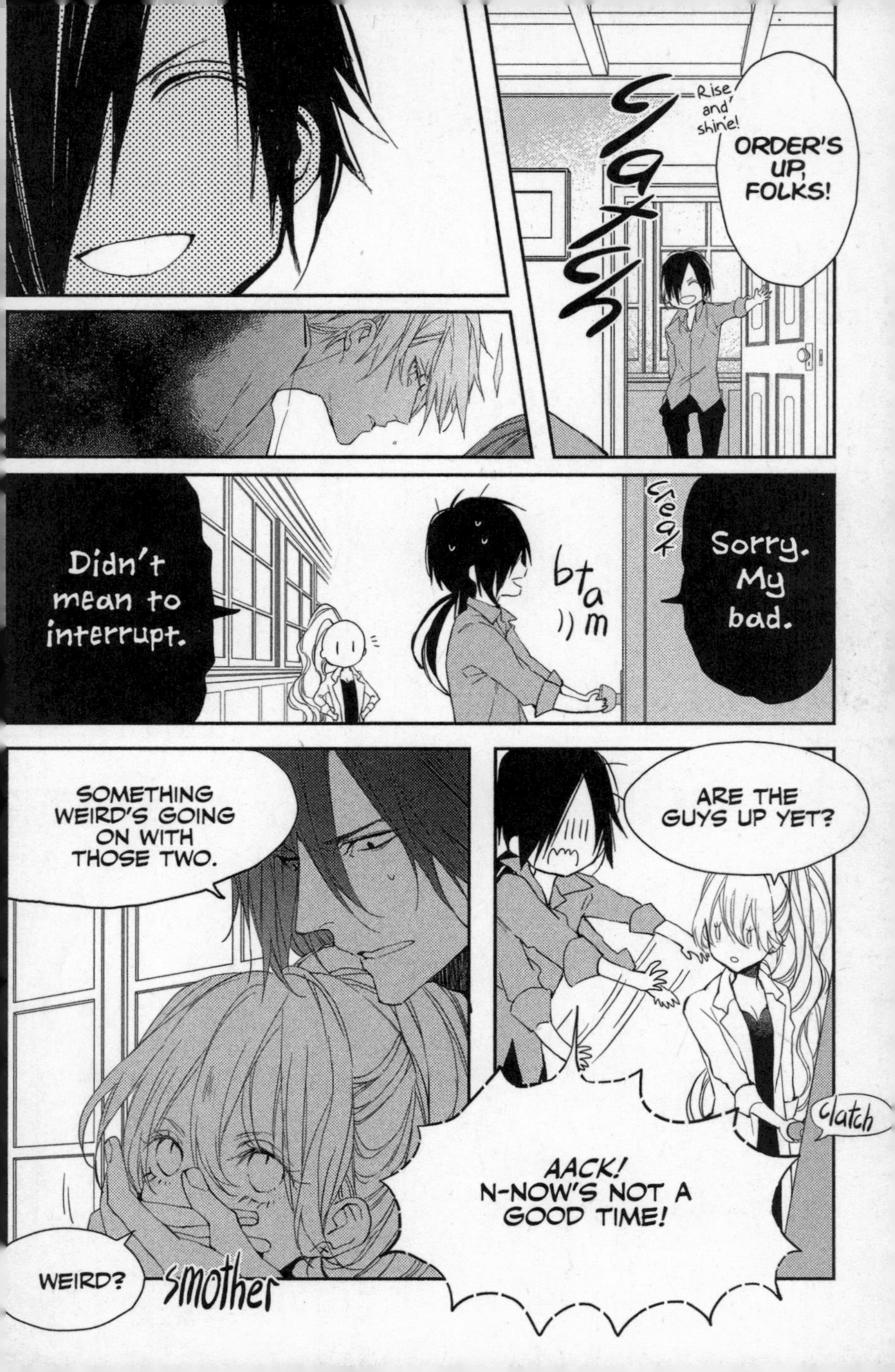
slatch
Rise and shine!
ORDER'S UP, FOLKS!
creak
Sorry. My bad.
btam
Didn't mean to interrupt.
ARE THE GUYS UP YET?
clatch
AACK! N-NOW'S NOT A GOOD TIME!
SOMETHING WEIRD'S GOING ON WITH THOSE TWO.
WEIRD?
smother

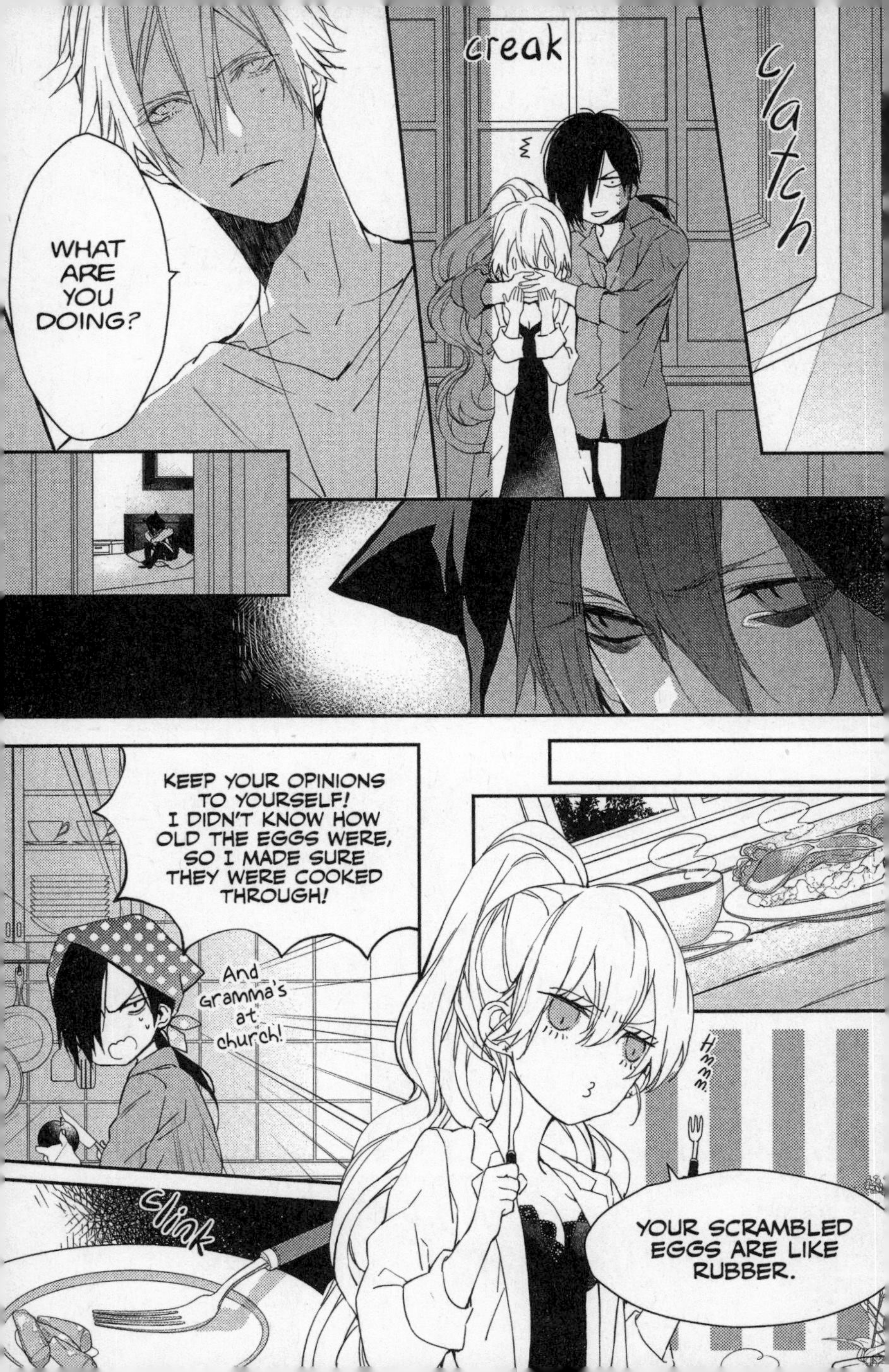
creak
clatch
WHAT ARE YOU DOING?
Hmmm
YOUR SCRAMBLED EGGS ARE LIKE RUBBER.
KEEP YOUR OPINIONS TO YOURSELF! I DIDN'T KNOW HOW OLD THE EGGS WERE, SO I MADE SURE THEY WERE COOKED THROUGH!
And Gramma's at church!
clink

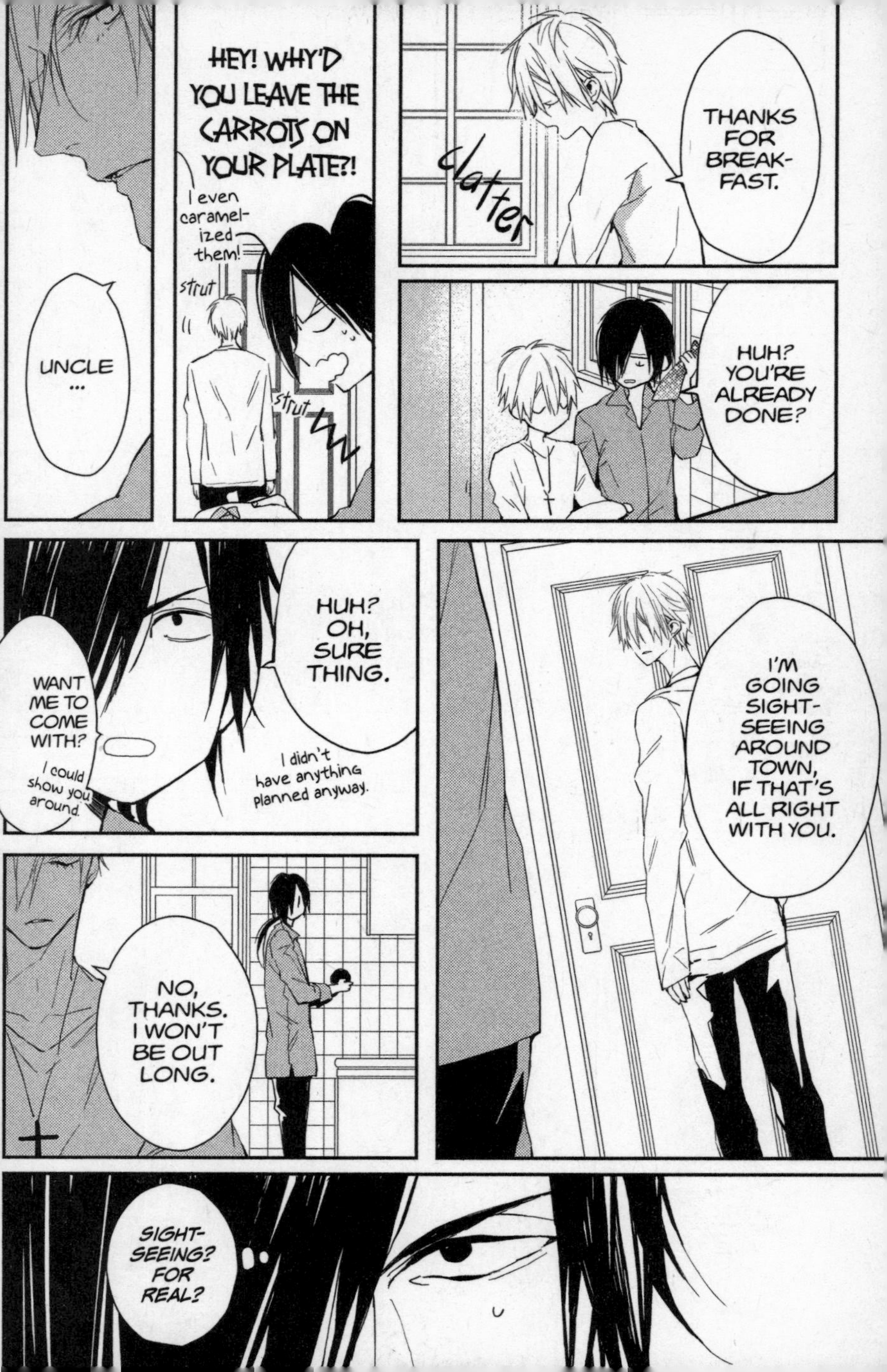
clatter
THANKS FOR BREAKFAST.
HUH? YOU'RE ALREADY DONE?
HEY! WHY'D YOU LEAVE THE CARROTS ON YOUR PLATE?!
I even caramelized them!
strut
strut
UNCLE ...
I'M GOING SIGHTSEEING AROUND TOWN, IF THAT'S ALL RIGHT WITH YOU.
HUH? OH, SURE THING.
I didn't have anything planned anyway.
WANT ME TO COME WITH?
I could show you around.
NO, THANKS. I WON'T BE OUT LONG.
SIGHTSEEING? FOR REAL?

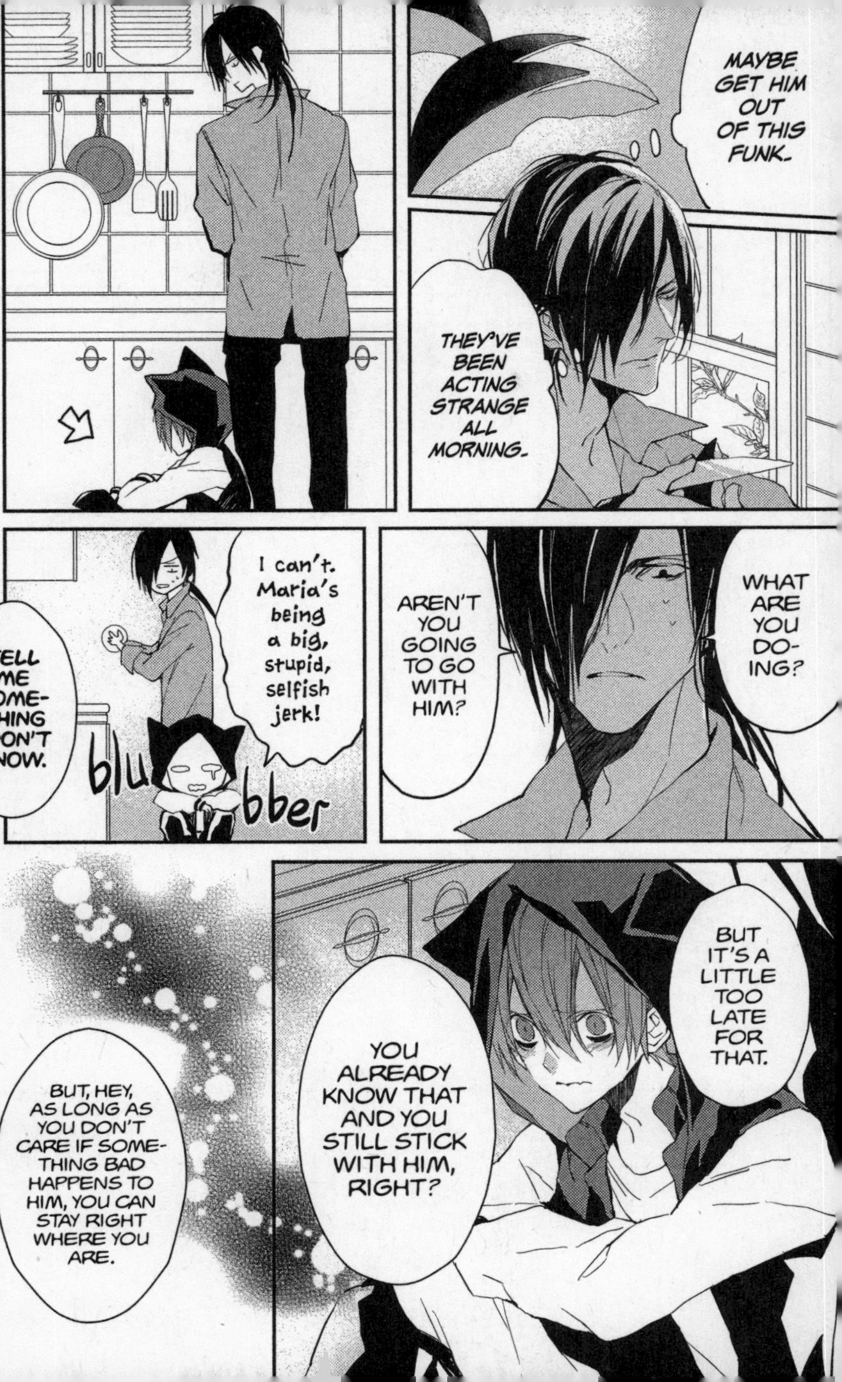
MAYBE GET HIM OUT OF THIS FUNK.
THEY'VE BEEN ACTING STRANGE ALL MORNING.
WHAT ARE YOU DO-ING?
AREN'T YOU GOING TO GO WITH HIM?
I can't. Maria's being a big, stupid, selfish jerk!
blubber
TELL ME SOME-THING I DON'T KNOW.
BUT IT'S A LITTLE TOO LATE FOR THAT.
YOU ALREADY KNOW THAT AND YOU STILL STICK WITH HIM, RIGHT?
BUT, HEY, AS LONG AS YOU DON'T CARE IF SOME-THING BAD HAPPENS TO HIM, YOU CAN STAY RIGHT WHERE YOU ARE.

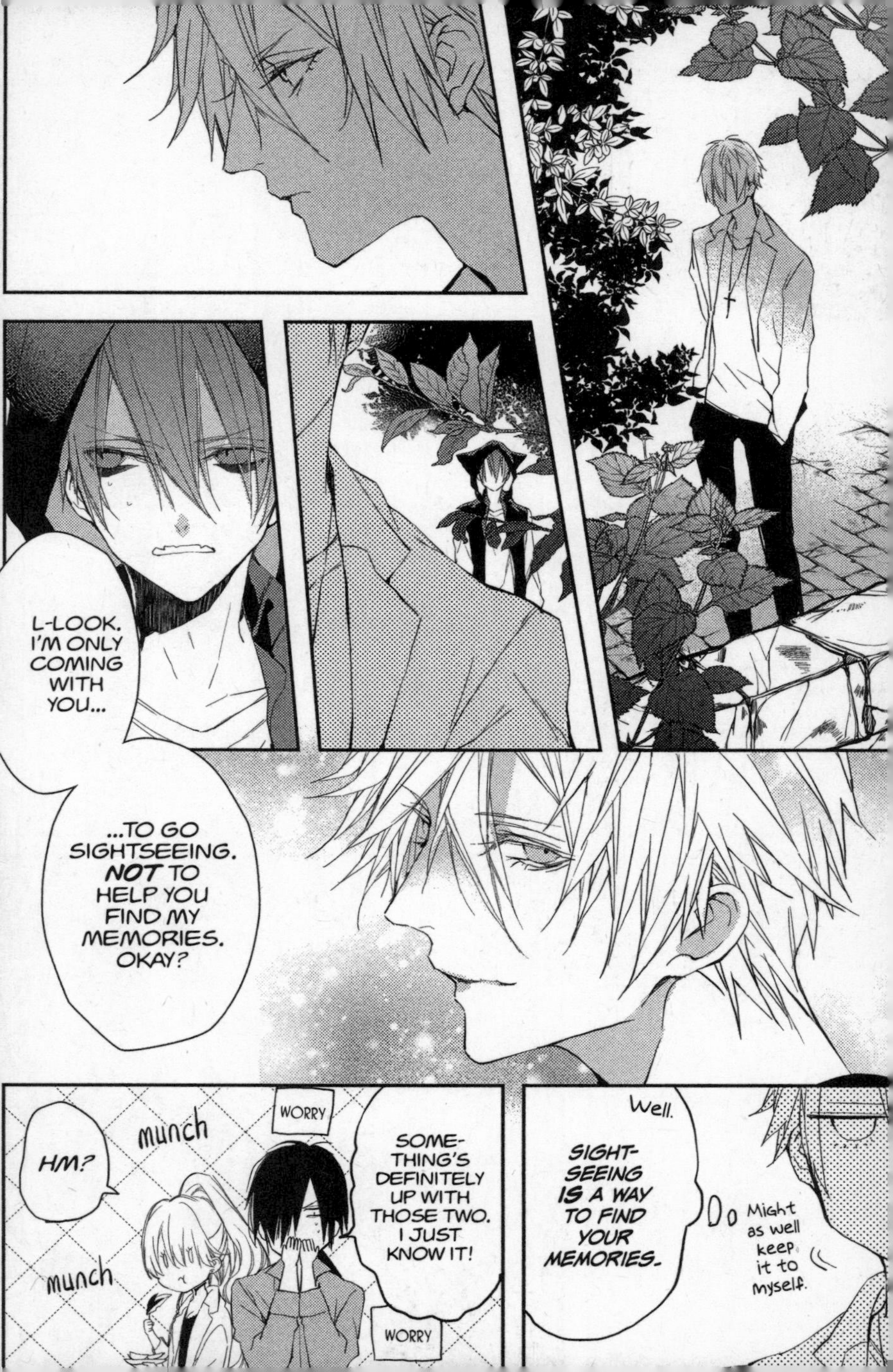
L-LOOK. I'M ONLY COMING WITH YOU...
...TO GO SIGHTSEEING. NOT TO HELP YOU FIND MY MEMORIES. OKAY?
Well.
SIGHT-SEEING IS A WAY TO FIND YOUR MEMORIES.
Might as well keep it to myself.
SOME-THING'S DEFINITELY UP WITH THOSE TWO. I JUST KNOW IT!
WORRY
munch
HM?
munch
WORRY

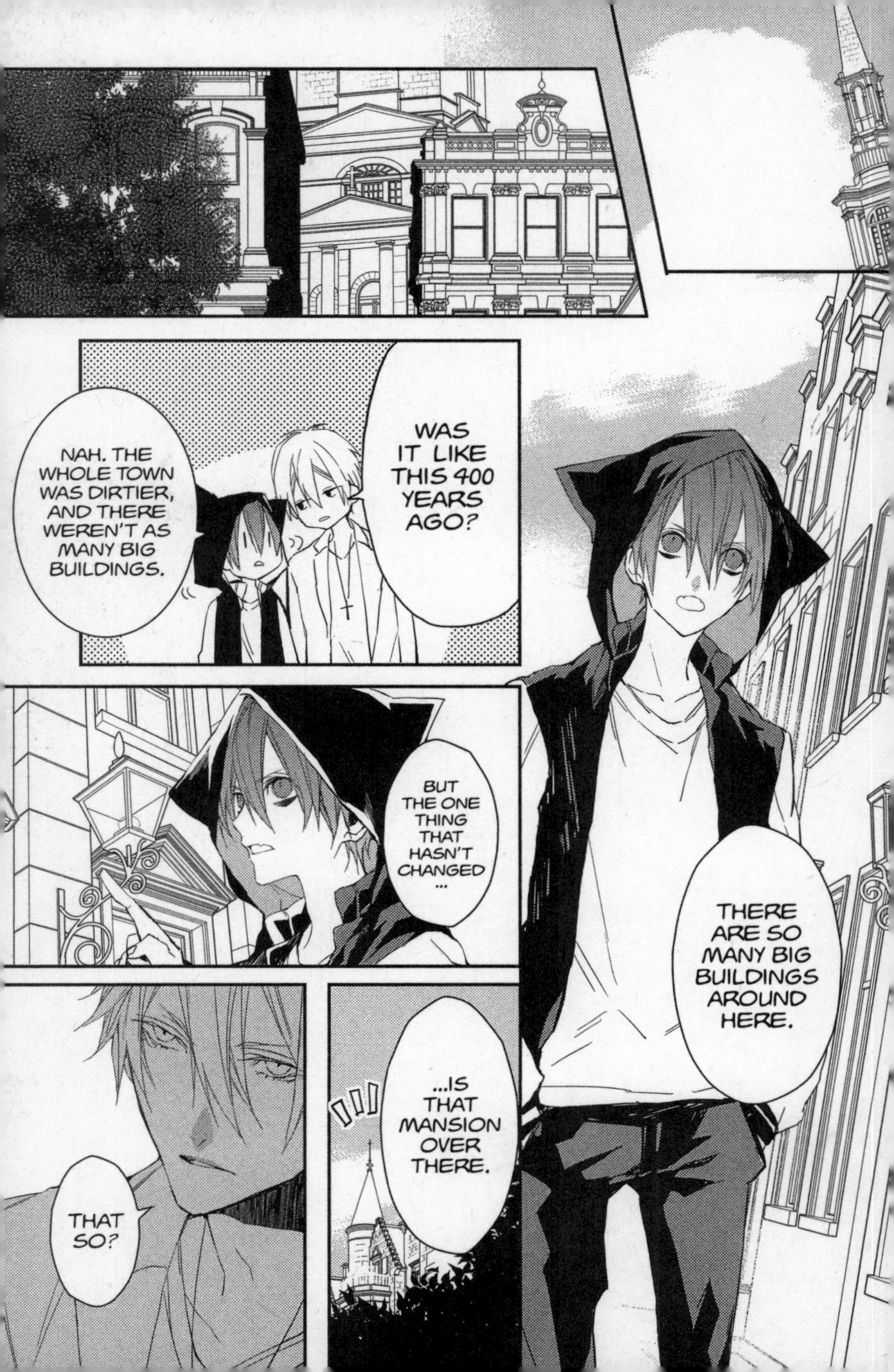
THERE ARE SO MANY BIG BUILDINGS AROUND HERE.
WAS IT LIKE THIS 400 YEARS AGO?
NAH. THE WHOLE TOWN WAS DIRTIER, AND THERE WEREN'T AS MANY BIG BUILDINGS.
BUT THE ONE THING THAT HASN'T CHANGED...
...IS THAT MANSION OVER THERE.
THAT SO?

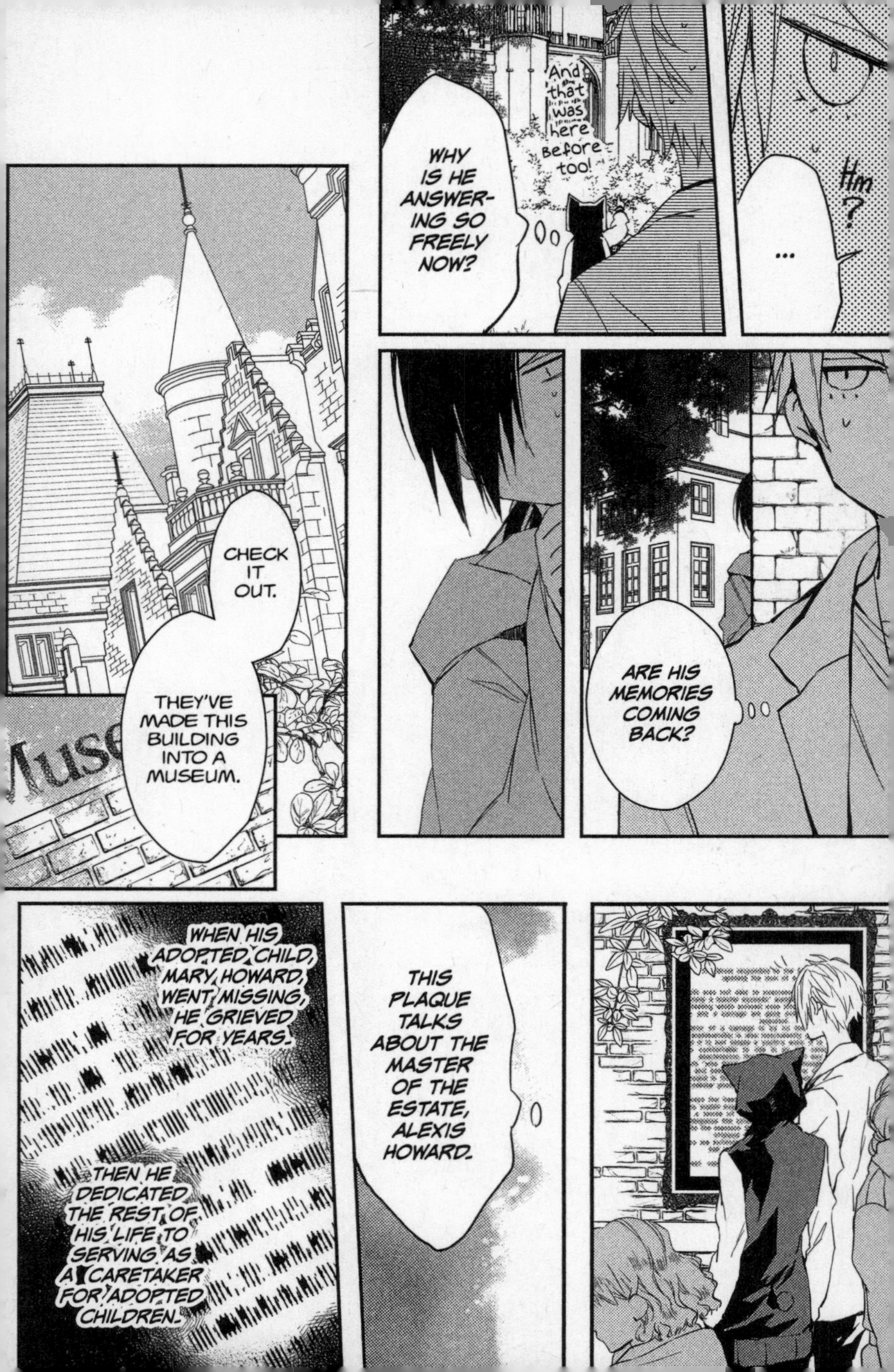
Hm?
...
And that was here before too!
WHY IS HE ANSWERING SO FREELY NOW?
ARE HIS MEMORIES COMING BACK?
CHECK IT OUT.
THEY'VE MADE THIS BUILDING INTO A MUSEUM.
THIS PLAQUE TALKS ABOUT THE MASTER OF THE ESTATE, ALEXIS HOWARD.
WHEN HIS ADOPTED CHILD, MARY HOWARD, WENT MISSING, HE GRIEVED FOR YEARS.
THEN HE DEDICATED THE REST OF HIS LIFE TO SERVING AS A CARETAKER FOR ADOPTED CHILDREN.

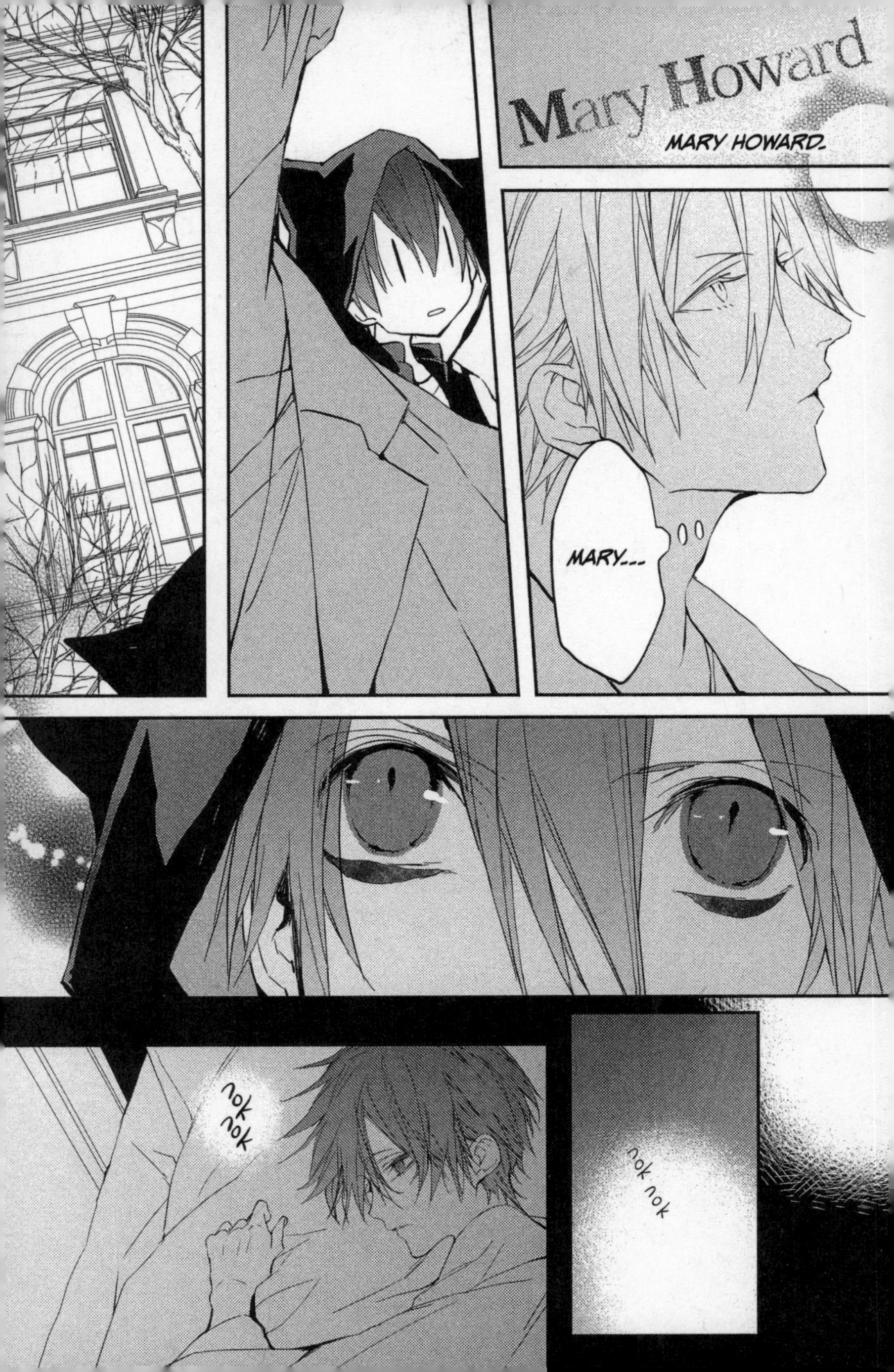
Mary Howard
MARY HOWARD.
MARY...
nok nok
nok nok

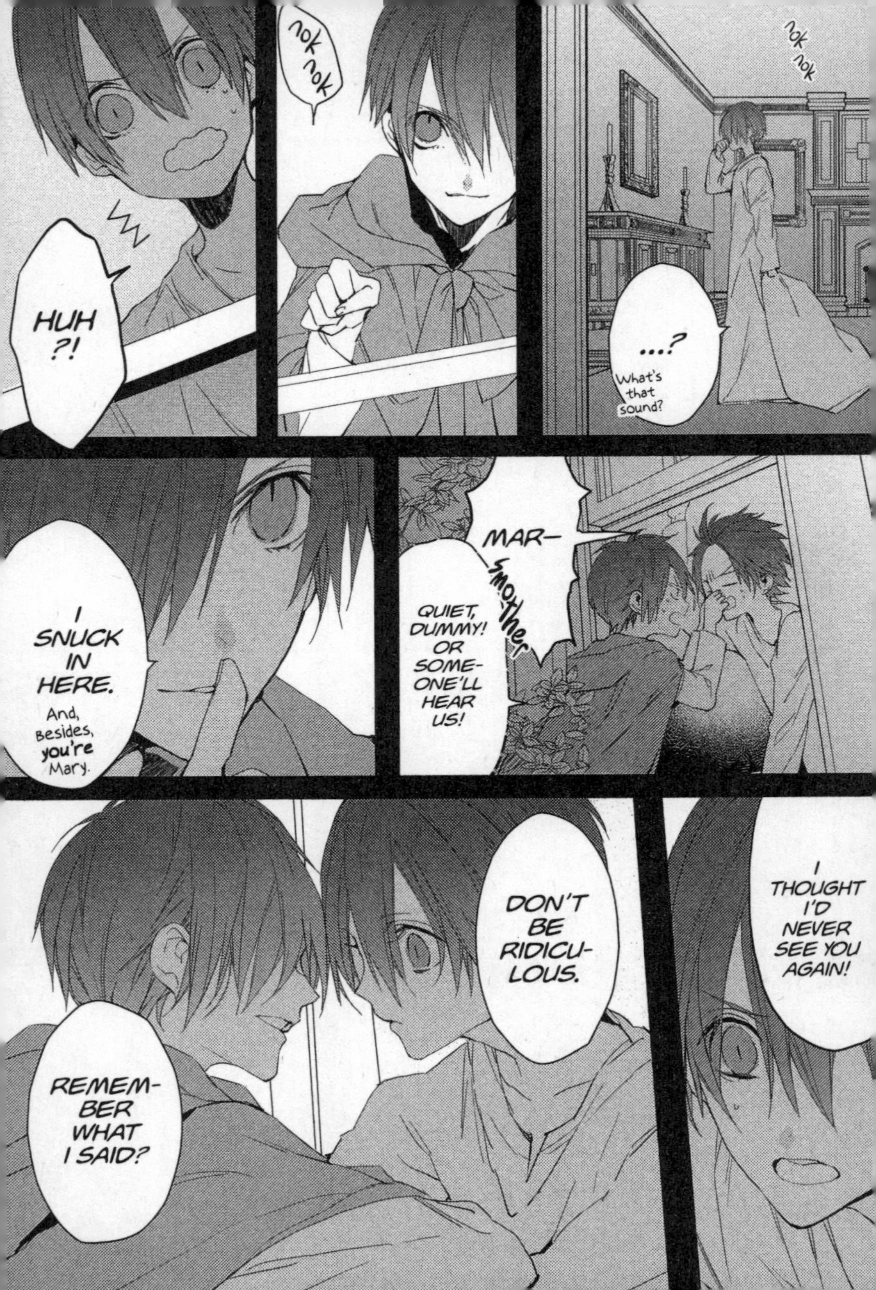
nok nok
...? What's that sound?
nok nok
HUH ?!
MAR—
smother
QUIET, DUMMY! OR SOME-ONE'LL HEAR US!
I SNUCK IN HERE.
And, besides, you're Mary.
I THOUGHT I'D NEVER SEE YOU AGAIN!
DON'T BE RIDICU-LOUS.
REMEM-BER WHAT I SAID?

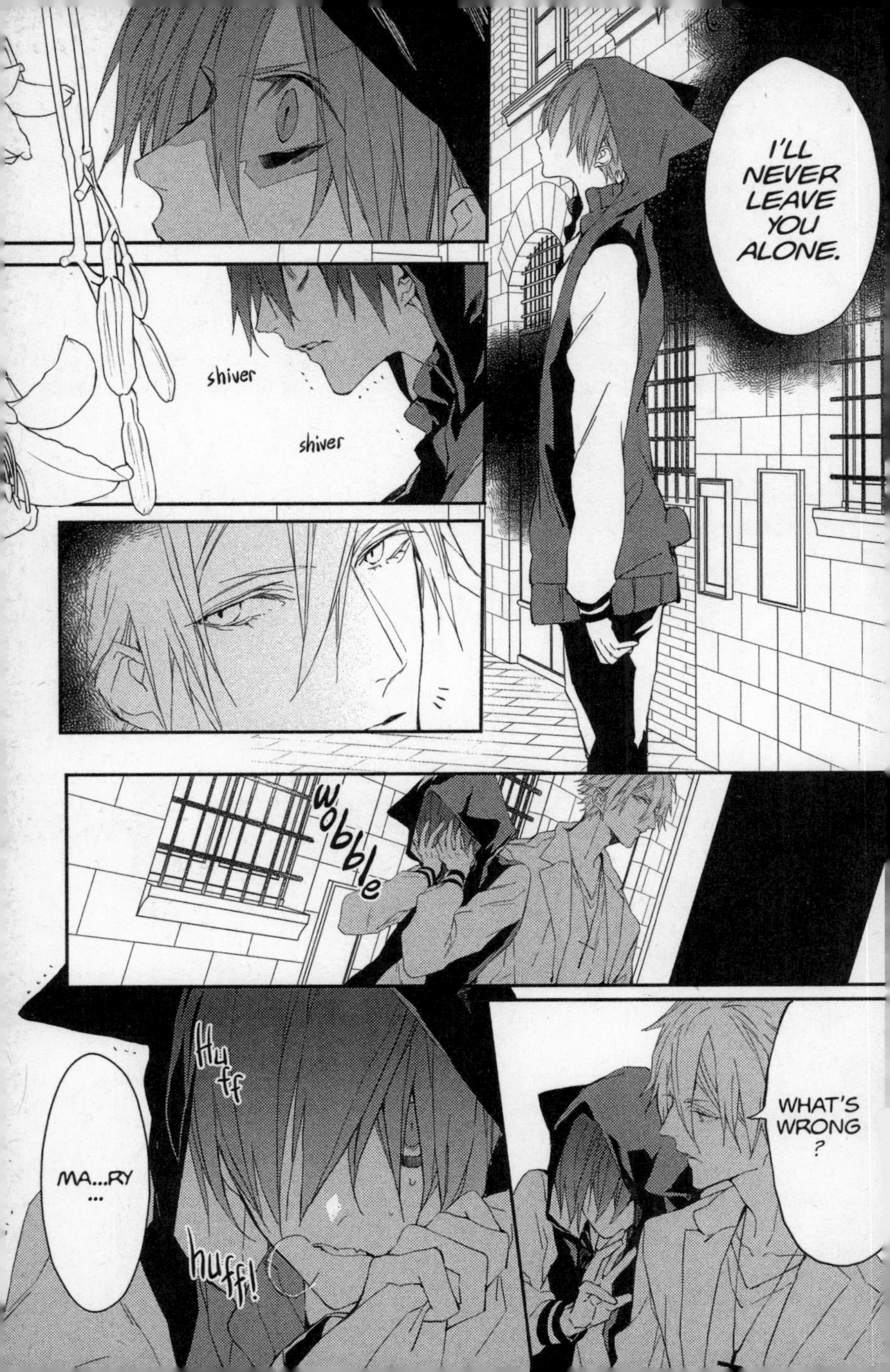
I'LL NEVER LEAVE YOU ALONE.
shiver
shiver
wobble
WHAT'S WRONG?
Huff
MA...RY...
huff!

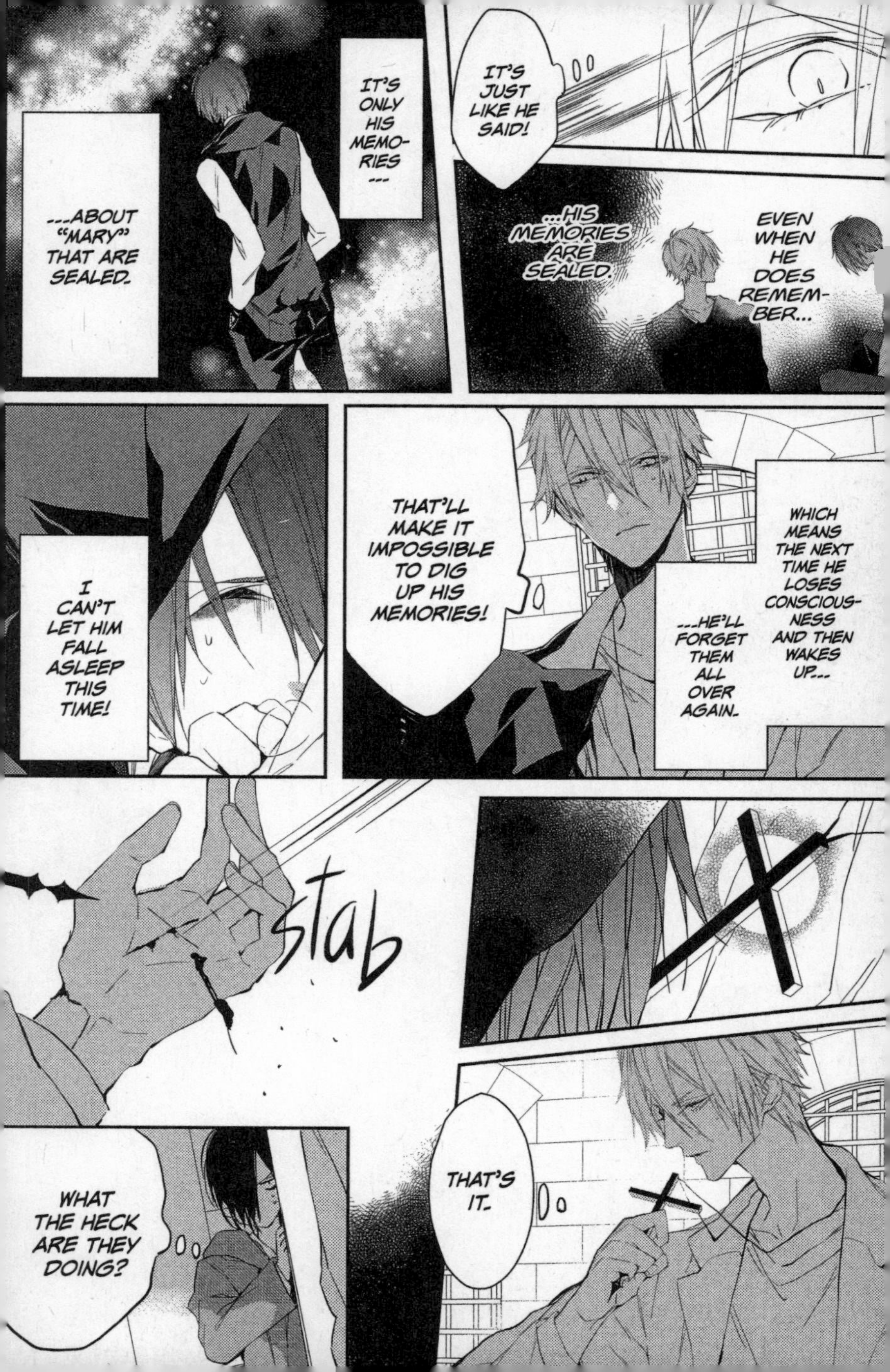
IT'S JUST LIKE HE SAID!
EVEN WHEN HE DOES REMEMBER...
...HIS MEMORIES ARE SEALED.
IT'S ONLY HIS MEMORIES---
---ABOUT "MARY" THAT ARE SEALED.
WHICH MEANS THE NEXT TIME HE LOSES CONSCIOUSNESS AND THEN WAKES UP...
...HE'LL FORGET THEM ALL OVER AGAIN.
THAT'LL MAKE IT IMPOSSIBLE TO DIG UP HIS MEMORIES!
I CAN'T LET HIM FALL ASLEEP THIS TIME!
THAT'S IT.
stab
WHAT THE HECK ARE THEY DOING?

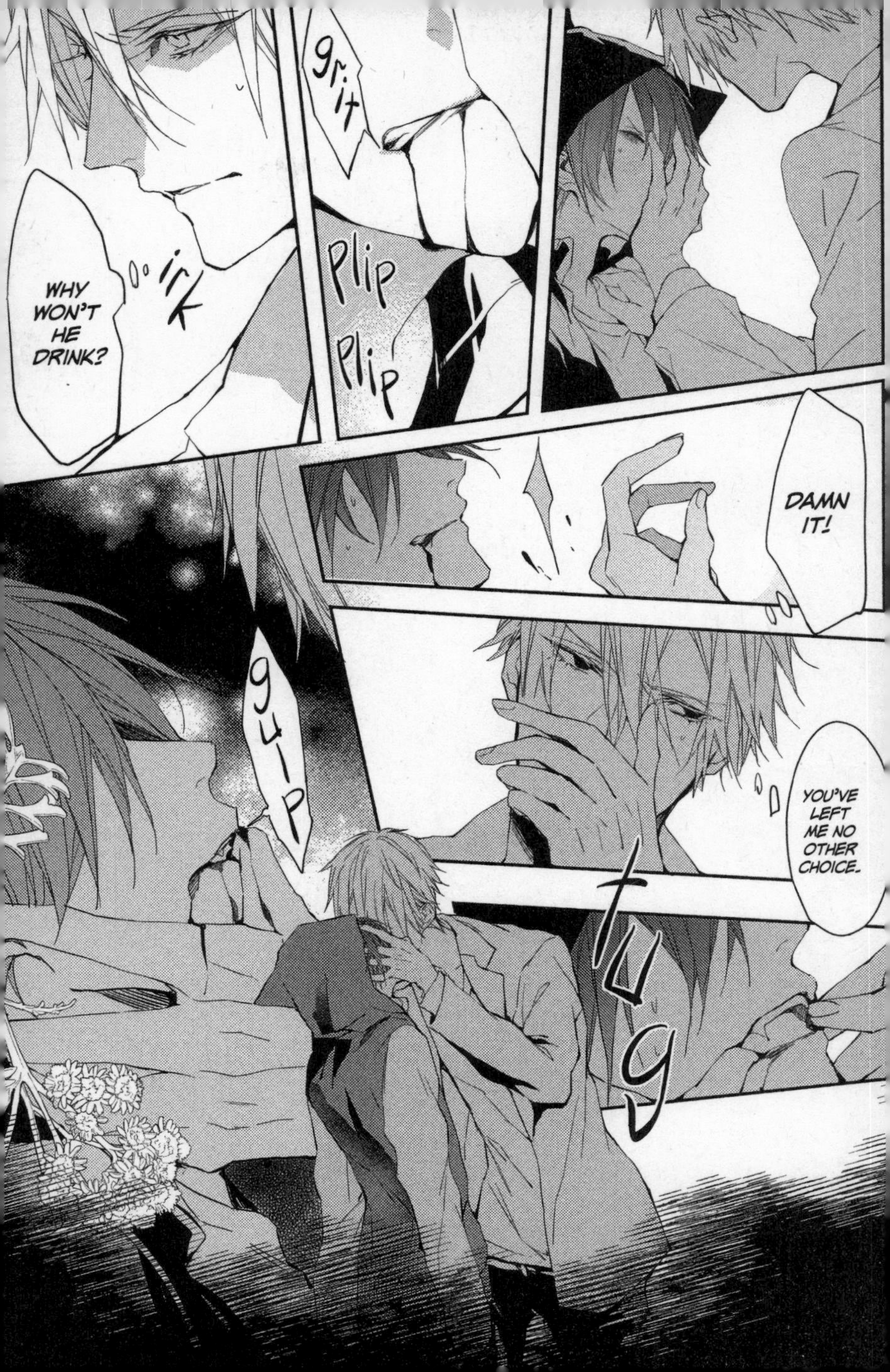
grit
plip plip
irk
WHY WON'T HE DRINK?
DAMN IT!
YOU'VE LEFT ME NO OTHER CHOICE.
tug
gulp

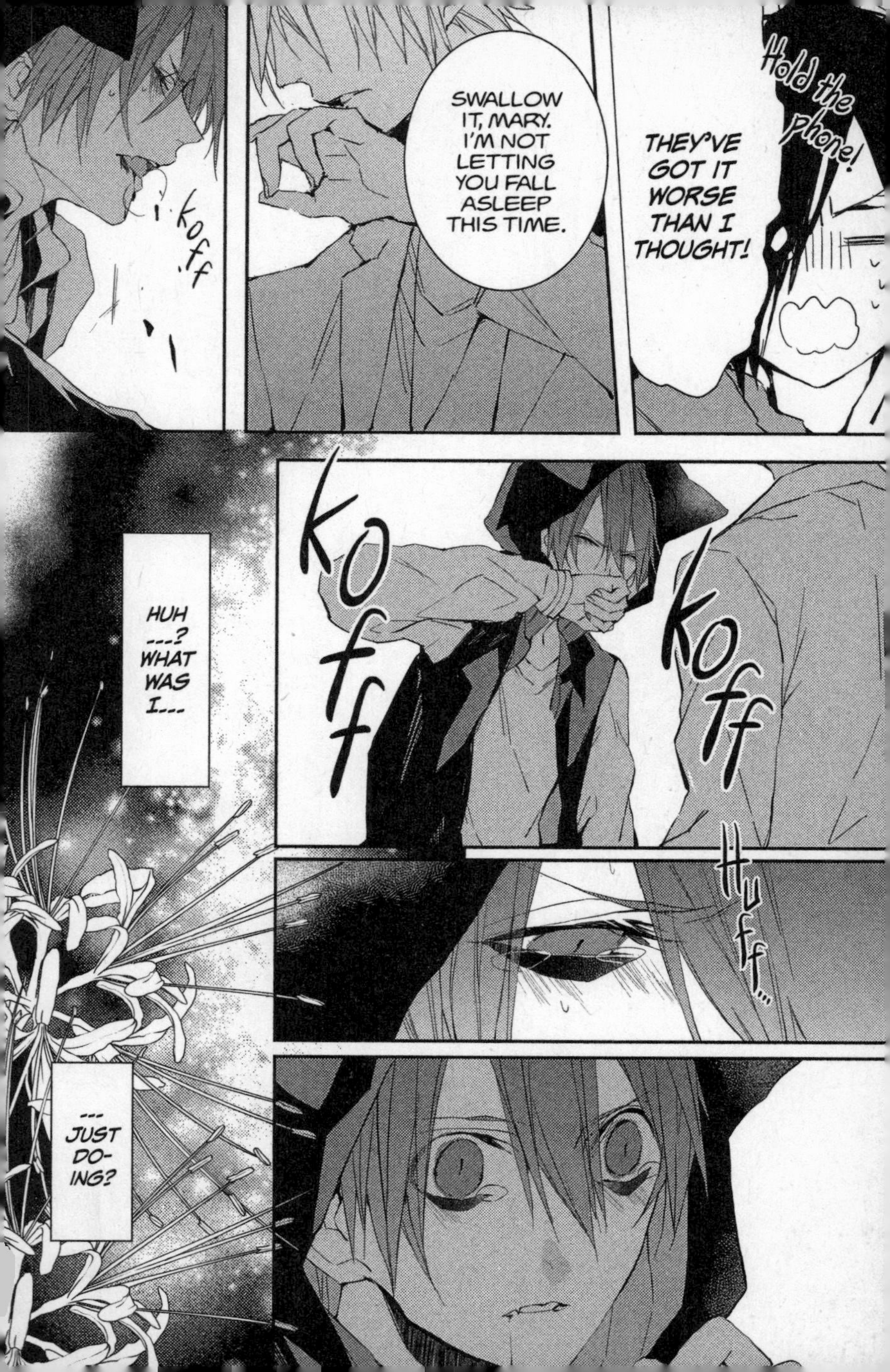
Hold the phone!
THEY'VE GOT IT WORSE THAN I THOUGHT!
SWALLOW IT, MARY. I'M NOT LETTING YOU FALL ASLEEP THIS TIME.
koff
koff
koff
Huff...
HUH---? WHAT WAS I---
---JUST DO-ING?

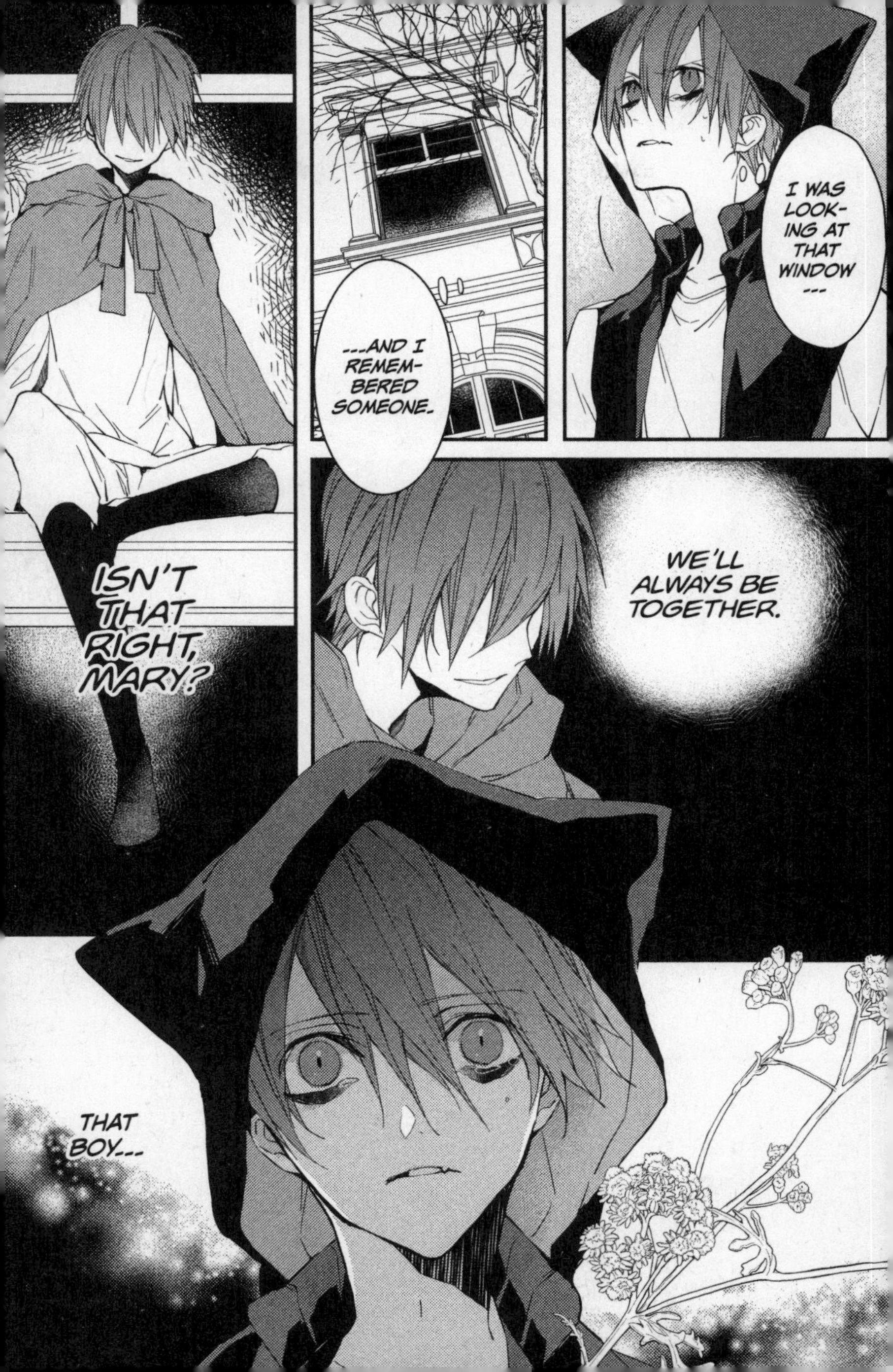
I WAS LOOKING AT THAT WINDOW---
---AND I REMEMBERED SOMEONE.
WE'LL ALWAYS BE TOGETHER.
ISN'T THAT RIGHT, MARY?
THAT BOY...

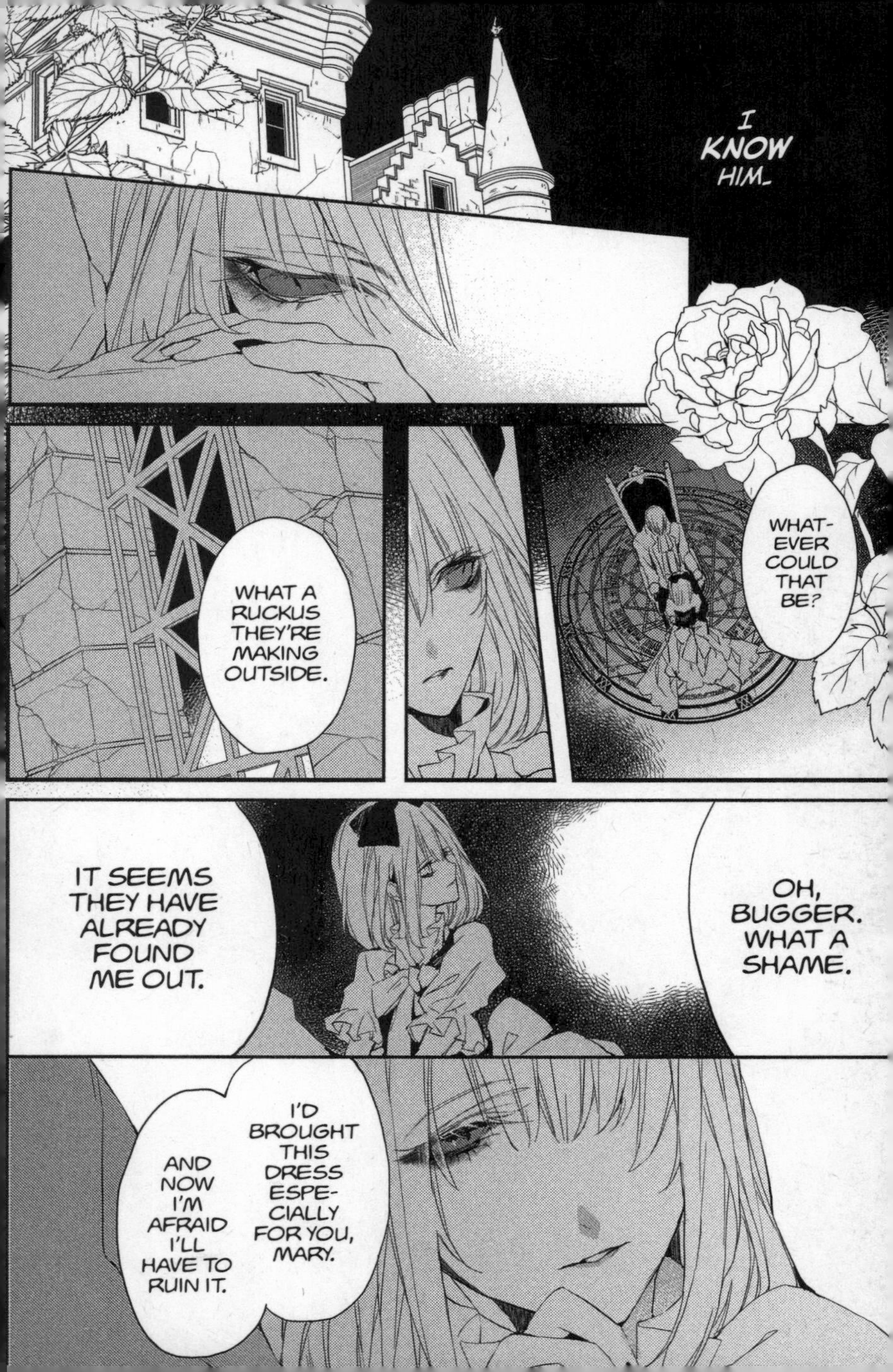
I KNOW HIM_
WHATEVER COULD THAT BE?
WHAT A RUCKUS THEY'RE MAKING OUTSIDE.
OH, BUGGER. WHAT A SHAME.
IT SEEMS THEY HAVE ALREADY FOUND ME OUT.
I'D BROUGHT THIS DRESS ESPECIALLY FOR YOU, MARY.
AND NOW I'M AFRAID I'LL HAVE TO RUIN IT.

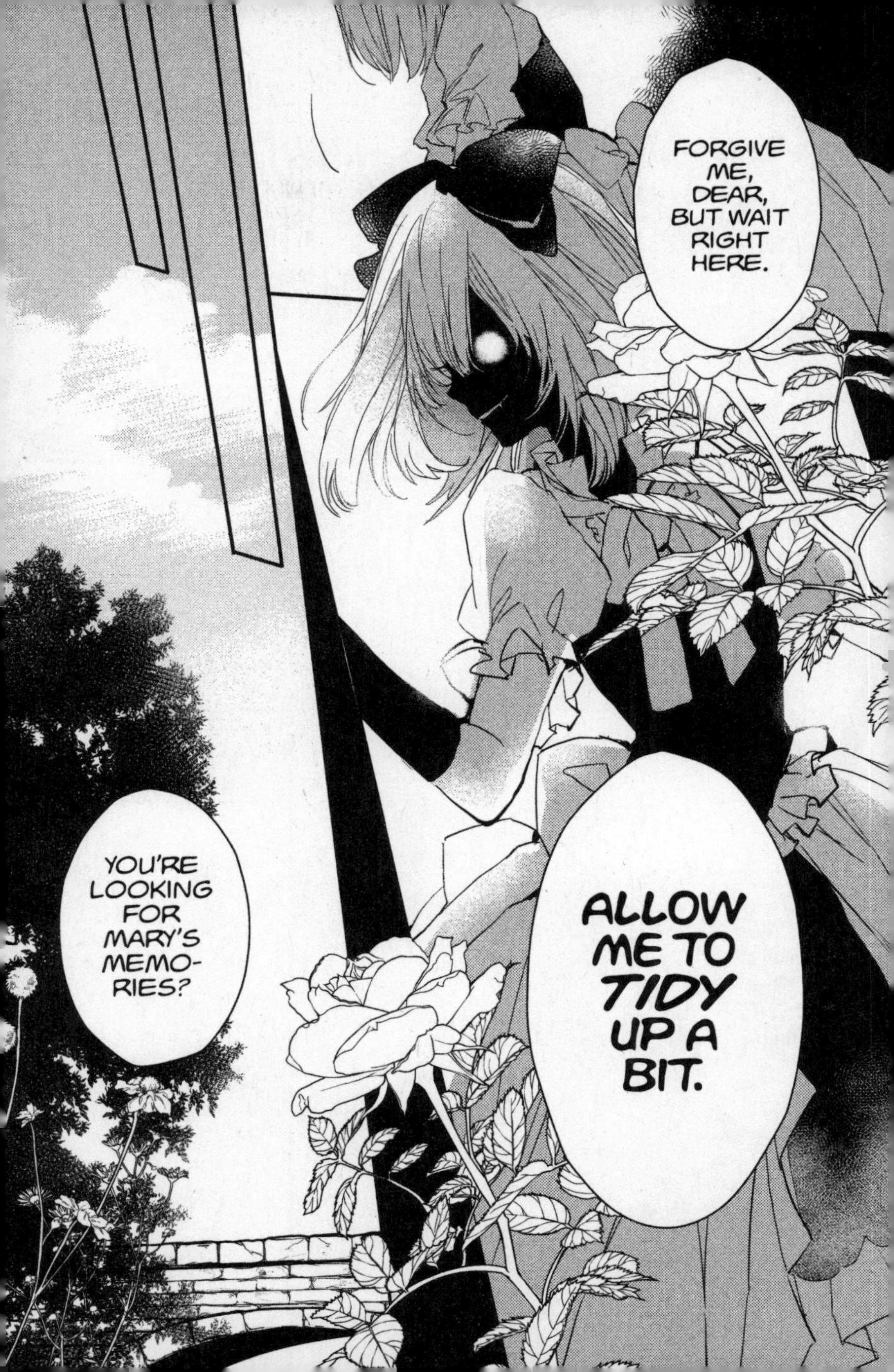
FORGIVE ME, DEAR, BUT WAIT RIGHT HERE.
ALLOW ME TO *TIDY* UP A BIT.
YOU'RE LOOKING FOR MARY'S MEMO-RIES?

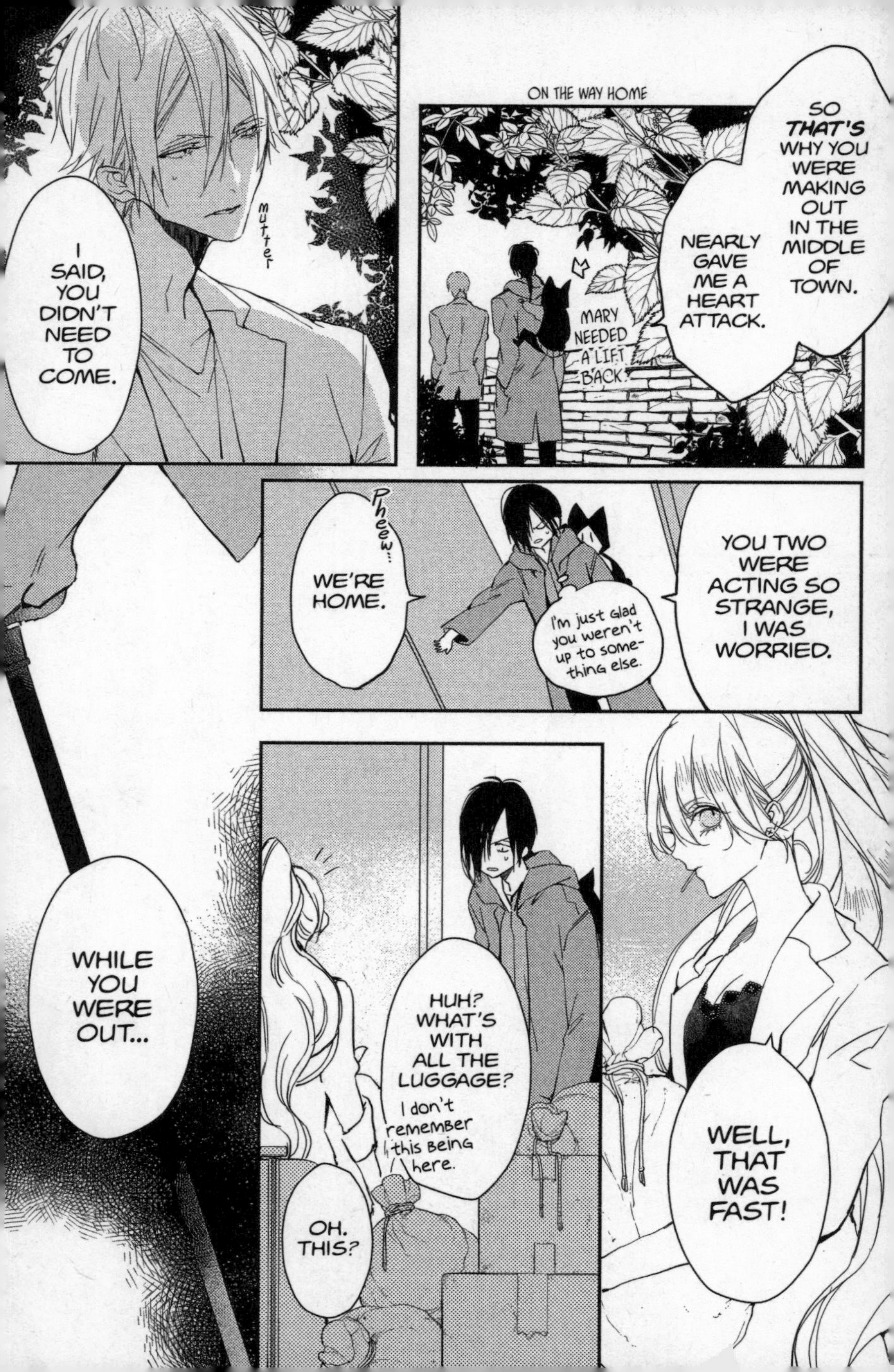
ON THE WAY HOME
SO *THAT'S* WHY YOU WERE MAKING OUT IN THE MIDDLE OF TOWN.
NEARLY GAVE ME A HEART ATTACK.
MARY NEEDED A LIFT BACK.
mutter
I SAID, YOU DIDN'T NEED TO COME.
YOU TWO WERE ACTING SO STRANGE, I WAS WORRIED.
I'm just glad you weren't up to something else.
Pheew...
WE'RE HOME.
WELL, THAT WAS FAST!
HUH? WHAT'S WITH ALL THE LUGGAGE?
I don't remember this being here.
OH. THIS?
WHILE YOU WERE OUT...

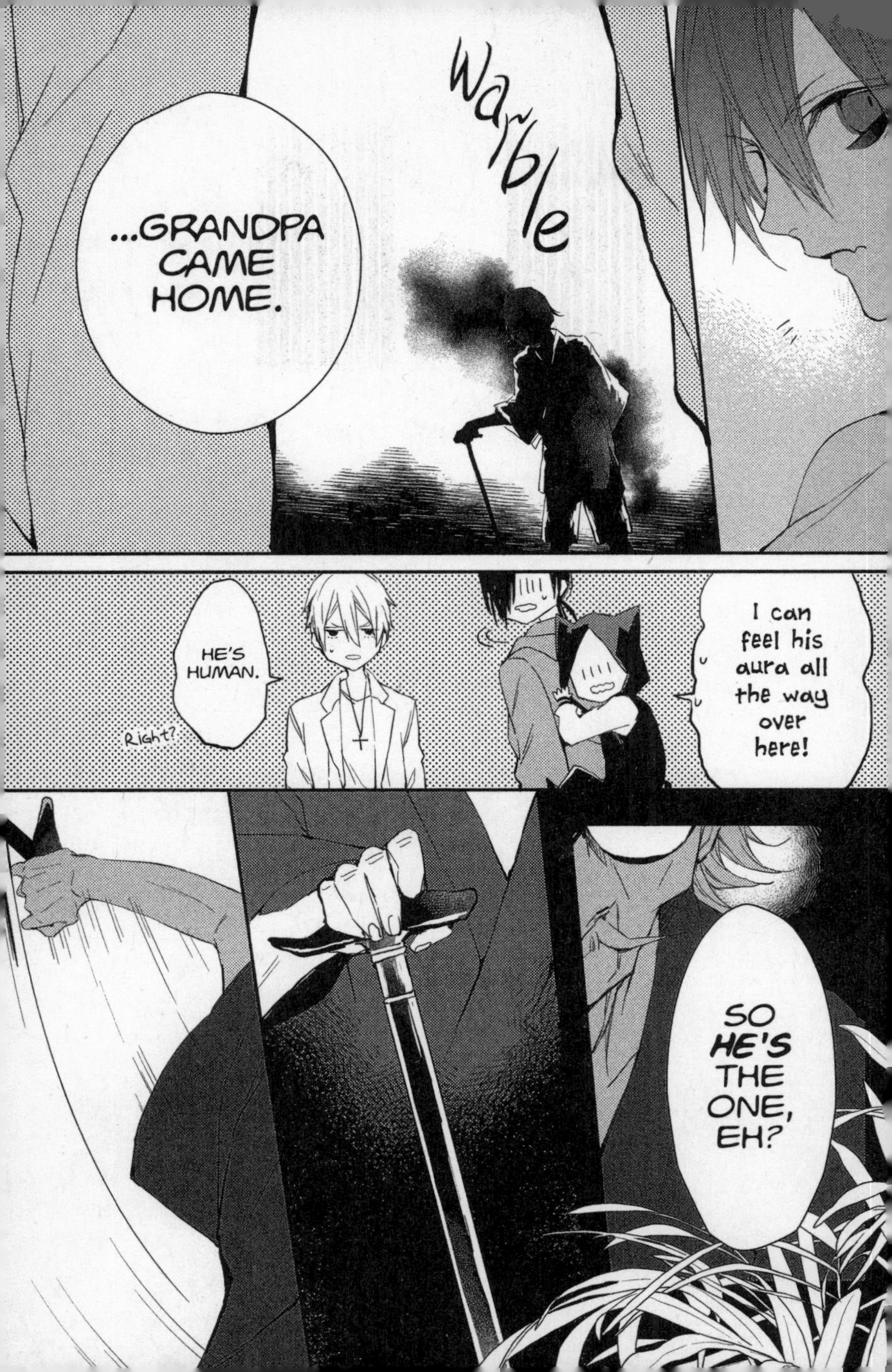

Warble
...GRANDPA CAME HOME.
I can feel his aura all the way over here!
HE'S HUMAN.
Right?
SO HE'S THE ONE, EH?

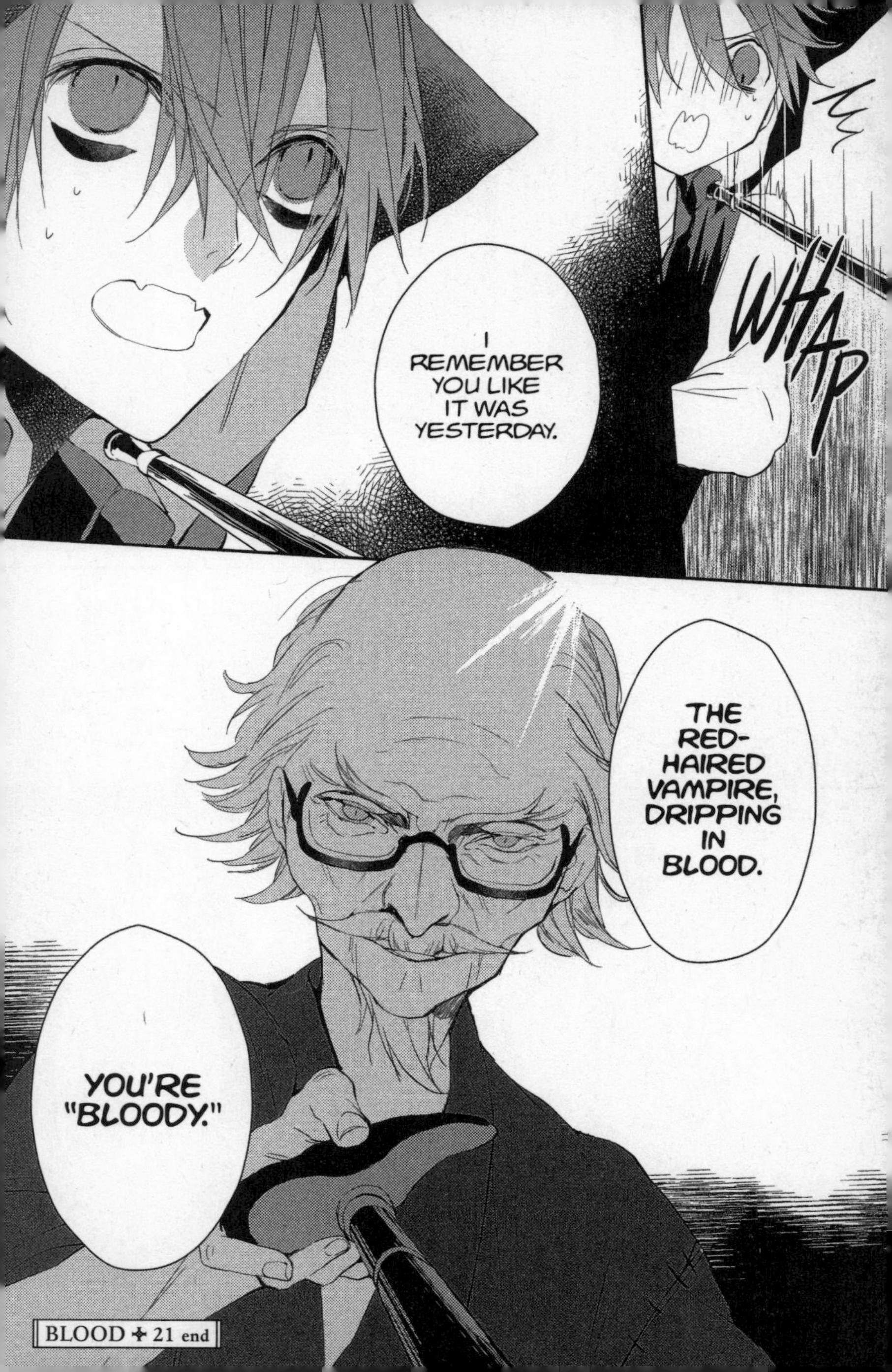
WHAP
I REMEMBER YOU LIKE IT WAS YESTERDAY.
THE RED-HAIRED VAMPIRE, DRIPPING IN BLOOD.
YOU'RE "BLOODY."
BLOOD ✣ 21 end

Bloody+Mary

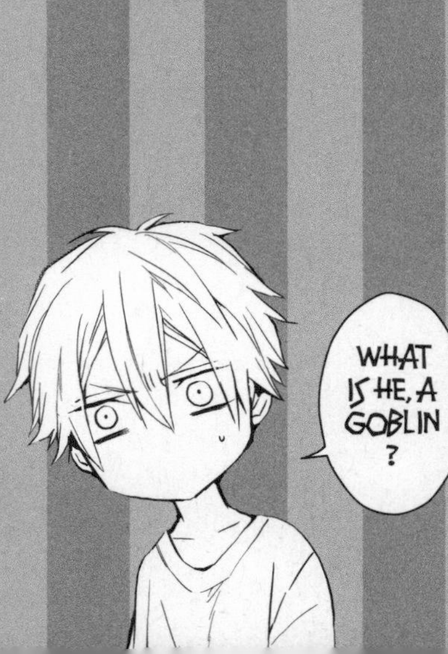
WHAT IS HE, A GOBLIN ?

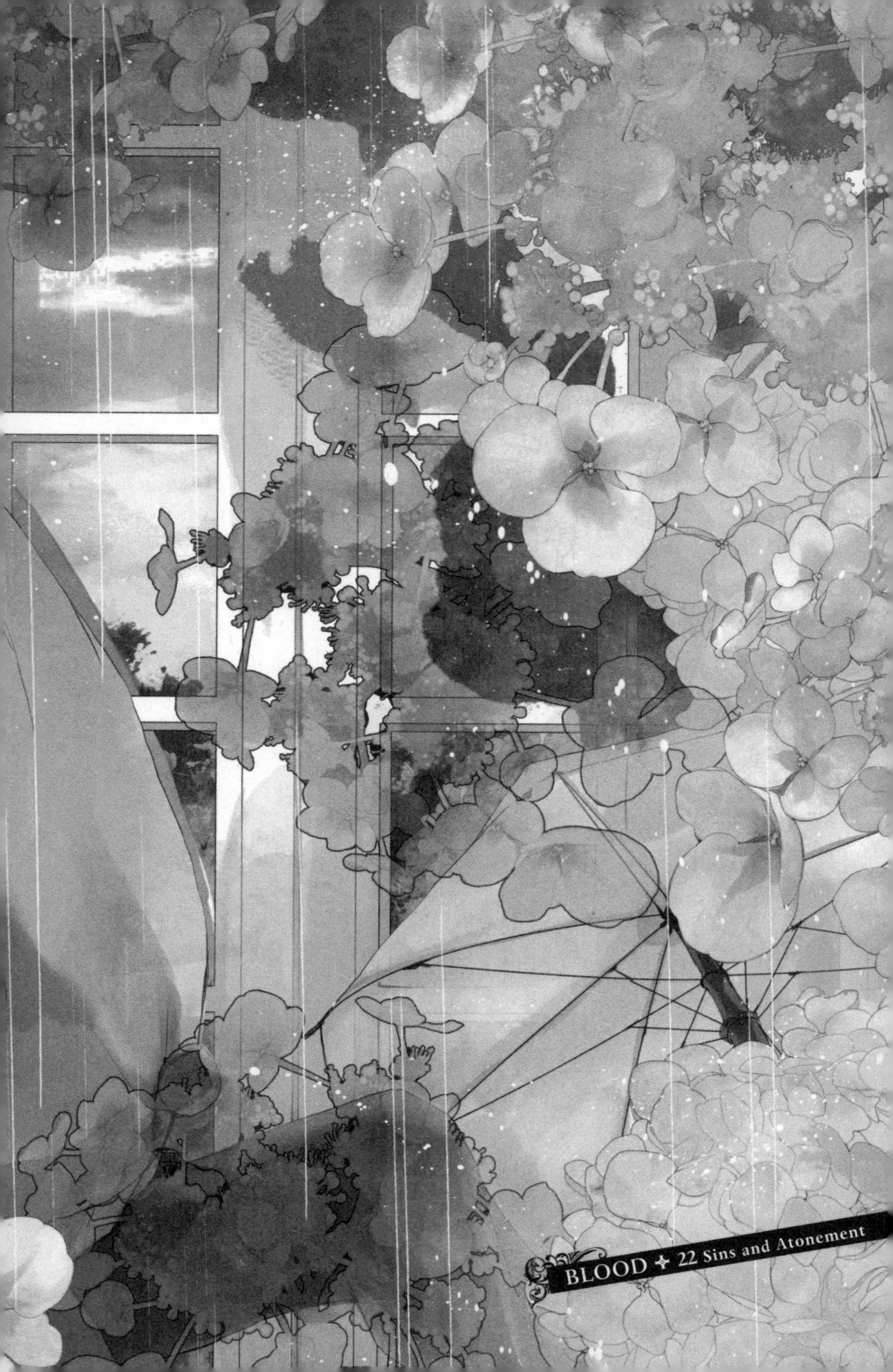
BLOOD ✦ 22 Sins and Atonement

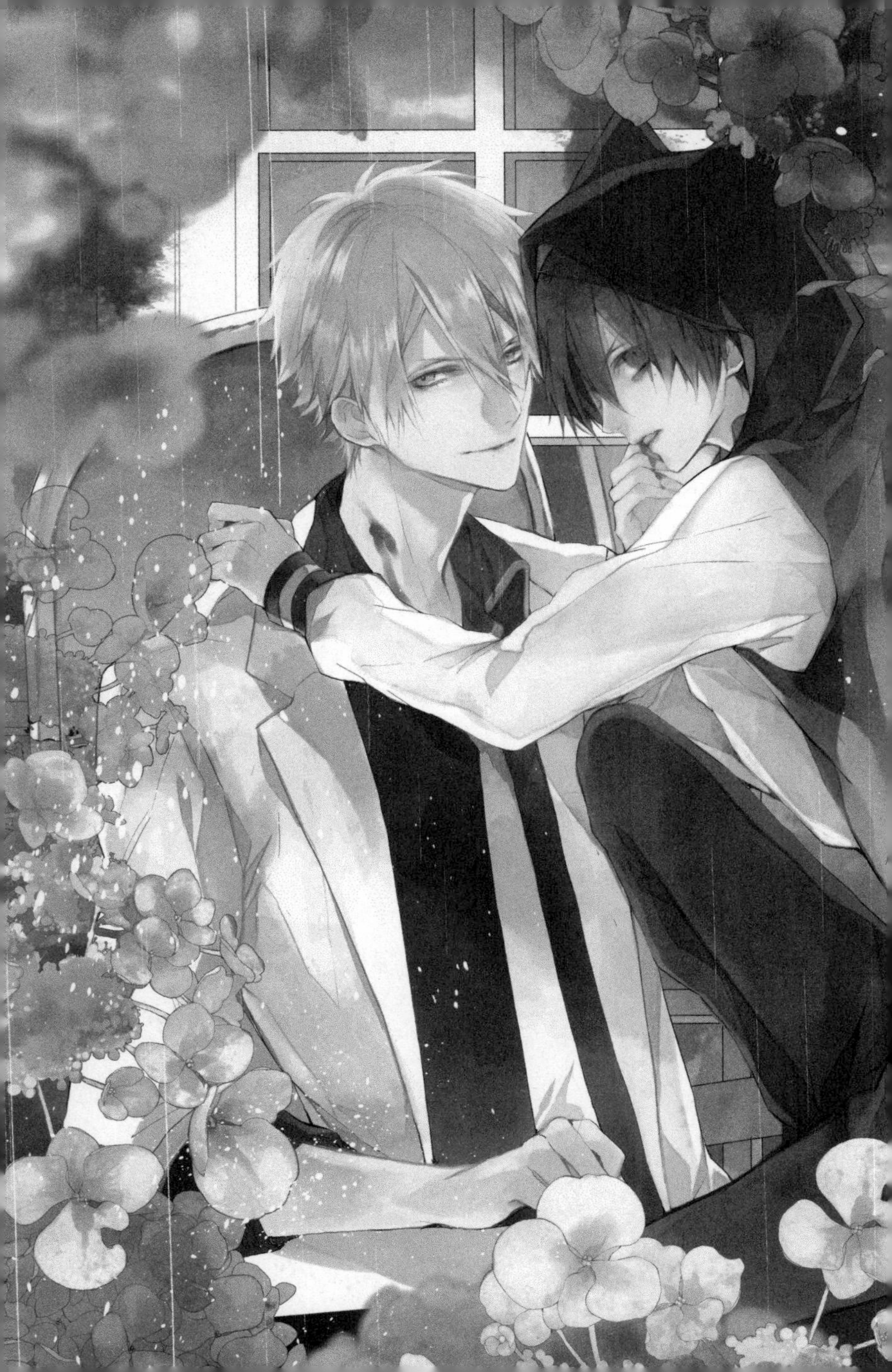

Bloody Mary

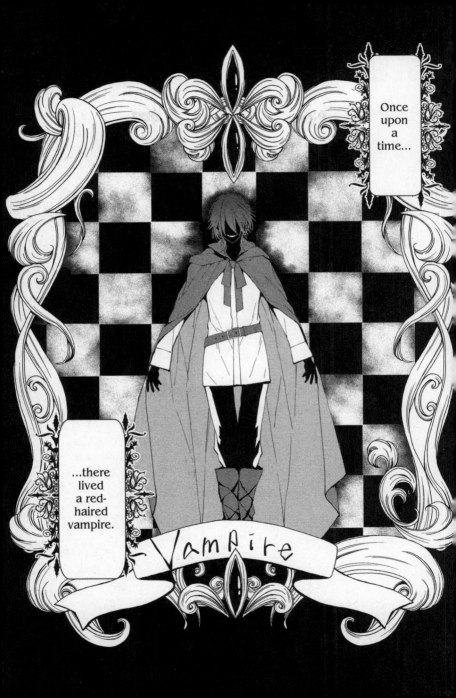

Once upon a time...

...there lived a red-haired vampire.

Vampire

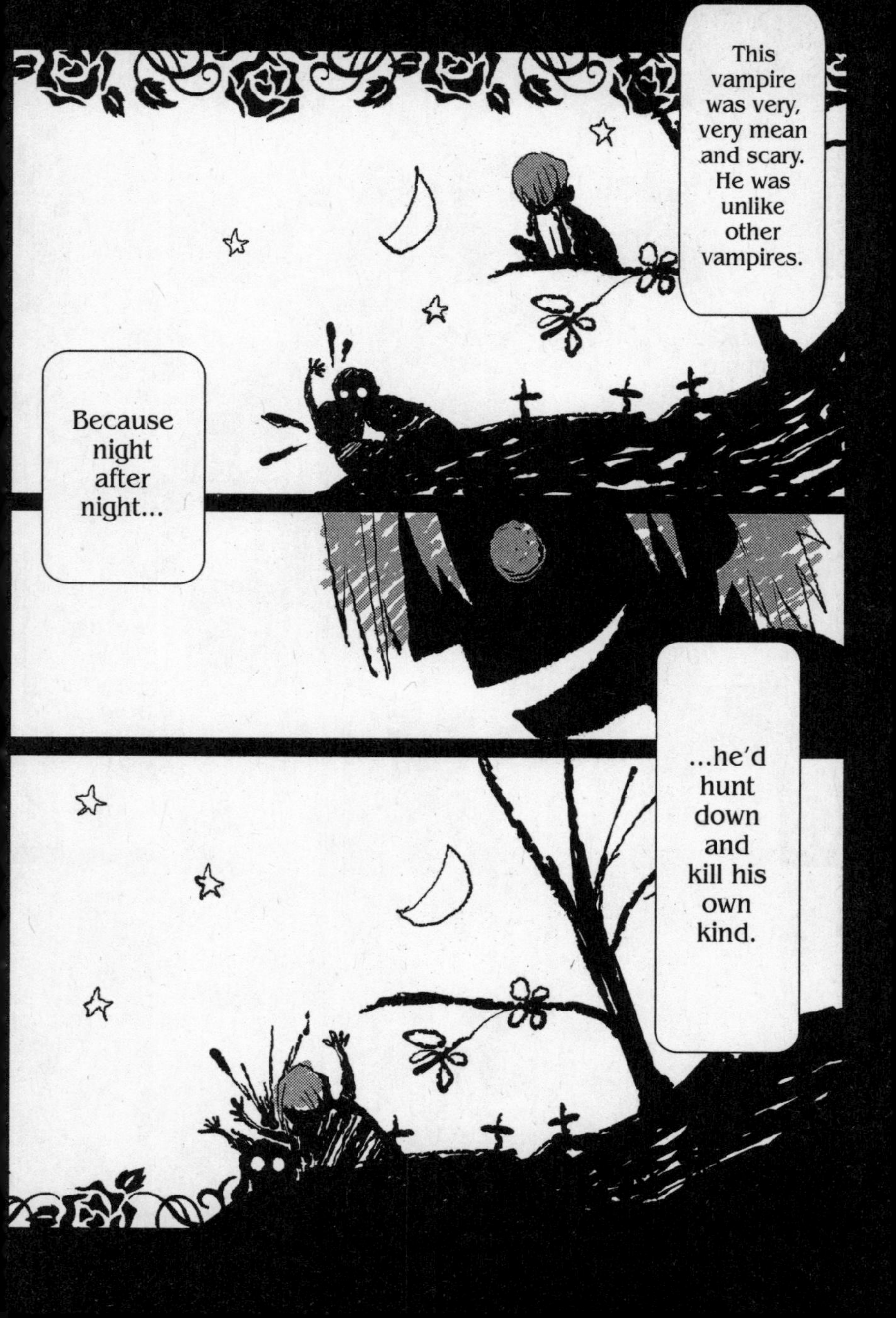
This vampire was very, very mean and scary. He was unlike other vampires.
Because night after night...
...he'd hunt down and kill his own kind.

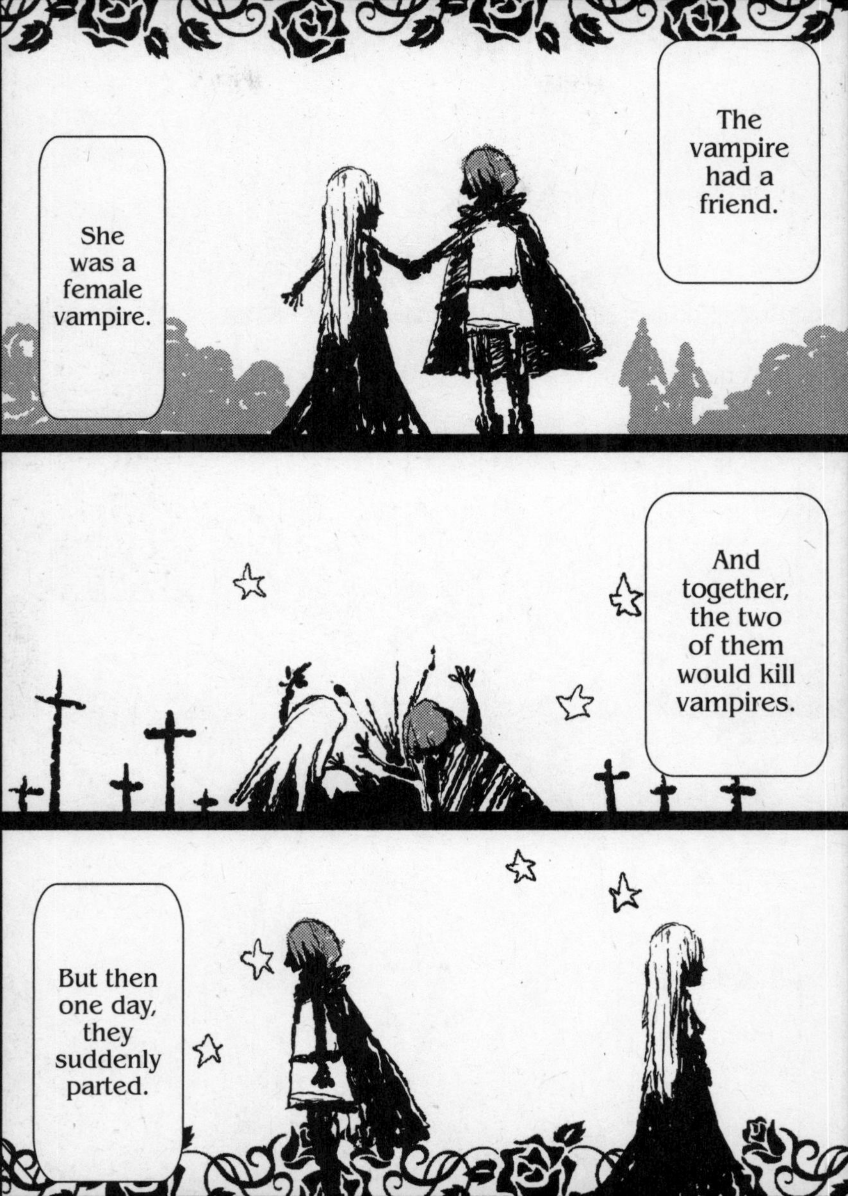
The vampire had a friend.
She was a female vampire.
And together, the two of them would kill vampires.
But then one day, they suddenly parted.

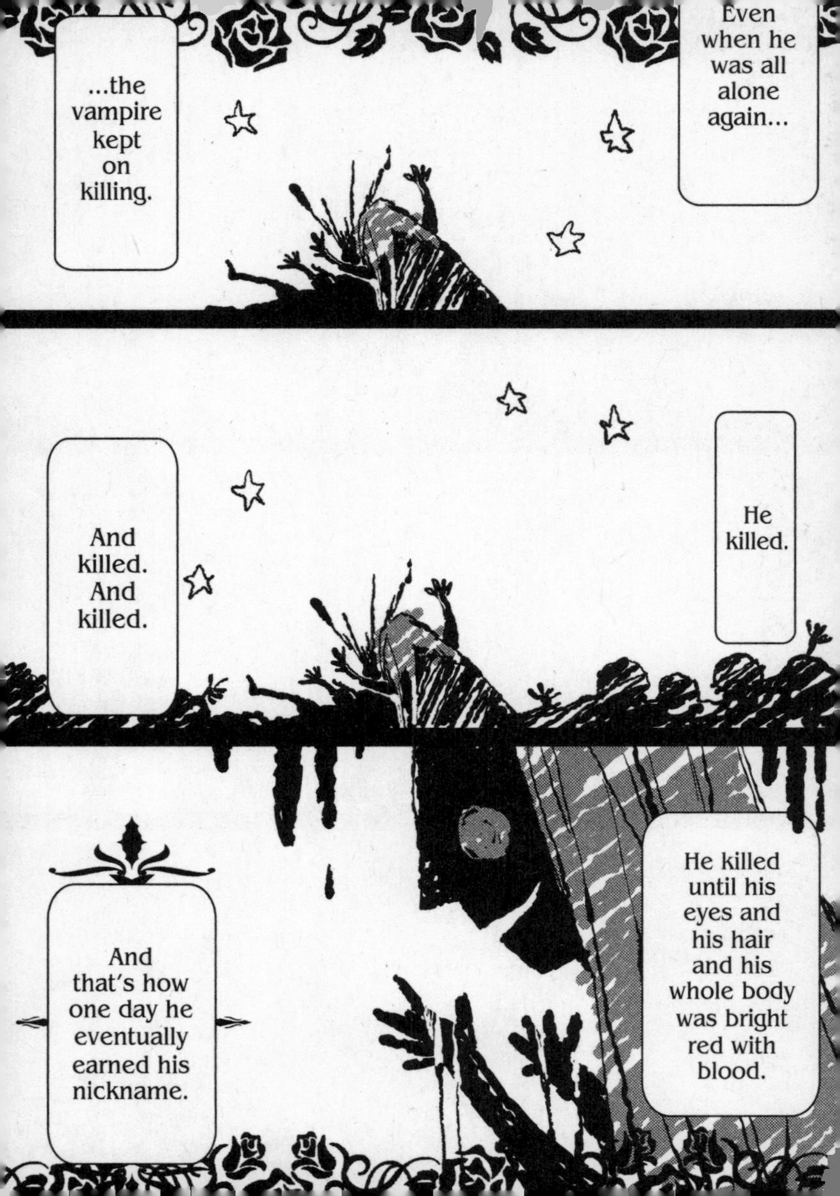
Even when he was all alone again...
...the vampire kept on killing.
He killed.
And killed. And killed.
He killed until his eyes and his hair and his whole body was bright red with blood.
And that's how one day he eventually earned his nickname.

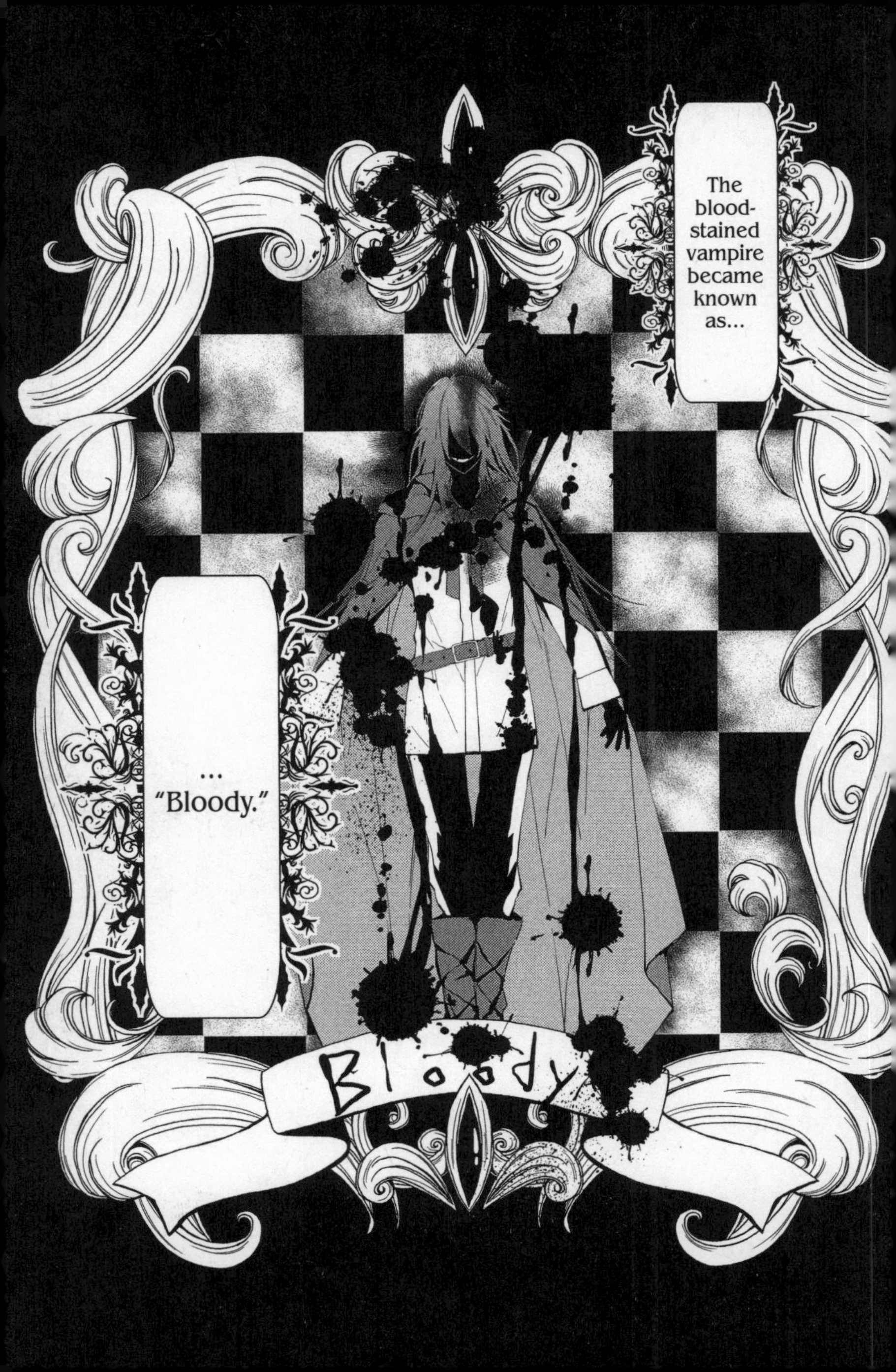
The blood-stained vampire became known as...
... "Bloody."
Bloody

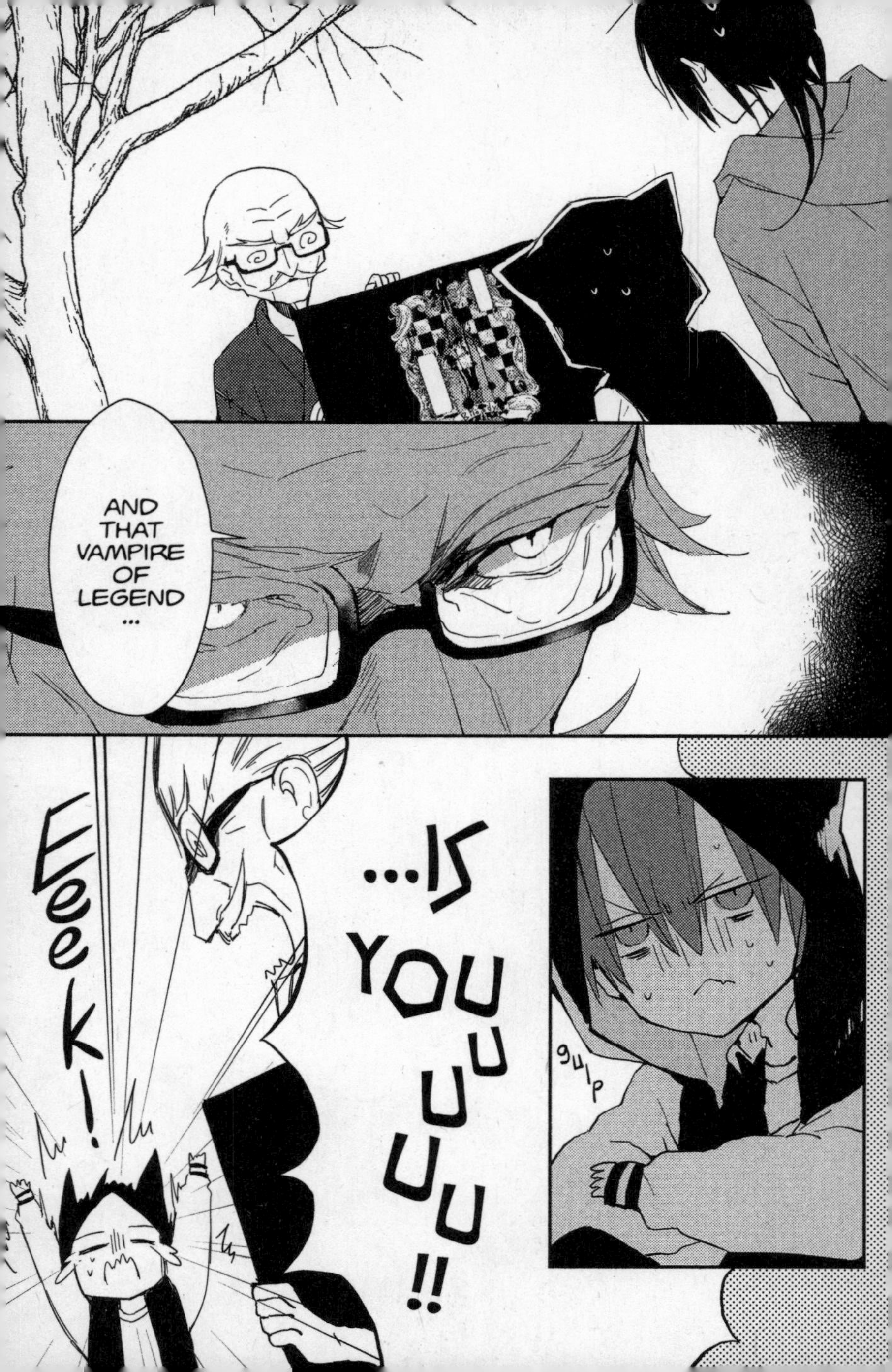
AND THAT VAMPIRE OF LEGEND ...
gulp
...IS YOUUUUU!!
Eeek!

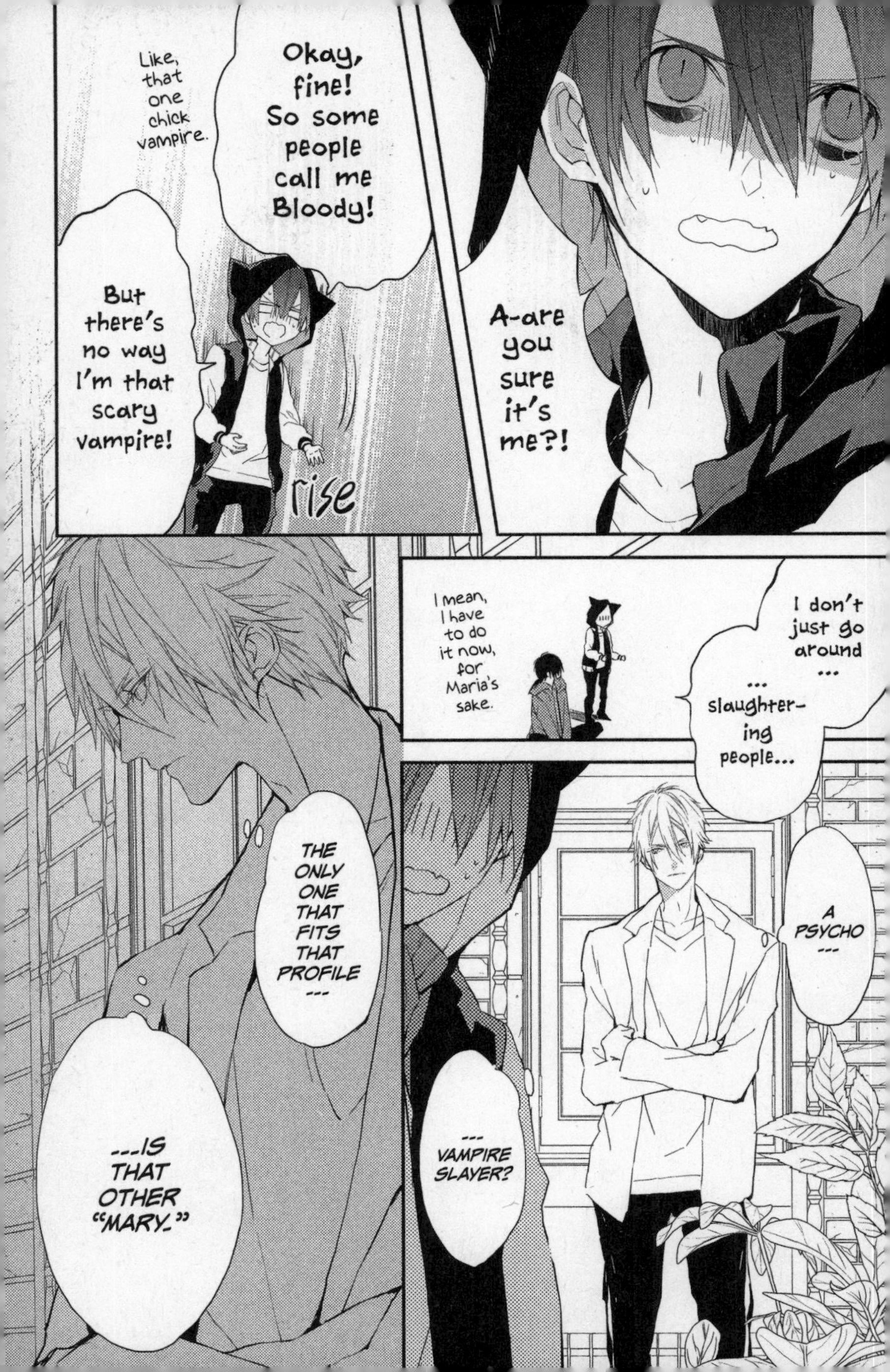
A-are you sure it's me?!
Okay, fine! So some people call me Bloody!
Like, that one chick vampire.
But there's no way I'm that scary vampire!
rise
I don't just go around ...
... slaughtering people...
I mean, I have to do it now, for Maria's sake.
A PSYCHO ---
--- VAMPIRE SLAYER?
THE ONLY ONE THAT FITS THAT PROFILE ---
---IS THAT OTHER "MARY."

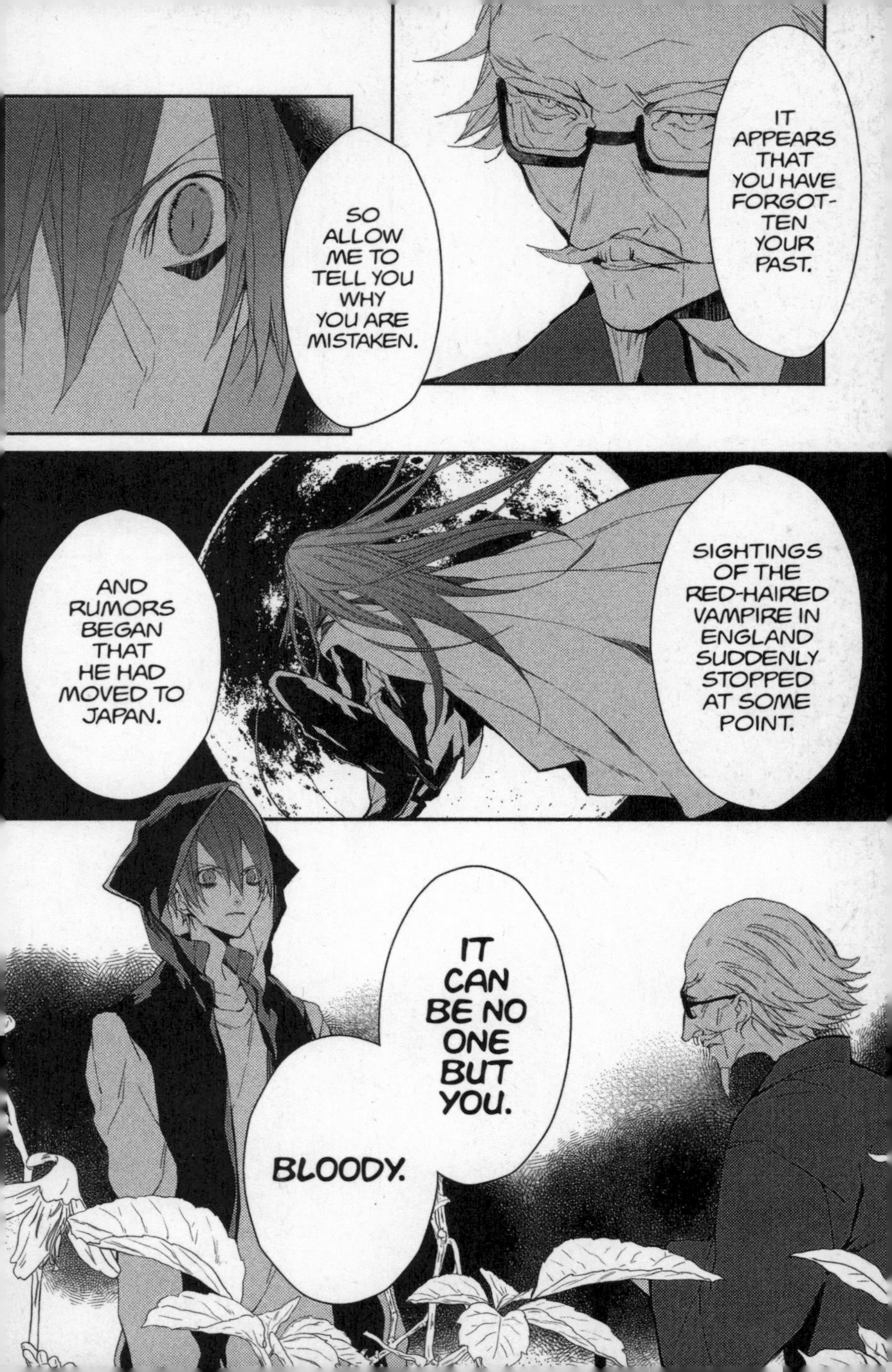
IT APPEARS THAT YOU HAVE FORGOT-TEN YOUR PAST.
SO ALLOW ME TO TELL YOU WHY YOU ARE MISTAKEN.
SIGHTINGS OF THE RED-HAIRED VAMPIRE IN ENGLAND SUDDENLY STOPPED AT SOME POINT.
AND RUMORS BEGAN THAT HE HAD MOVED TO JAPAN.
IT CAN BE NO ONE BUT YOU.
BLOODY.

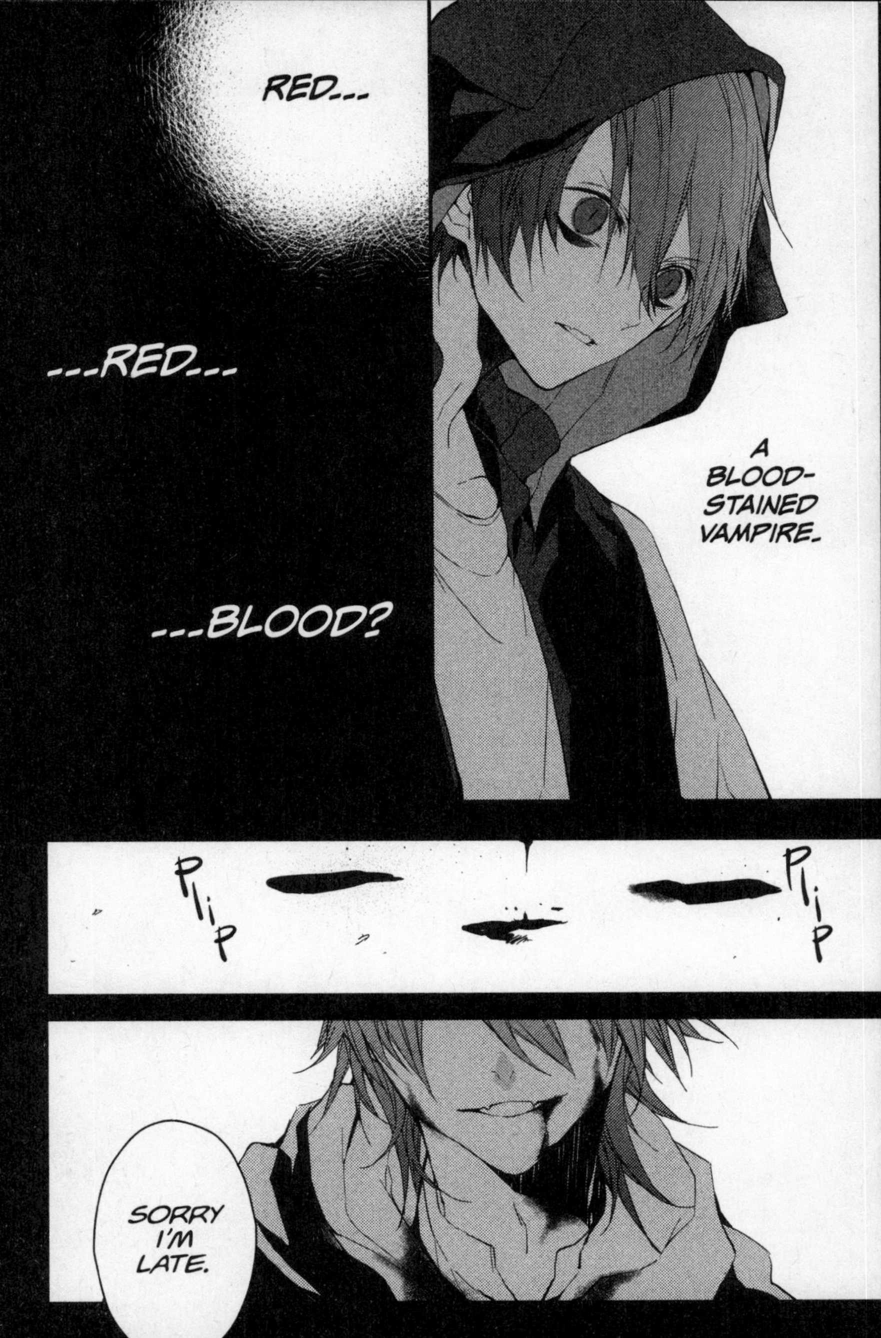
A BLOOD-STAINED VAMPIRE...
RED...
...RED...
...BLOOD?
Plip
Plip
SORRY I'M LATE.

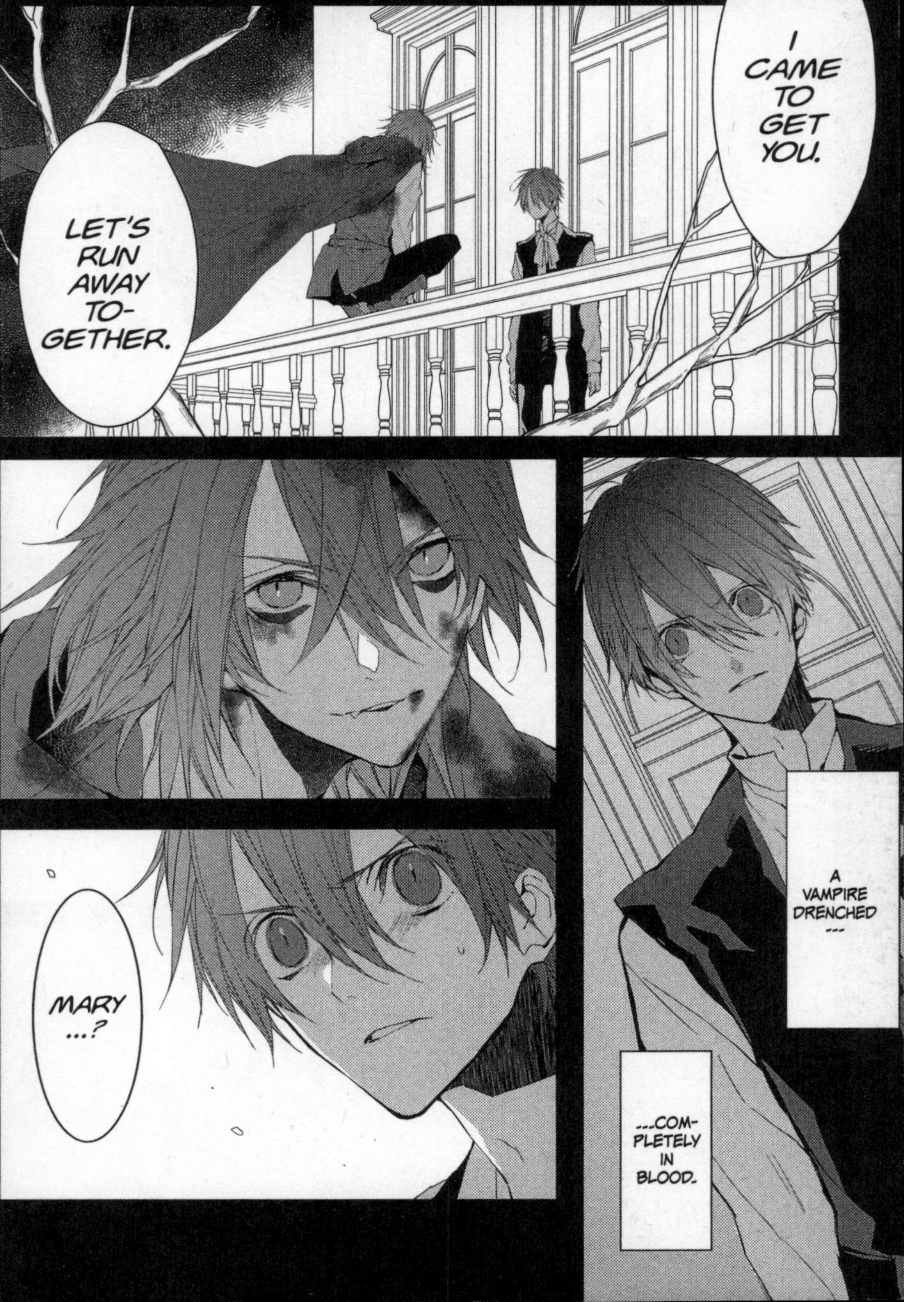
I CAME TO GET YOU.
LET'S RUN AWAY TO-GETHER.
A VAMPIRE DRENCHED---
---COM-PLETELY IN BLOOD.
MARY ...?

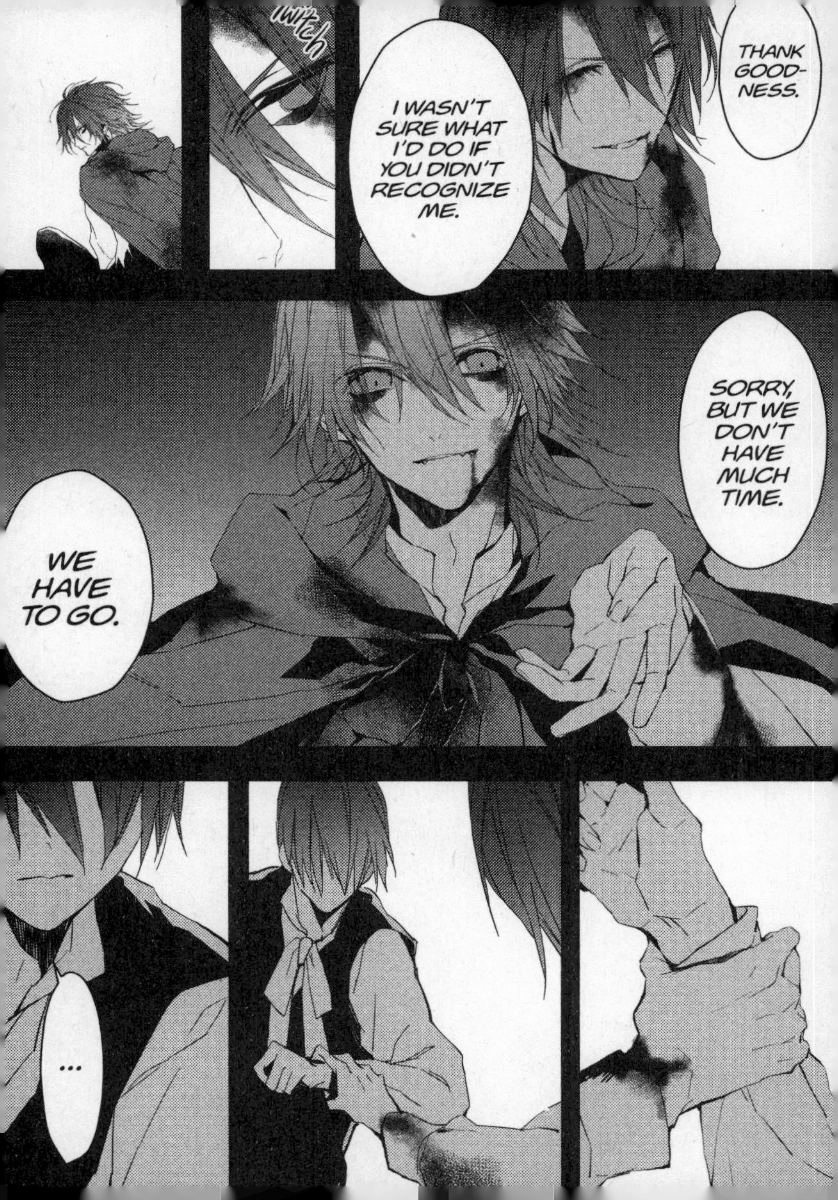
THANK GOODNESS.
I WASN'T SURE WHAT I'D DO IF YOU DIDN'T RECOGNIZE ME.
twitch
SORRY, BUT WE DON'T HAVE MUCH TIME.
WE HAVE TO GO.
...

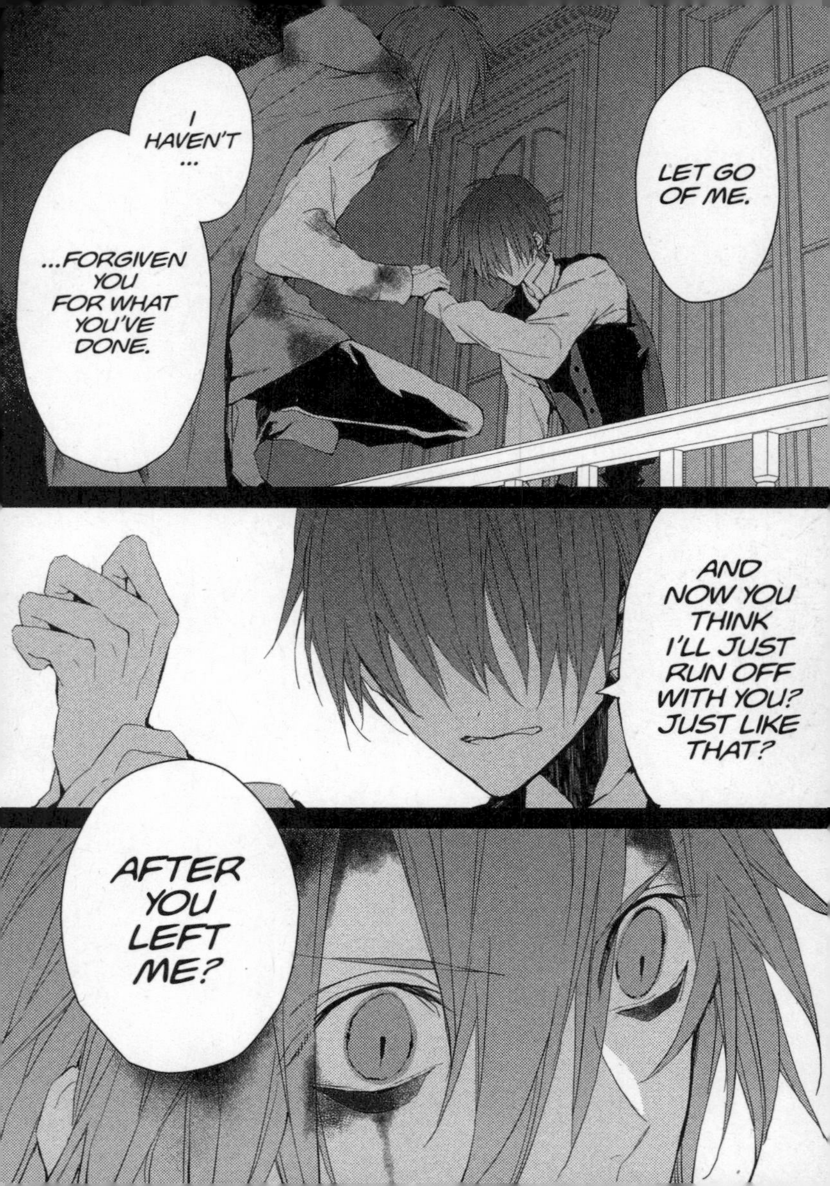
LET GO OF ME.
I HAVEN'T ...
...FORGIVEN YOU FOR WHAT YOU'VE DONE.
AND NOW YOU THINK I'LL JUST RUN OFF WITH YOU? JUST LIKE THAT?
AFTER YOU LEFT ME?

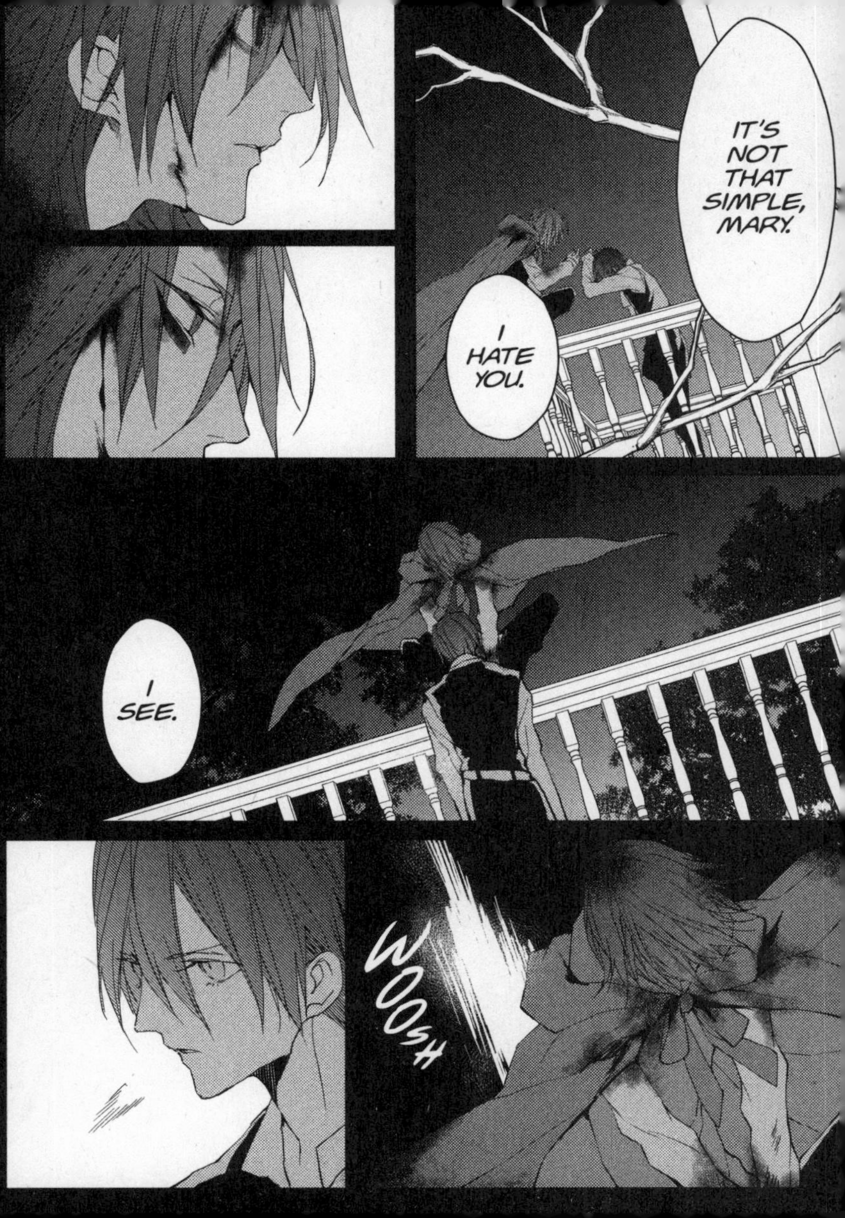
IT'S NOT THAT SIMPLE, MARY.
I HATE YOU.
I SEE.
WOOSH

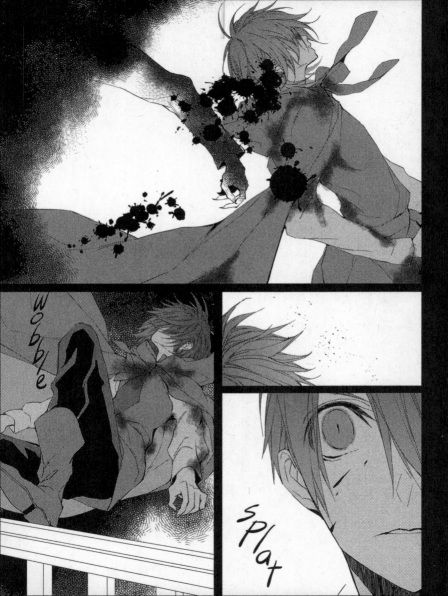

Wobble

Splat

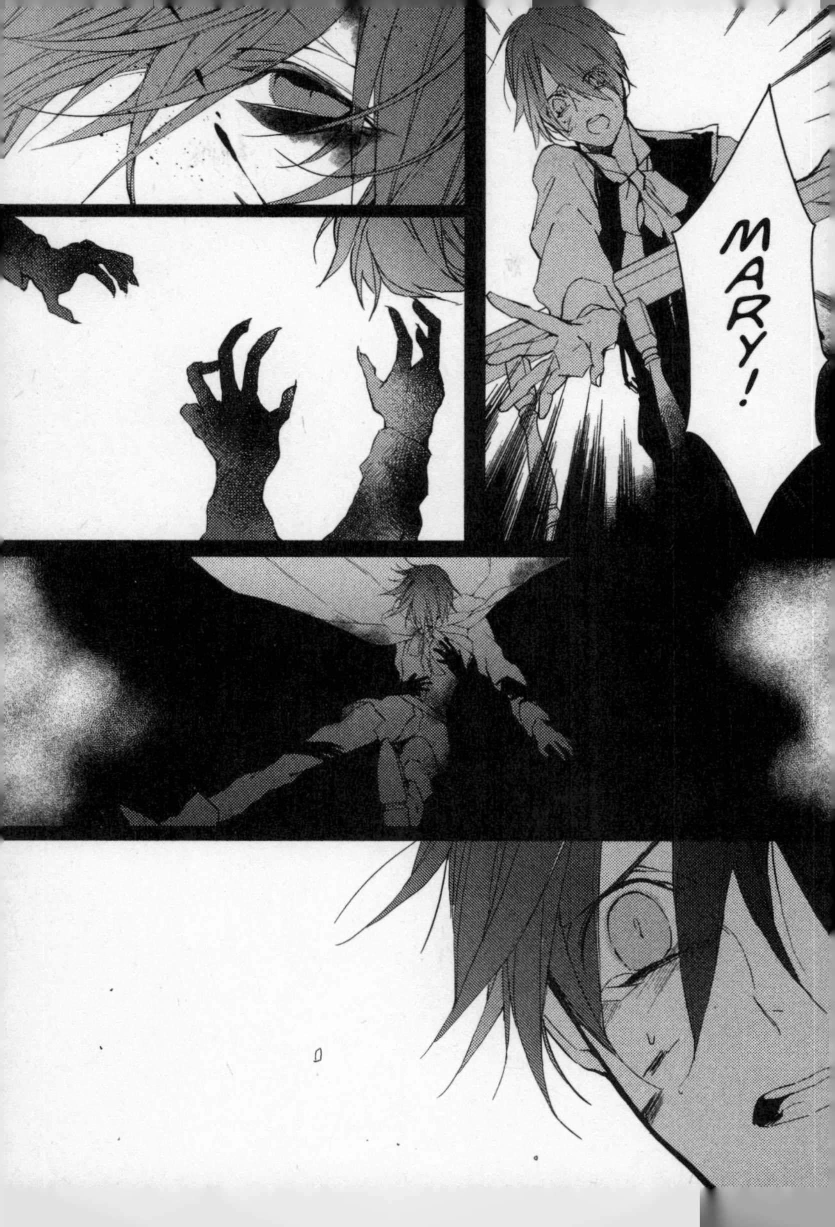
MARY!

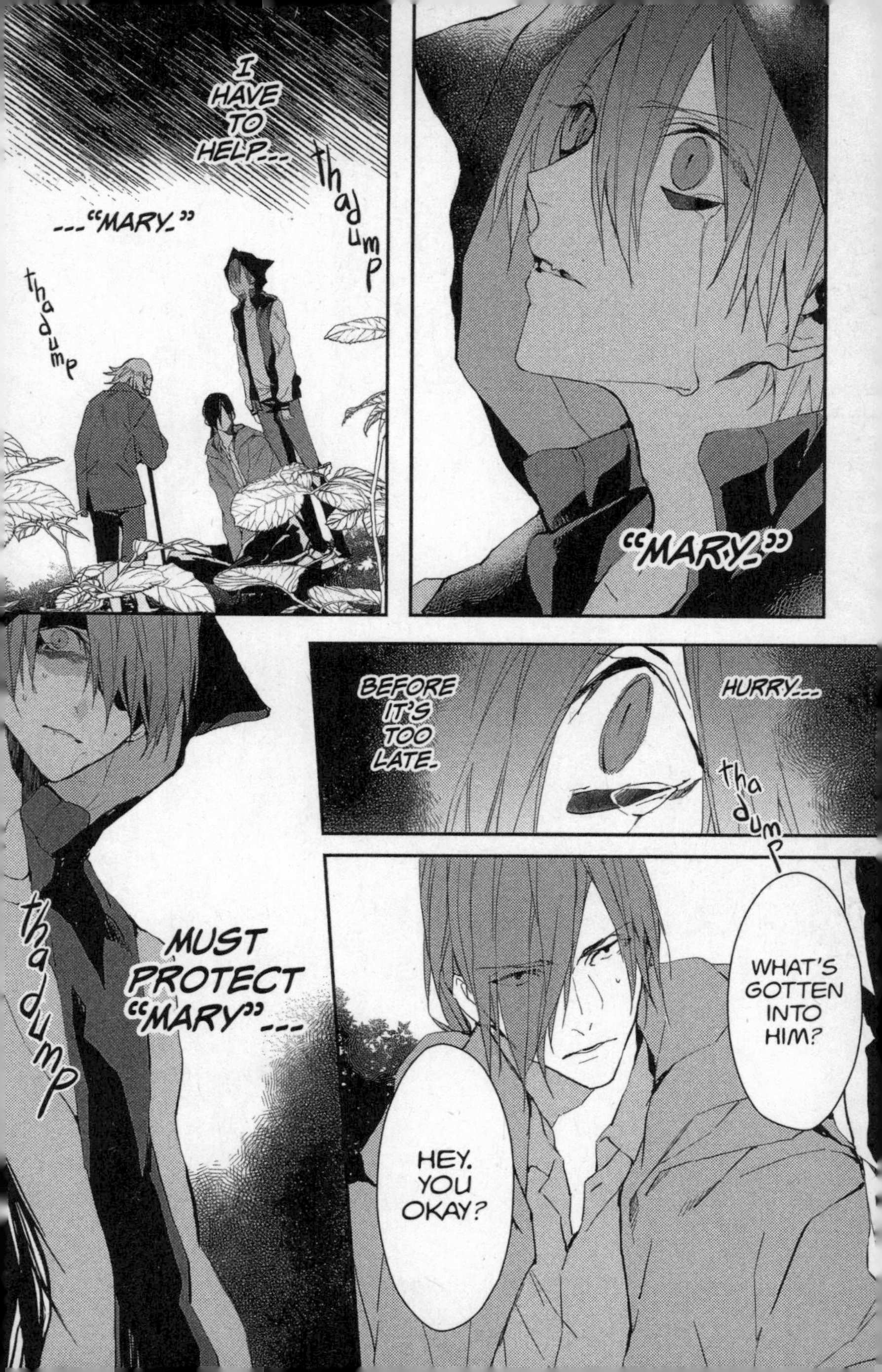
"MARY."
I HAVE TO HELP...
thadump
..."MARY."
thadump
HURRY...
BEFORE IT'S TOO LATE.
thadump
WHAT'S GOTTEN INTO HIM?
HEY. YOU OKAY?
MUST PROTECT "MARY"...
thadump

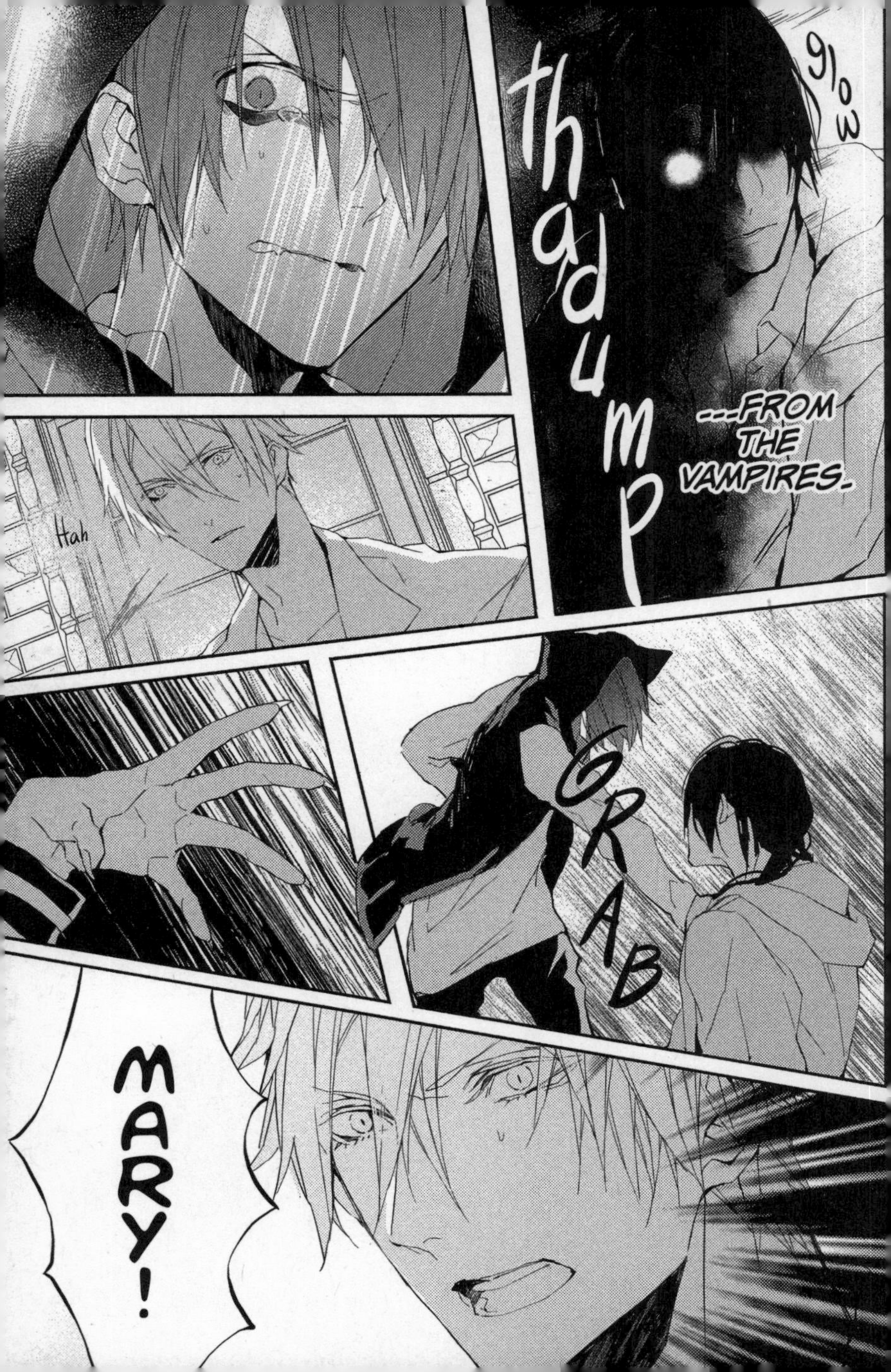
thadump
...FROM THE VAMPIRES.
Hah
GRAB
MARY!

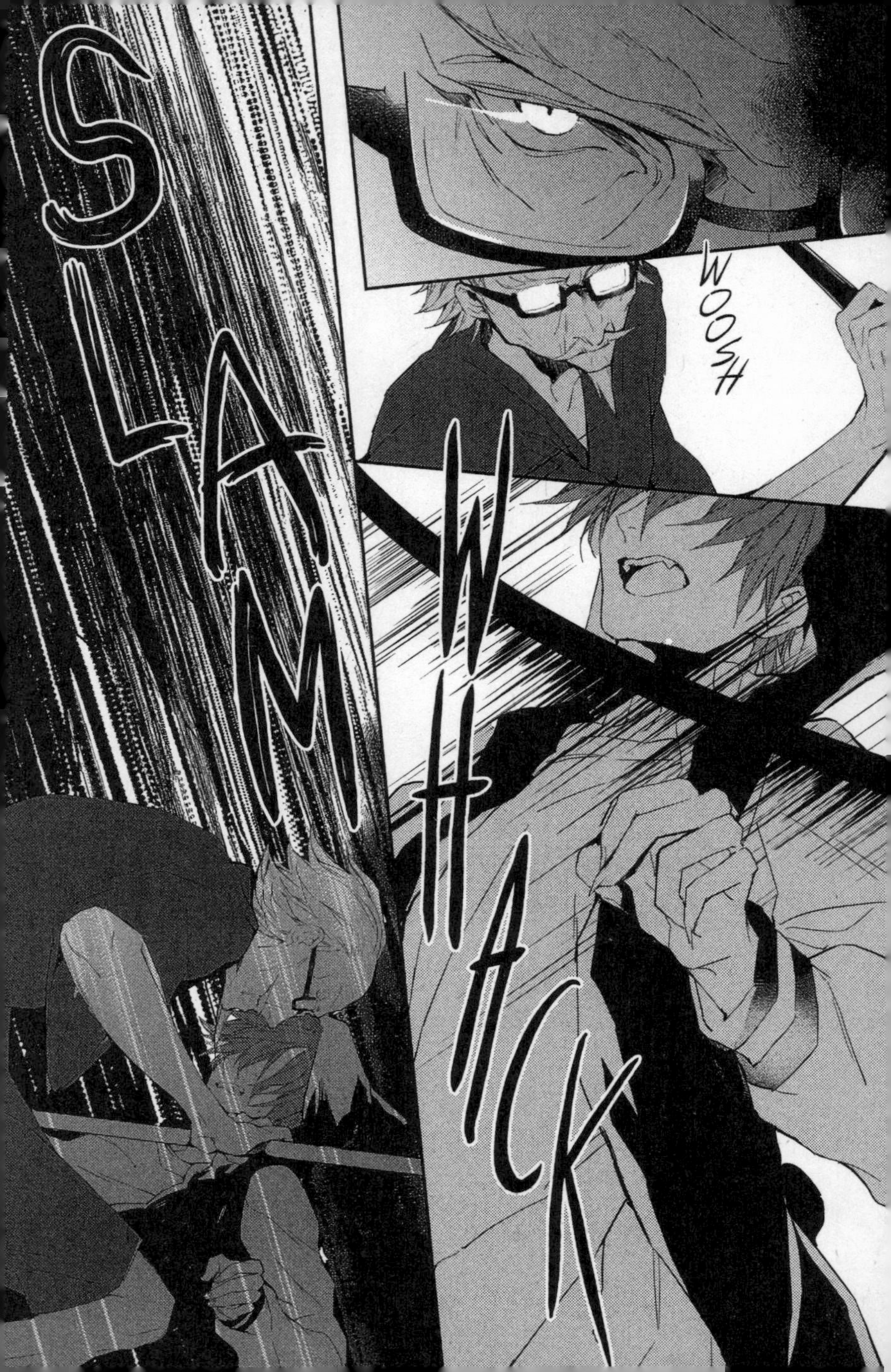
WOOSH
WHACK
SLAM

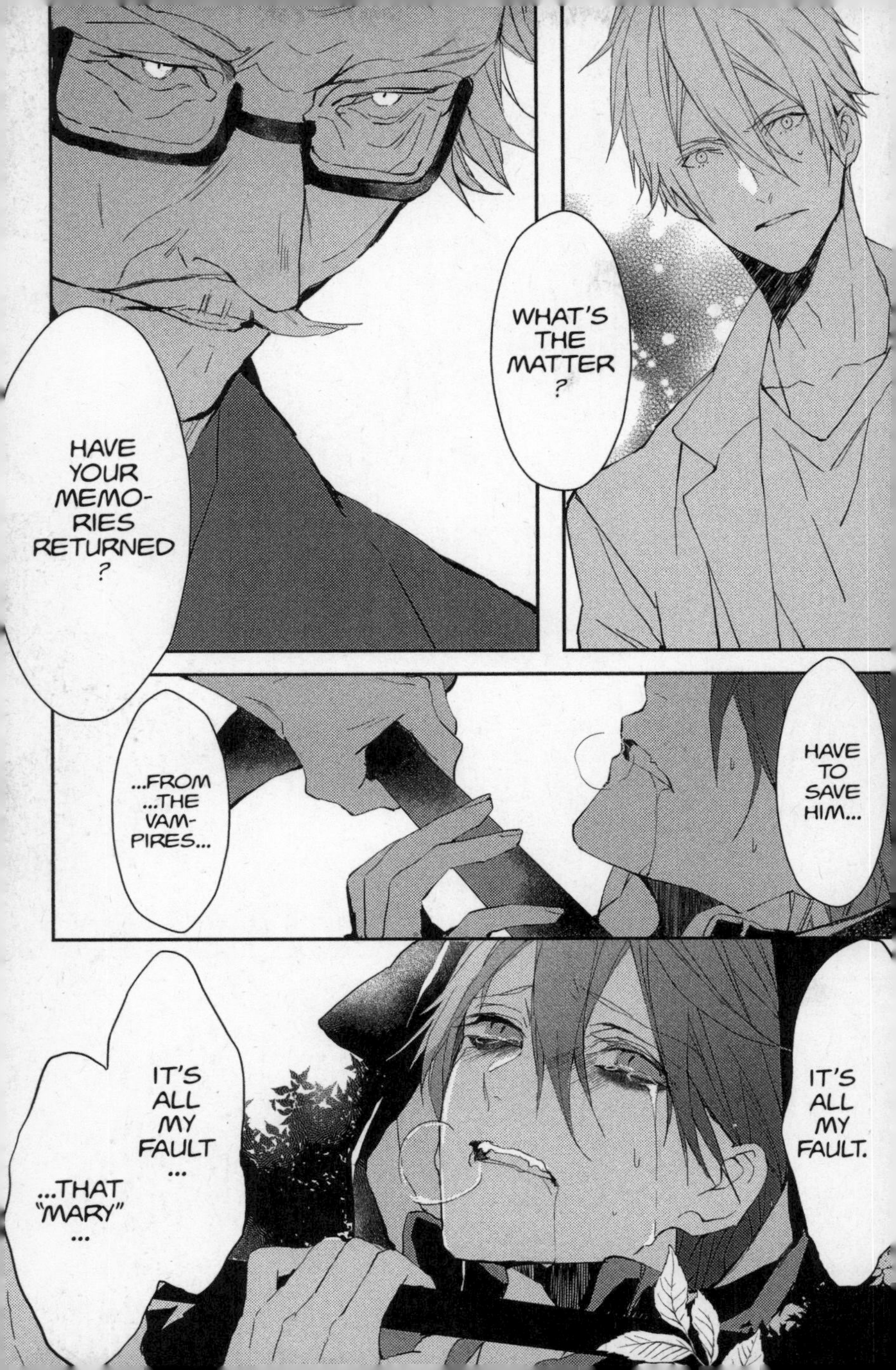
WHAT'S THE MATTER?
HAVE YOUR MEMORIES RETURNED?
HAVE TO SAVE HIM...
...FROM ...THE VAMPIRES...
IT'S ALL MY FAULT.
IT'S ALL MY FAULT...
...THAT "MARY"...

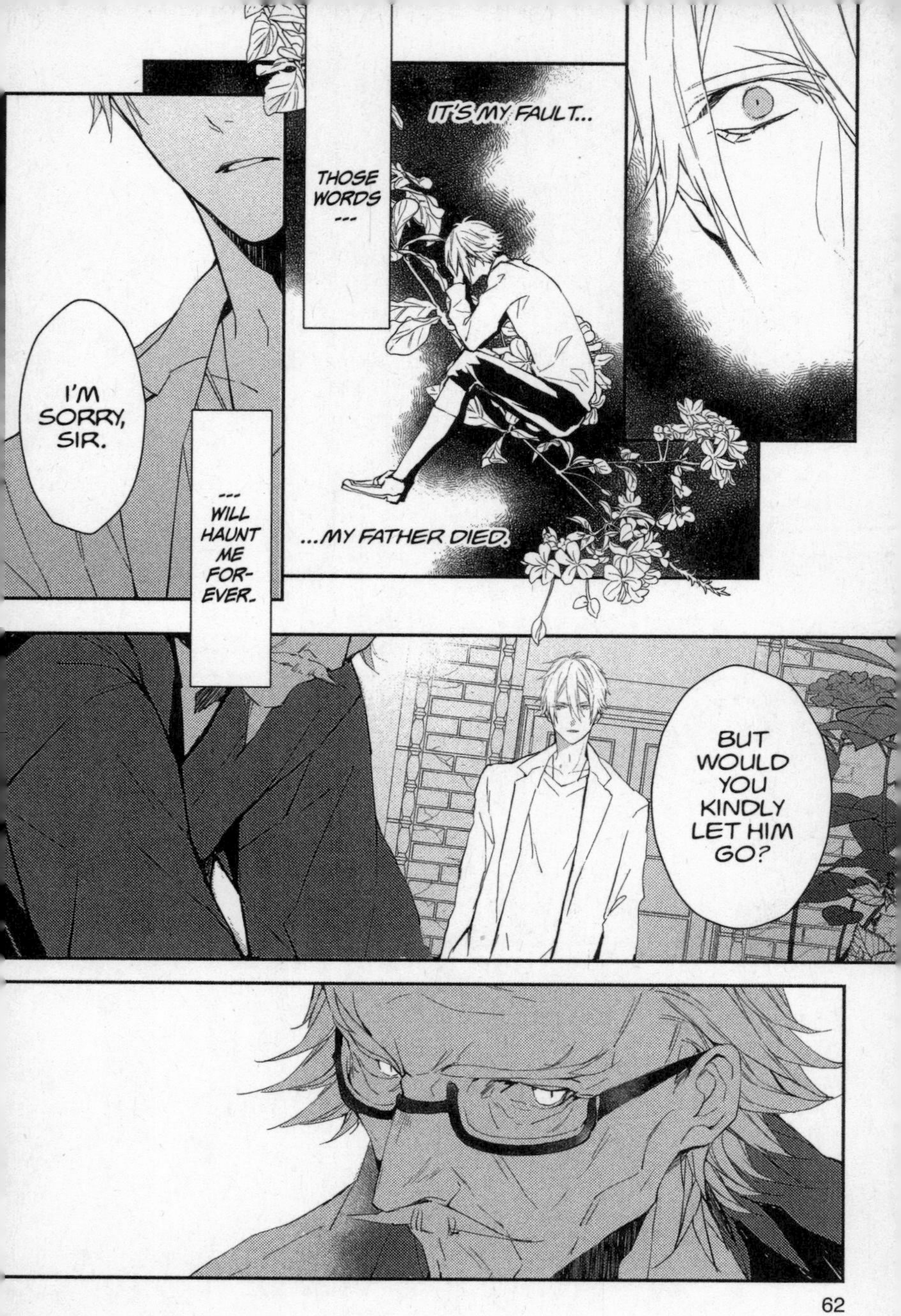
IT'S MY FAULT...
...MY FATHER DIED.
THOSE WORDS ---
--- WILL HAUNT ME FOR-EVER.
I'M SORRY, SIR.
BUT WOULD YOU KINDLY LET HIM GO?

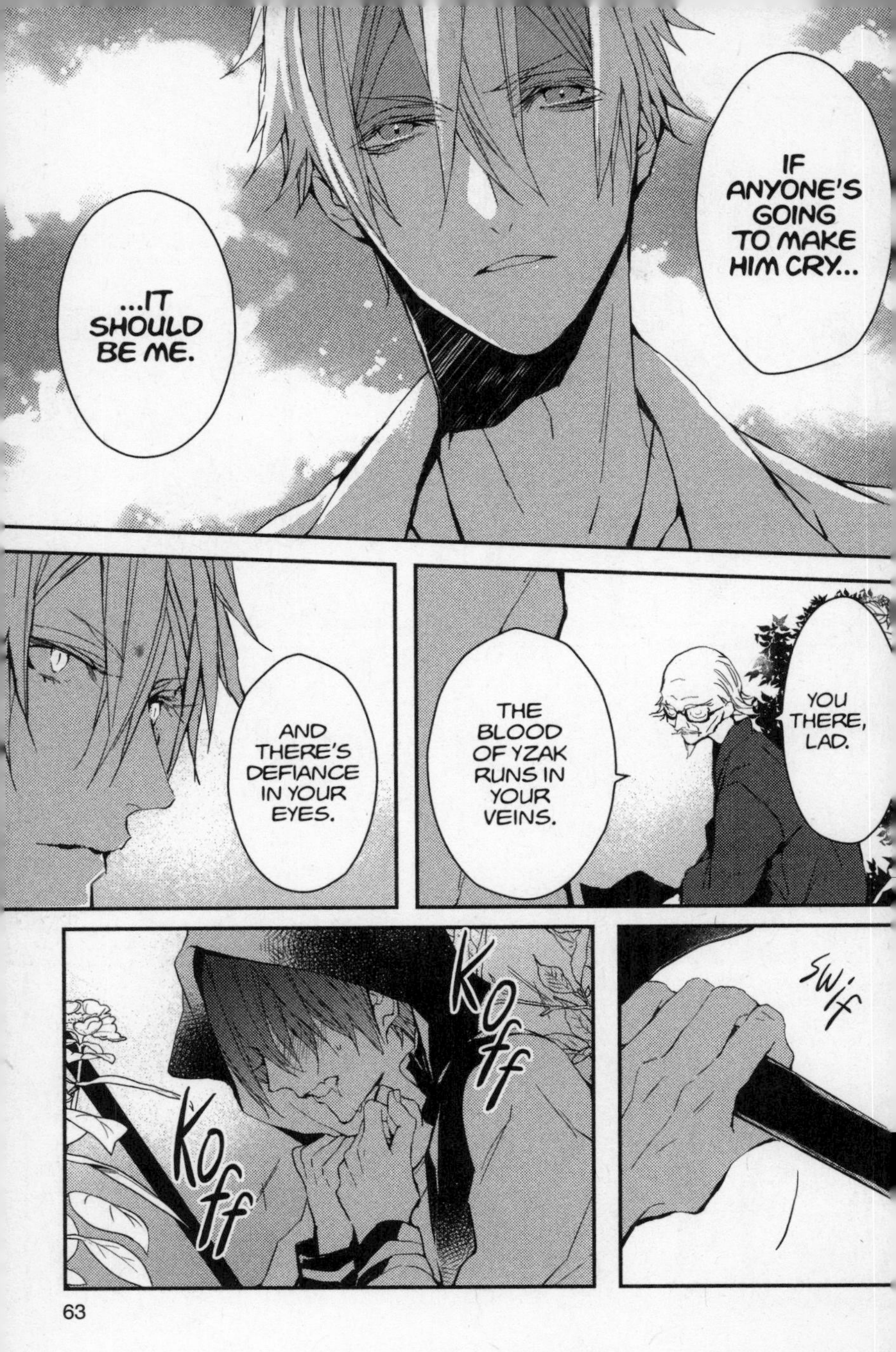
IF ANYONE'S GOING TO MAKE HIM CRY...
...IT SHOULD BE ME.
YOU THERE, LAD.
THE BLOOD OF YZAK RUNS IN YOUR VEINS.
AND THERE'S DEFIANCE IN YOUR EYES.
SWIF
KOFF
KOFF

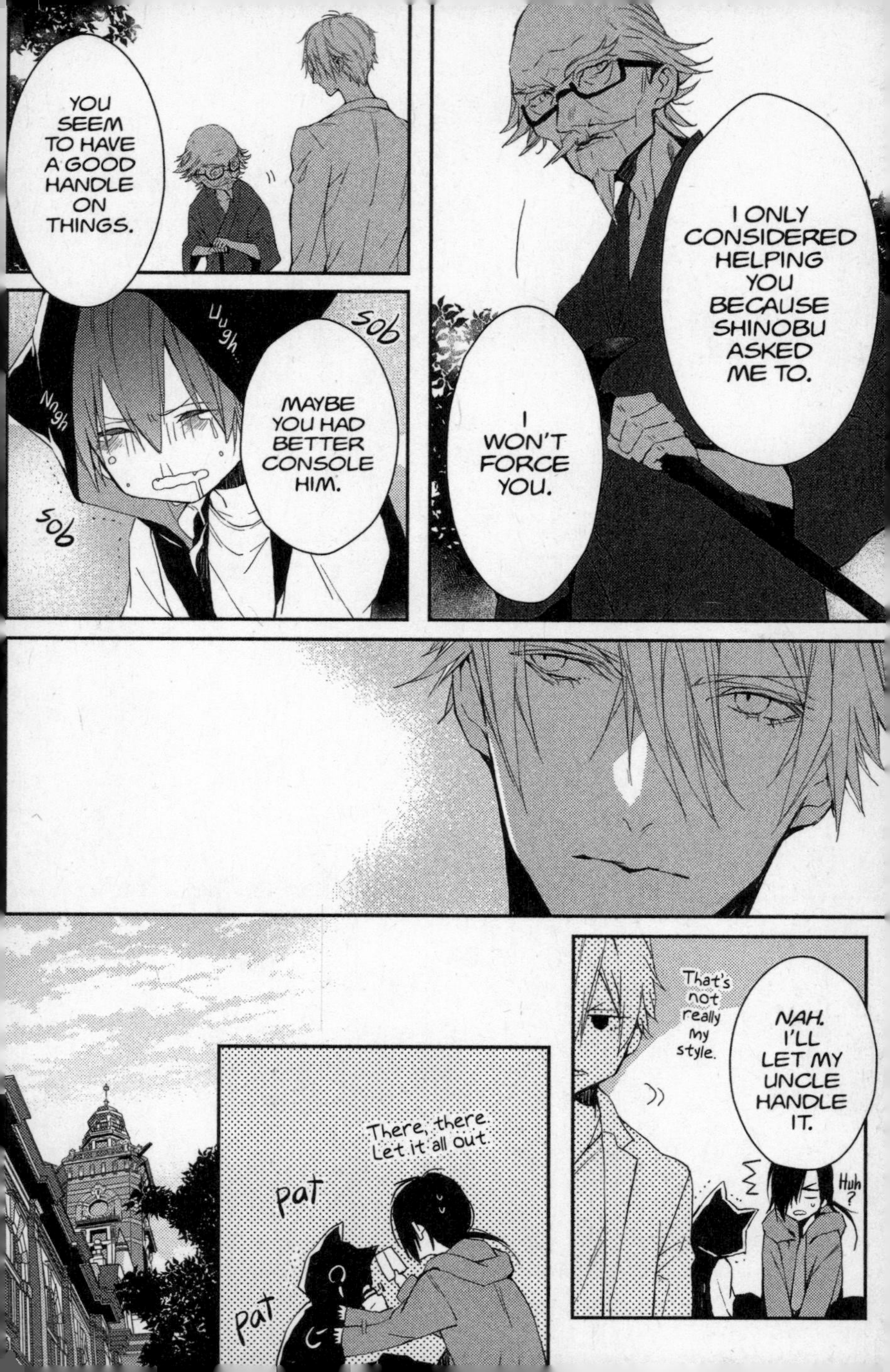
I ONLY CONSIDERED HELPING YOU BECAUSE SHINOBU ASKED ME TO.
I WON'T FORCE YOU.
YOU SEEM TO HAVE A GOOD HANDLE ON THINGS.
sob
Uugh...
MAYBE YOU HAD BETTER CONSOLE HIM.
Nngh
sob
NAH. I'LL LET MY UNCLE HANDLE IT.
That's not really my style.
Huh?
There, there Let it all out.
pat
pat

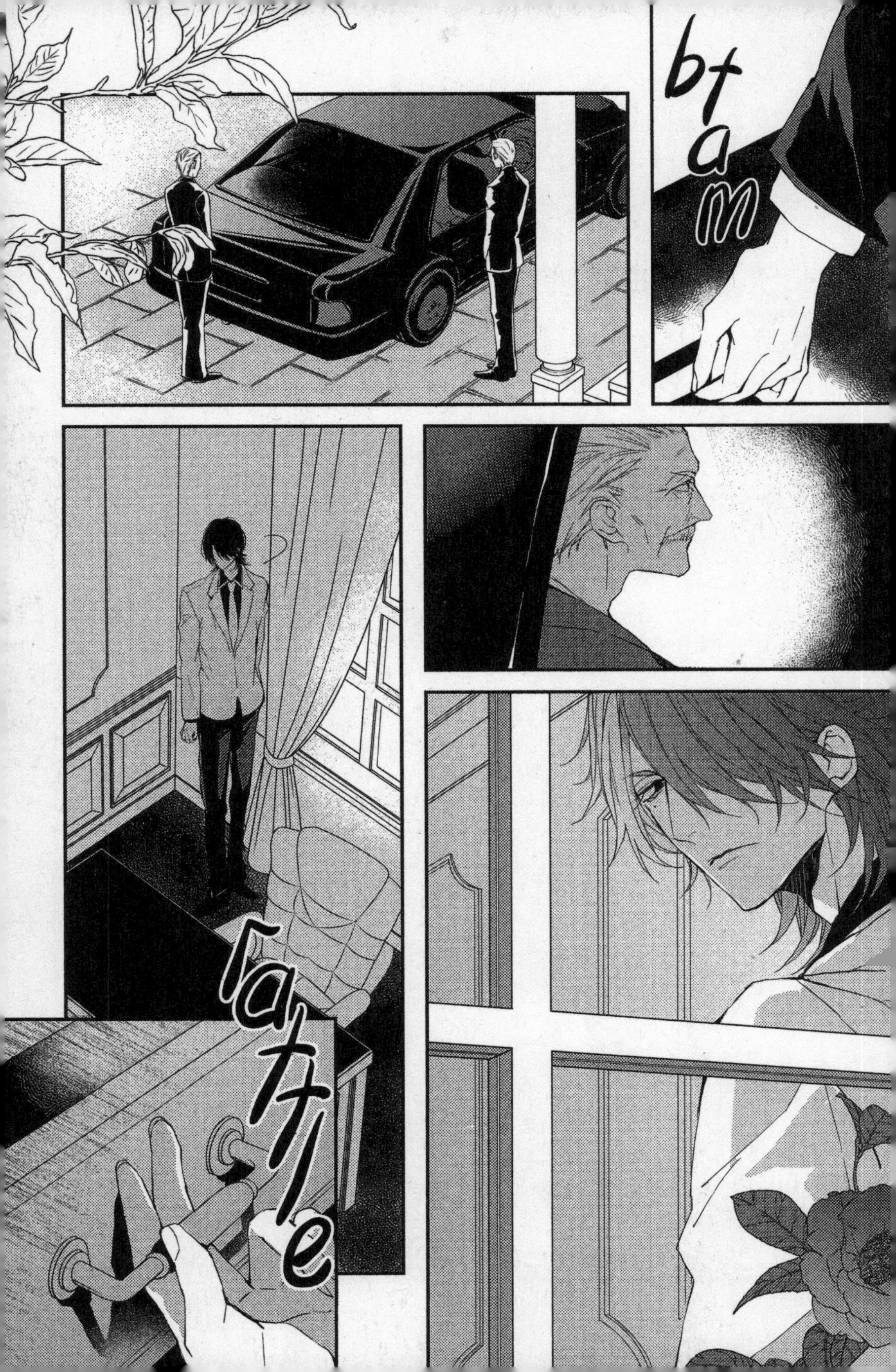
btam
rattle

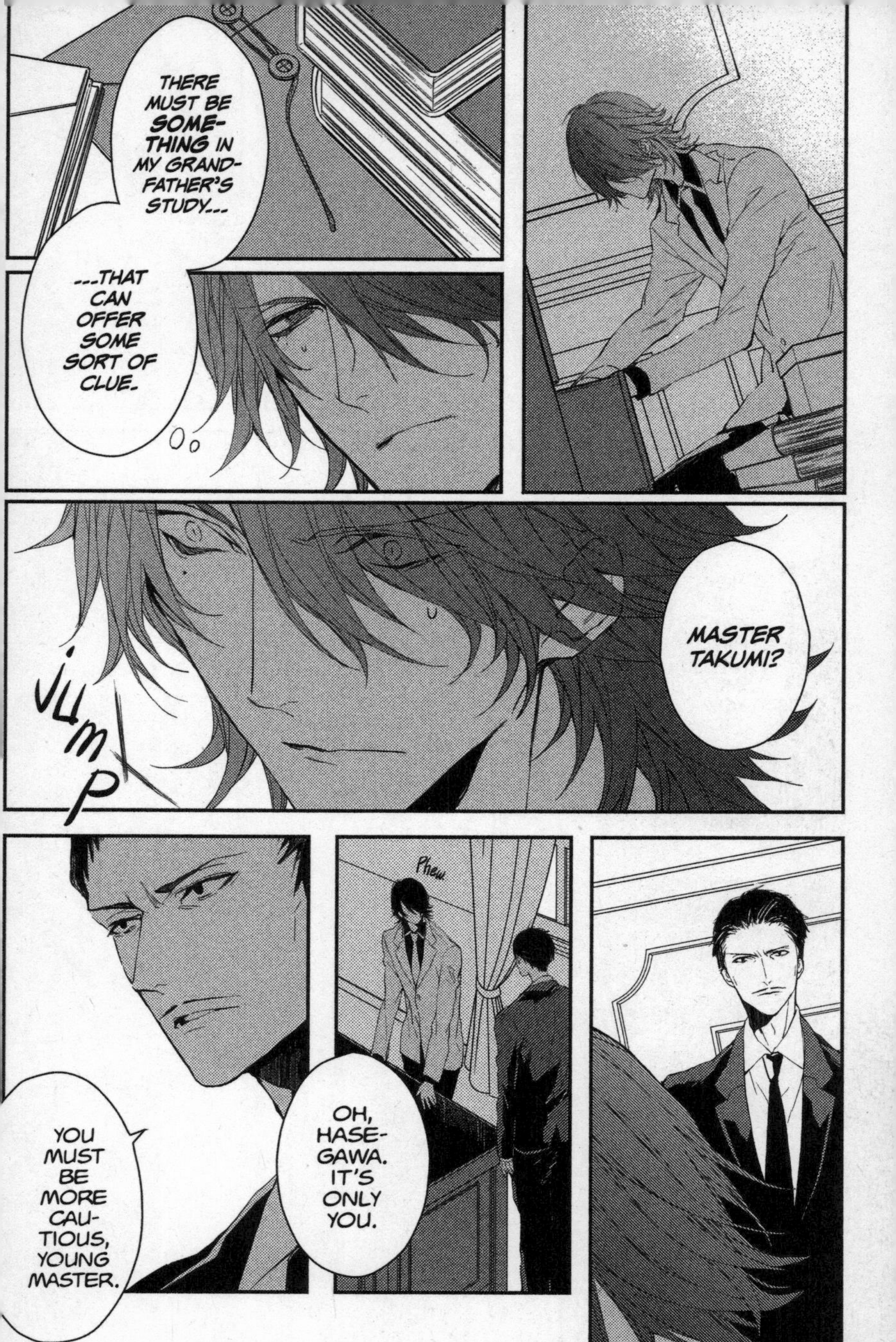
THERE MUST BE SOMETHING IN MY GRANDFATHER'S STUDY...
...THAT CAN OFFER SOME SORT OF CLUE.
MASTER TAKUMI?
JUMP
Phew
OH, HASEGAWA. IT'S ONLY YOU.
YOU MUST BE MORE CAUTIOUS, YOUNG MASTER.

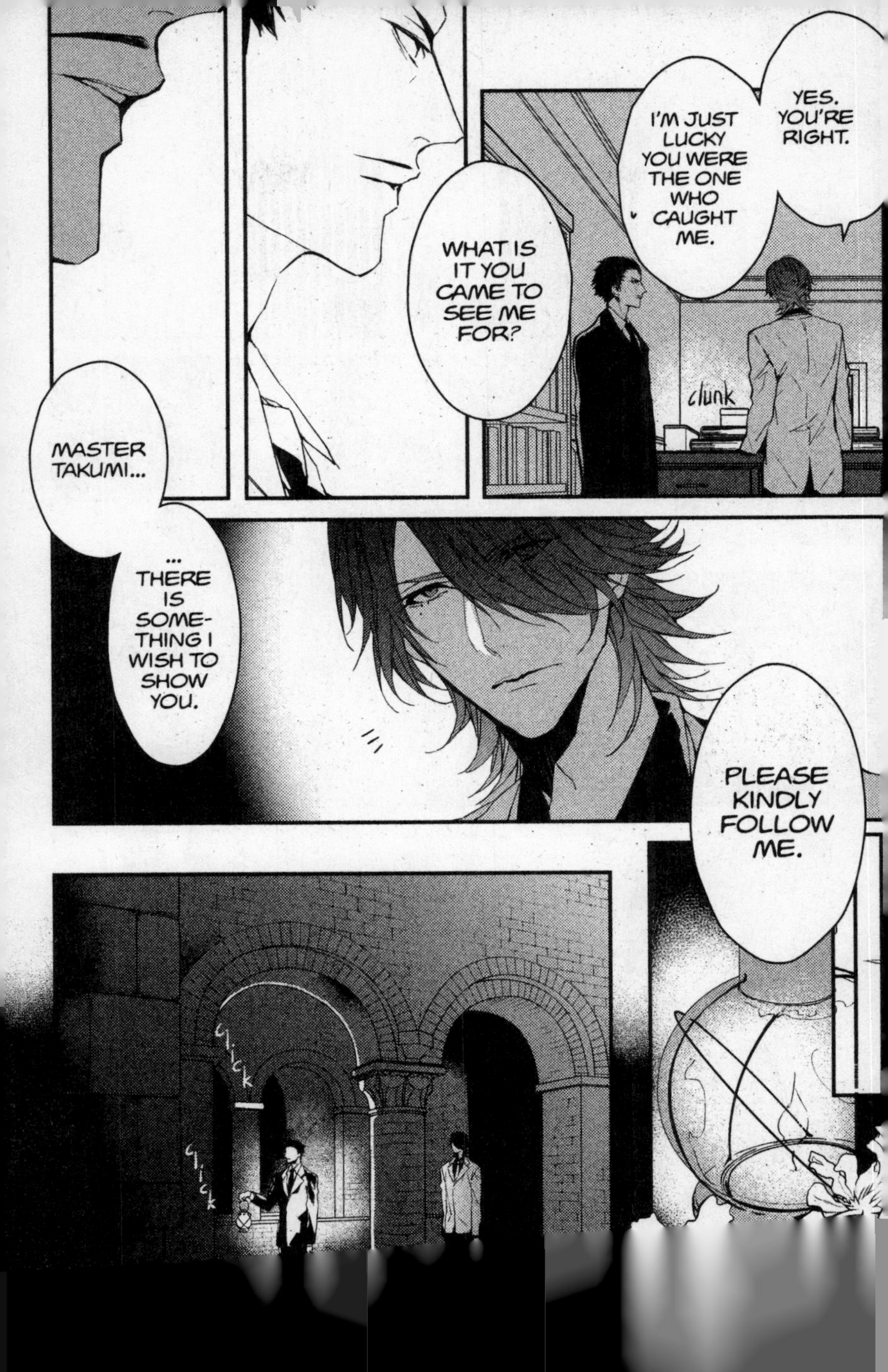
YES. YOU'RE RIGHT.
I'M JUST LUCKY YOU WERE THE ONE WHO CAUGHT ME.
clunk
WHAT IS IT YOU CAME TO SEE ME FOR?
MASTER TAKUMI...
... THERE IS SOME-THING I WISH TO SHOW YOU.
PLEASE KINDLY FOLLOW ME.
click
click

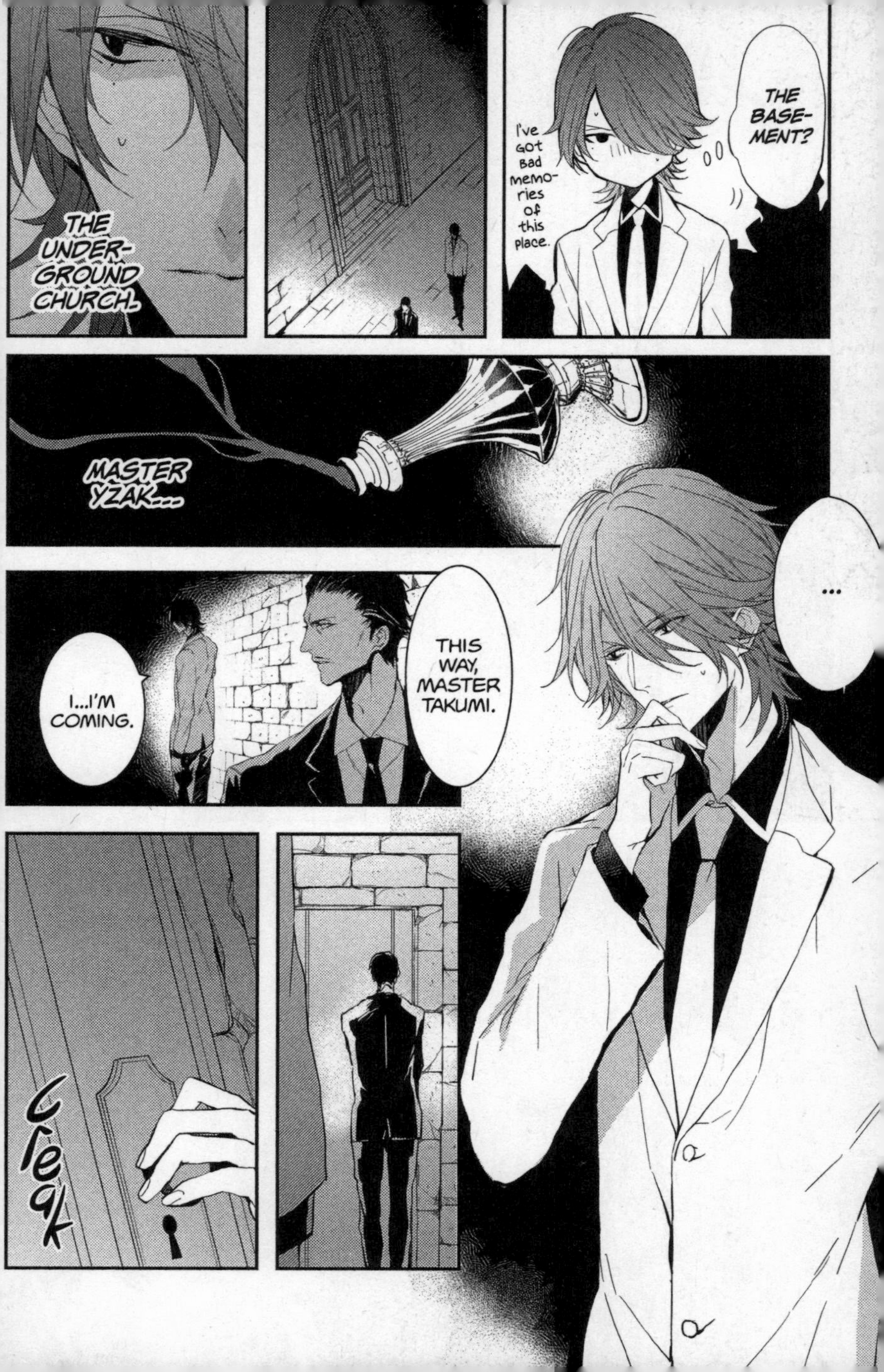
THE BASE-MENT?
I've got bad memo-ries of this place.
THE UNDER-GROUND CHURCH.
...
MASTER YZAK...
THIS WAY, MASTER TAKUMI.
I...I'M COMING.
Creak

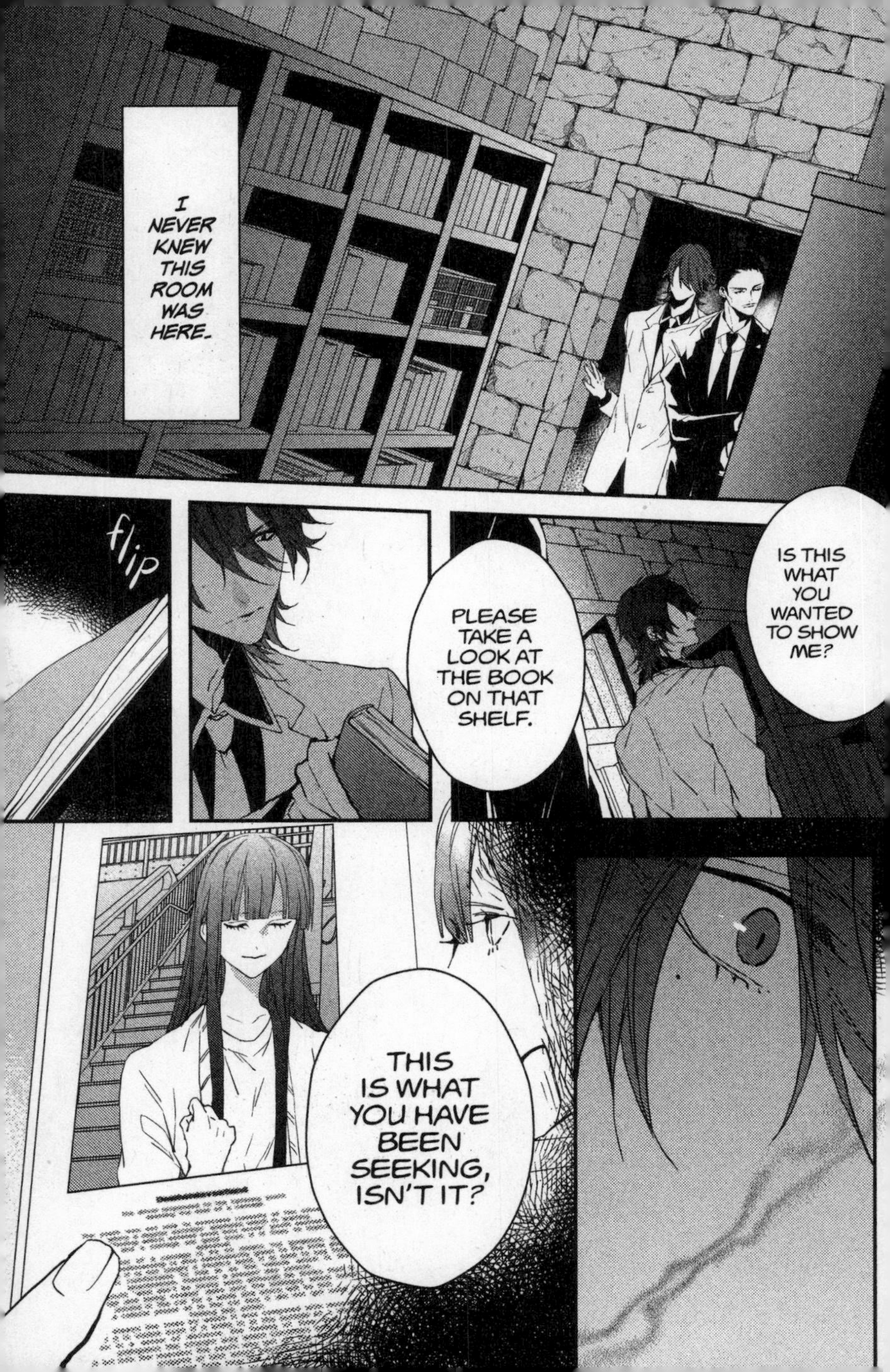
I NEVER KNEW THIS ROOM WAS HERE…
IS THIS WHAT YOU WANTED TO SHOW ME?
PLEASE TAKE A LOOK AT THE BOOK ON THAT SHELF.
flip
THIS IS WHAT YOU HAVE BEEN SEEKING, ISN'T IT?

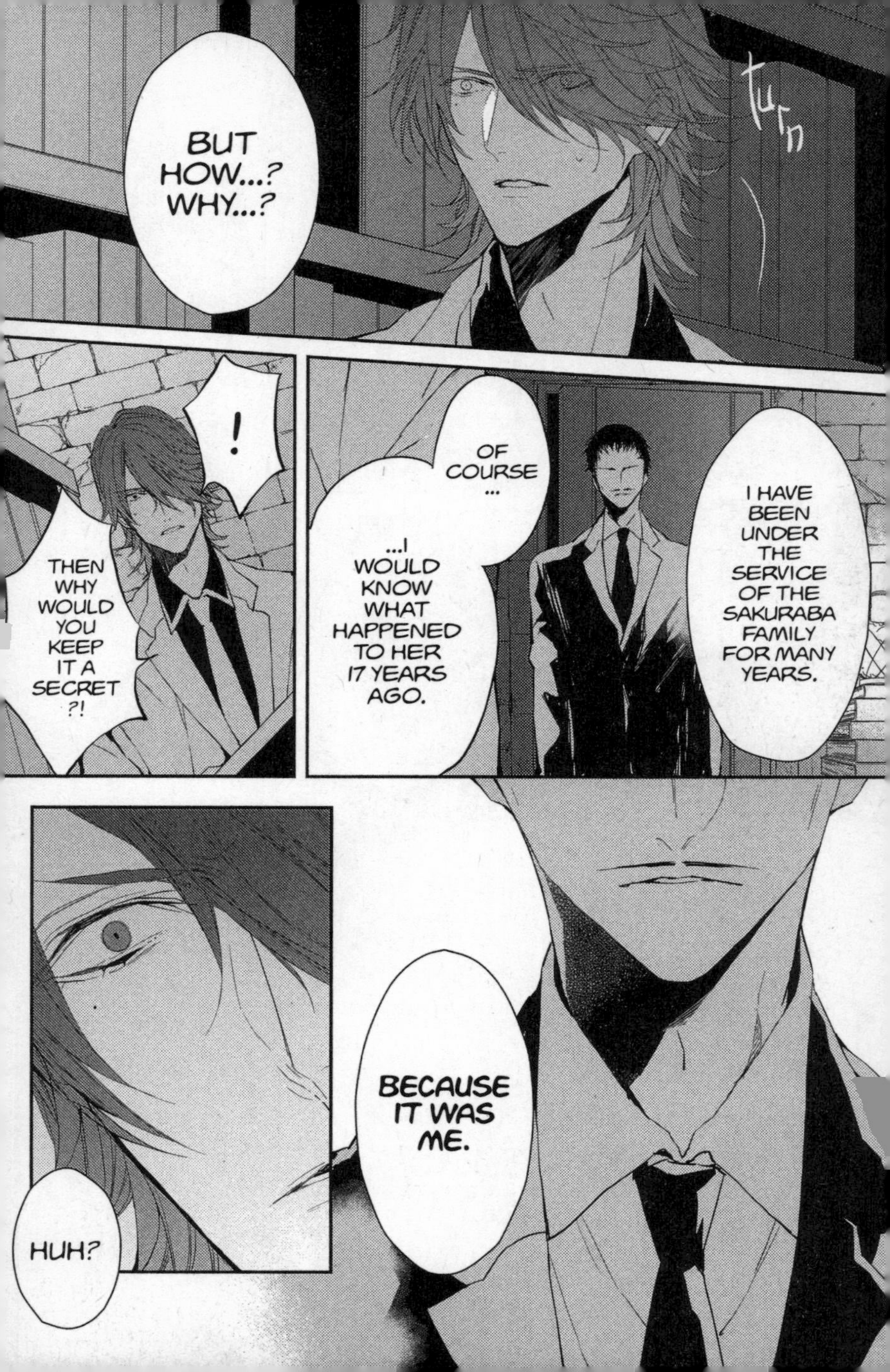
turn
BUT HOW...? WHY...?
I HAVE BEEN UNDER THE SERVICE OF THE SAKURABA FAMILY FOR MANY YEARS.
OF COURSE...
...I WOULD KNOW WHAT HAPPENED TO HER 17 YEARS AGO.
!
THEN WHY WOULD YOU KEEP IT A SECRET?!
BECAUSE IT WAS ME.
HUH?

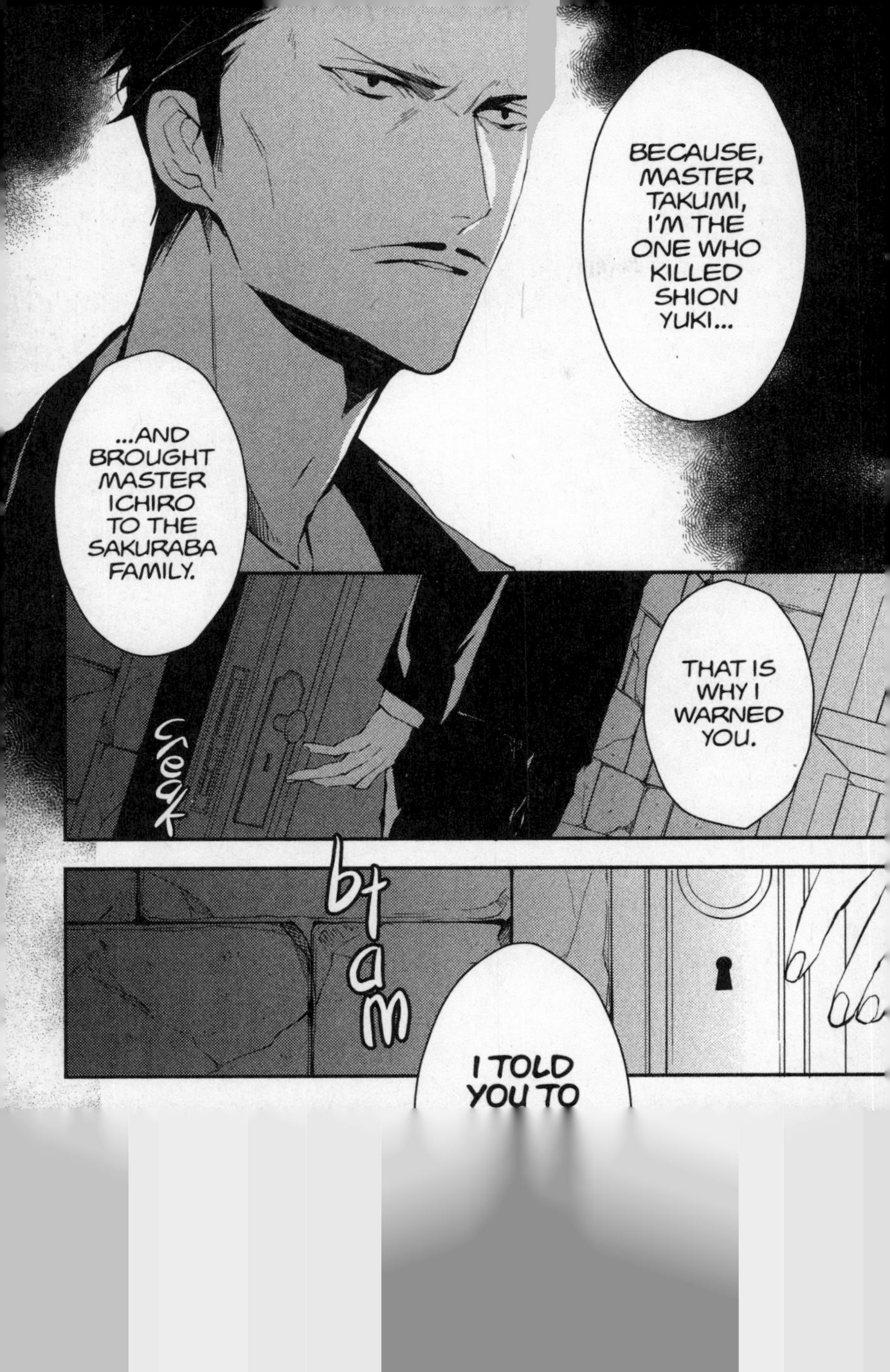
BECAUSE, MASTER TAKUMI, I'M THE ONE WHO KILLED SHION YUKI...
...AND BROUGHT MASTER ICHIRO TO THE SAKURABA FAMILY.
THAT IS WHY I WARNED YOU.
creak
I TOLD YOU TO

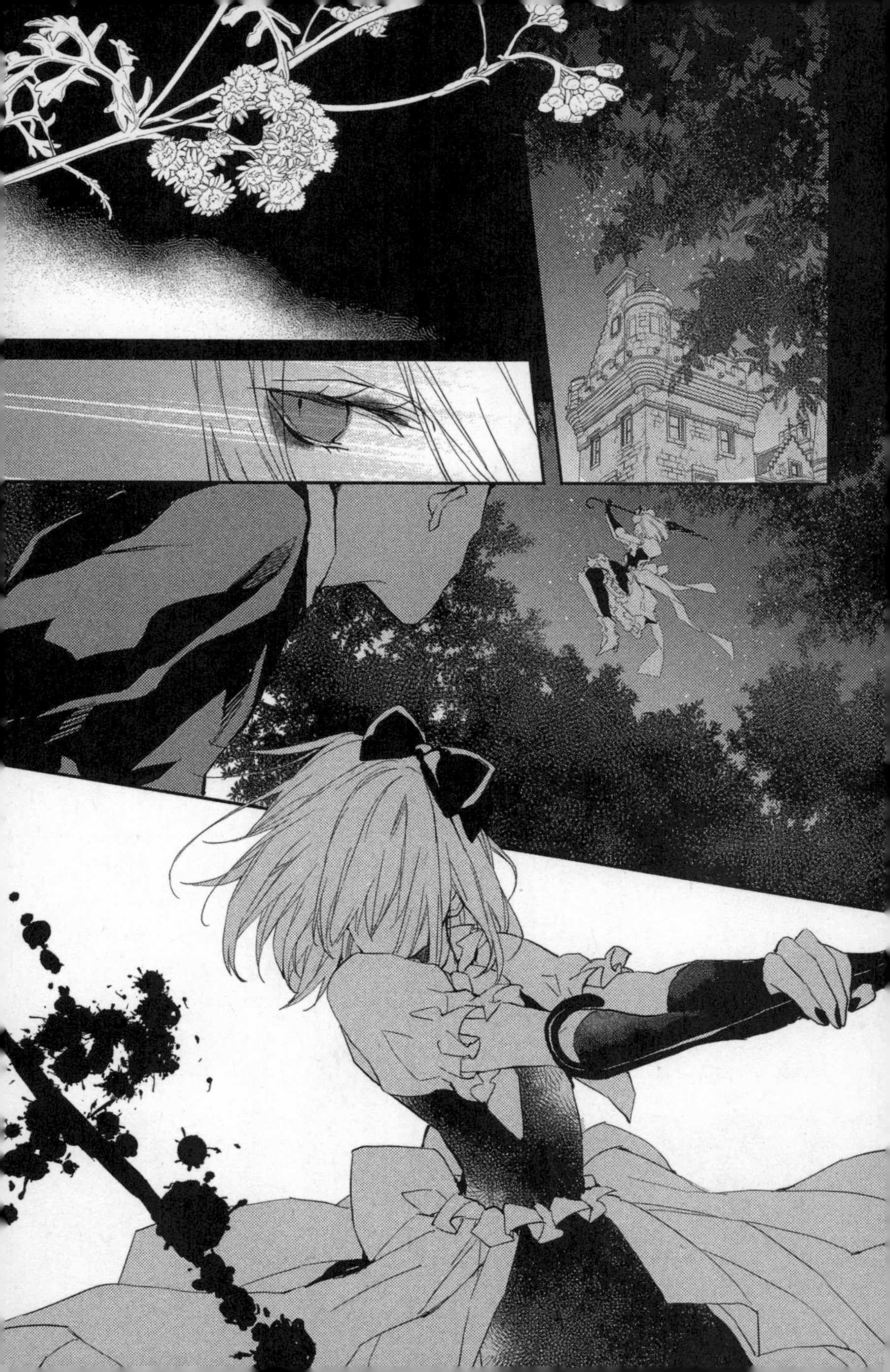

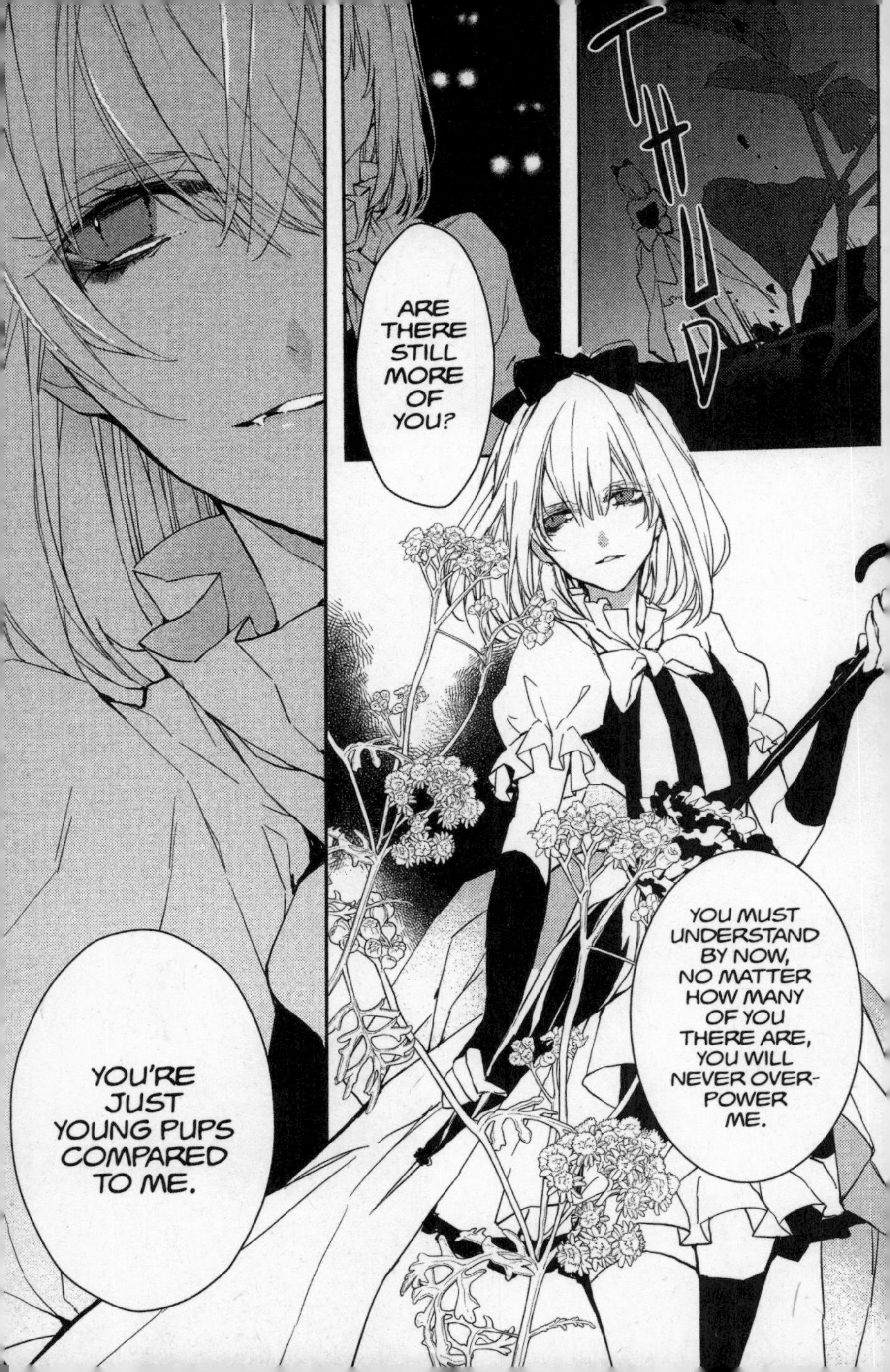
THUD
ARE THERE STILL MORE OF YOU?
YOU MUST UNDERSTAND BY NOW, NO MATTER HOW MANY OF YOU THERE ARE, YOU WILL NEVER OVER-POWER ME.
YOU'RE JUST YOUNG PUPS COMPARED TO ME.

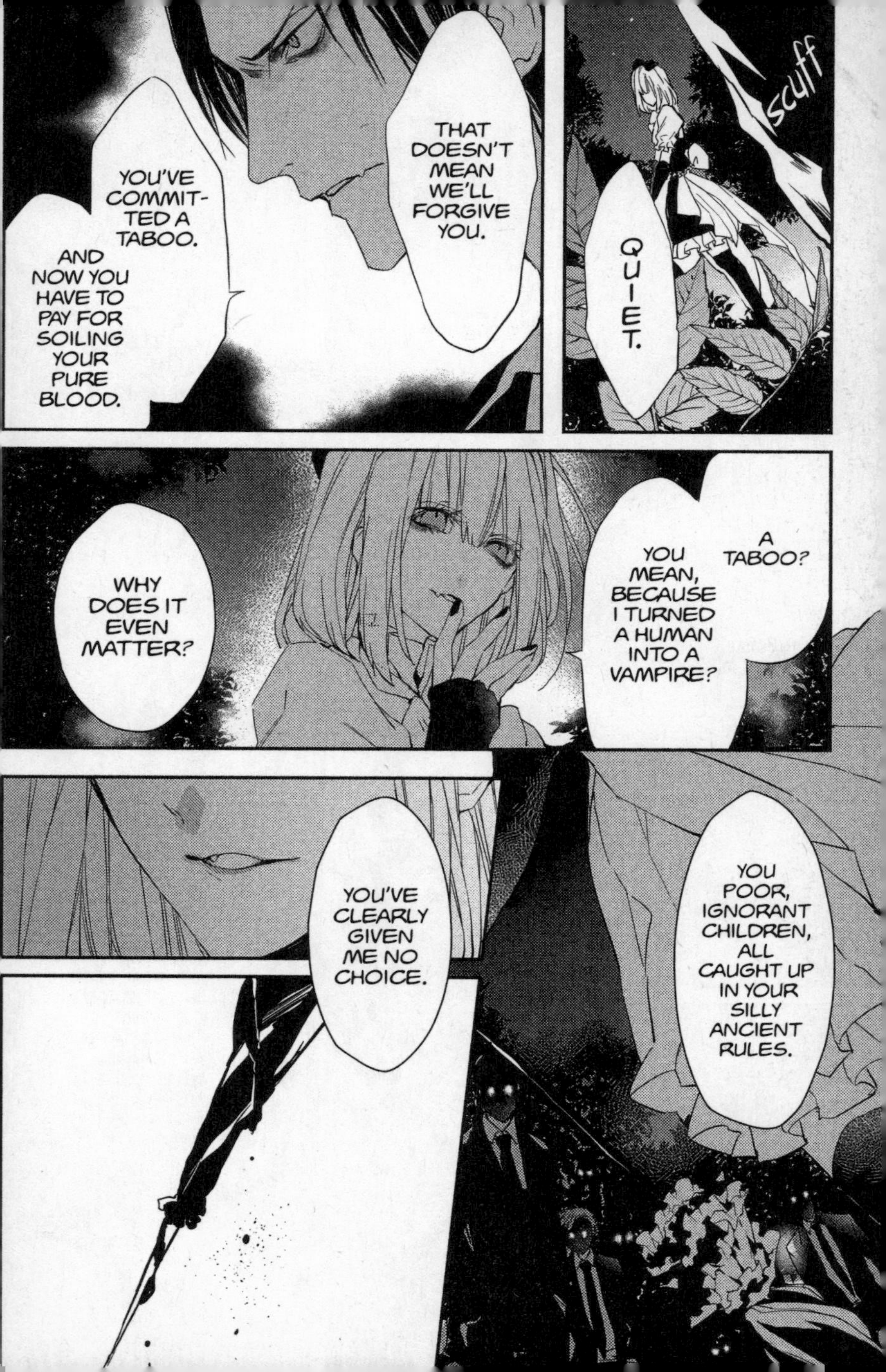
scuff
QUIET.
THAT DOESN'T MEAN WE'LL FORGIVE YOU.
YOU'VE COMMITTED A TABOO.
AND NOW YOU HAVE TO PAY FOR SOILING YOUR PURE BLOOD.
A TABOO?
YOU MEAN, BECAUSE I TURNED A HUMAN INTO A VAMPIRE?
WHY DOES IT EVEN MATTER?
YOU POOR, IGNORANT CHILDREN, ALL CAUGHT UP IN YOUR SILLY ANCIENT RULES.
YOU'VE CLEARLY GIVEN ME NO CHOICE.

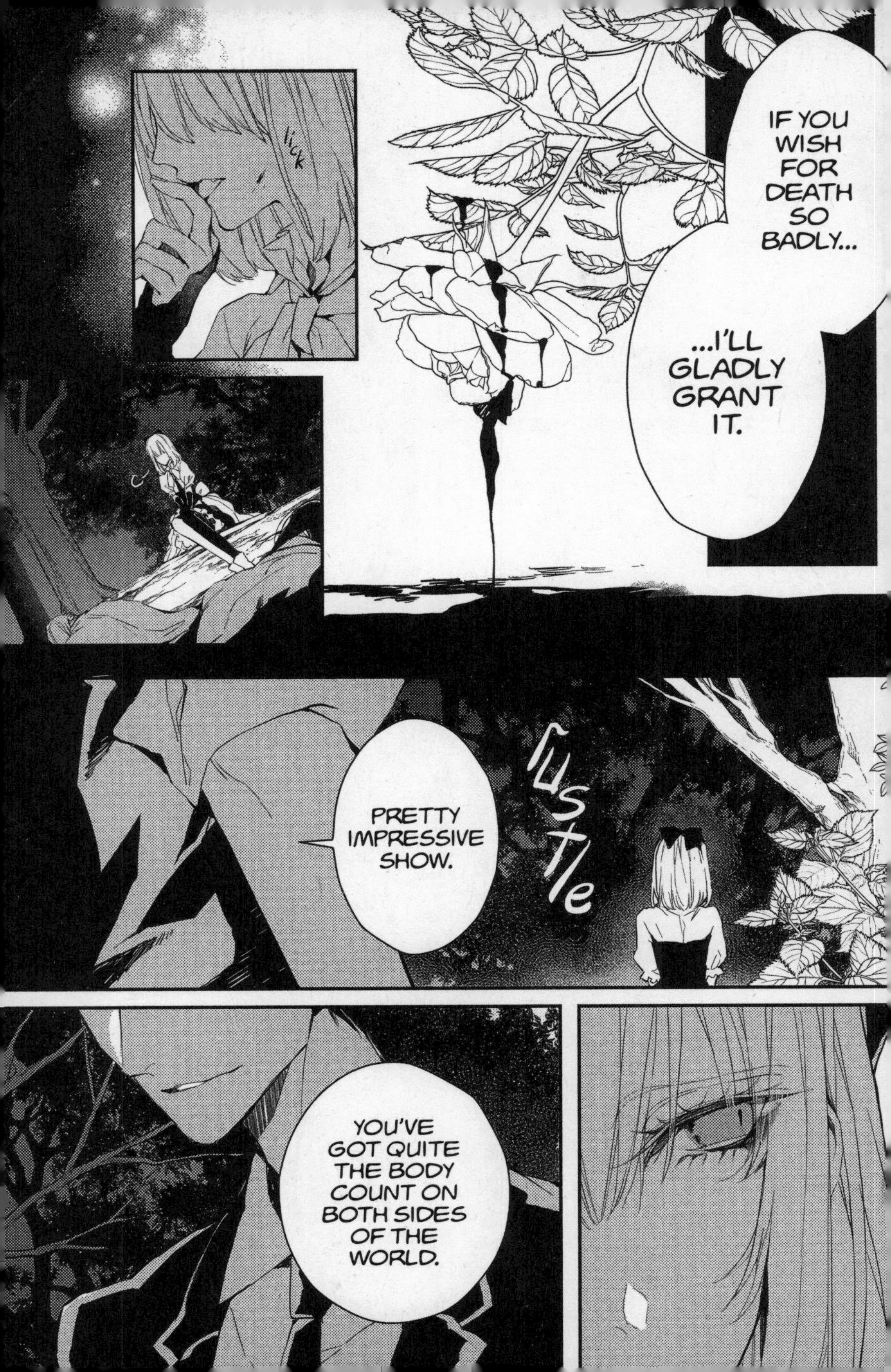
IF YOU WISH FOR DEATH SO BADLY...
...I'LL GLADLY GRANT IT.
lick
rustle
PRETTY IMPRESSIVE SHOW.
YOU'VE GOT QUITE THE BODY COUNT ON BOTH SIDES OF THE WORLD.

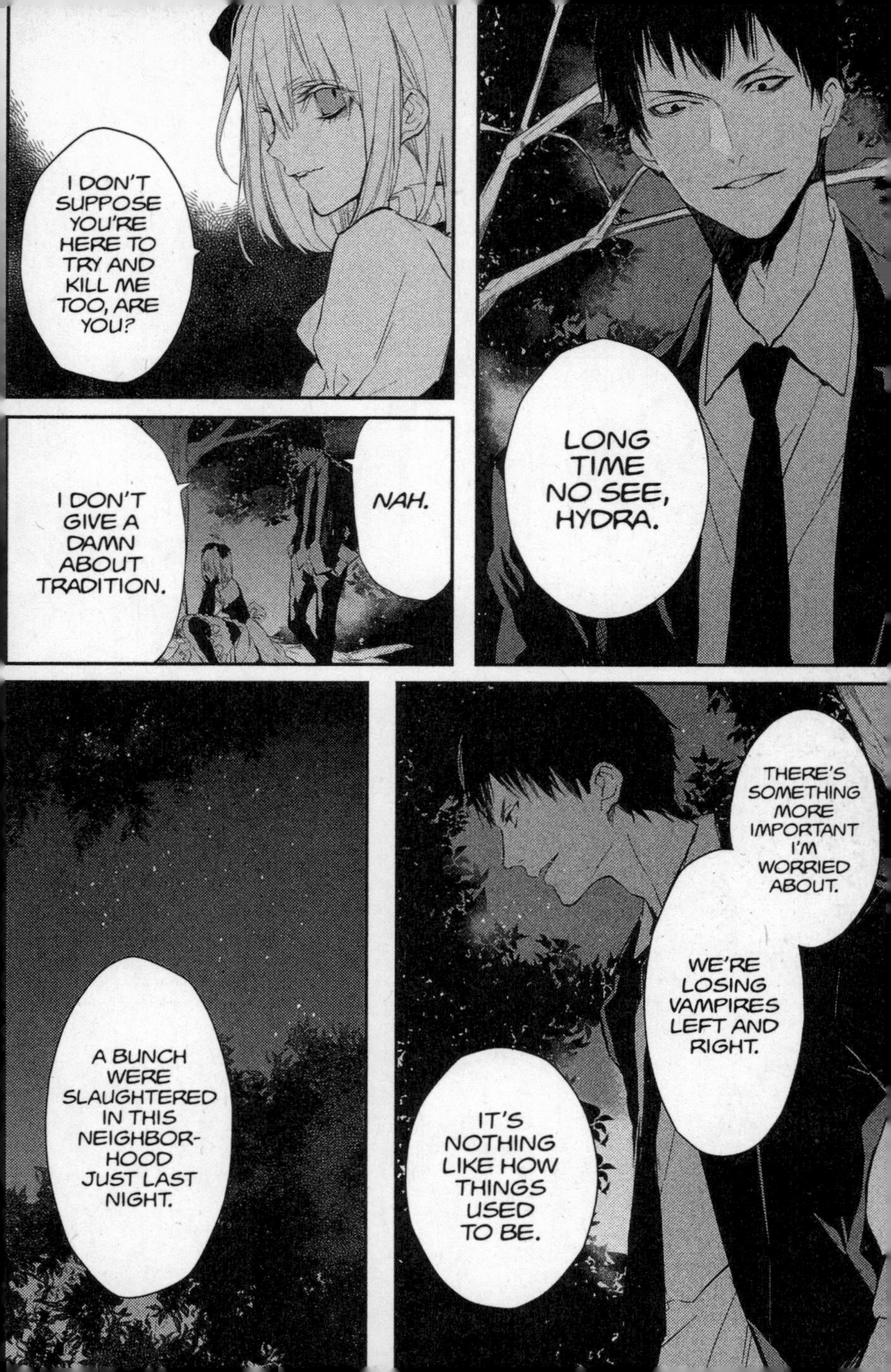
LONG TIME NO SEE, HYDRA.
I DON'T SUPPOSE YOU'RE HERE TO TRY AND KILL ME TOO, ARE YOU?
NAH.
I DON'T GIVE A DAMN ABOUT TRADITION.
THERE'S SOMETHING MORE IMPORTANT I'M WORRIED ABOUT.
WE'RE LOSING VAMPIRES LEFT AND RIGHT.
IT'S NOTHING LIKE HOW THINGS USED TO BE.
A BUNCH WERE SLAUGHTERED IN THIS NEIGHBOR-HOOD JUST LAST NIGHT.

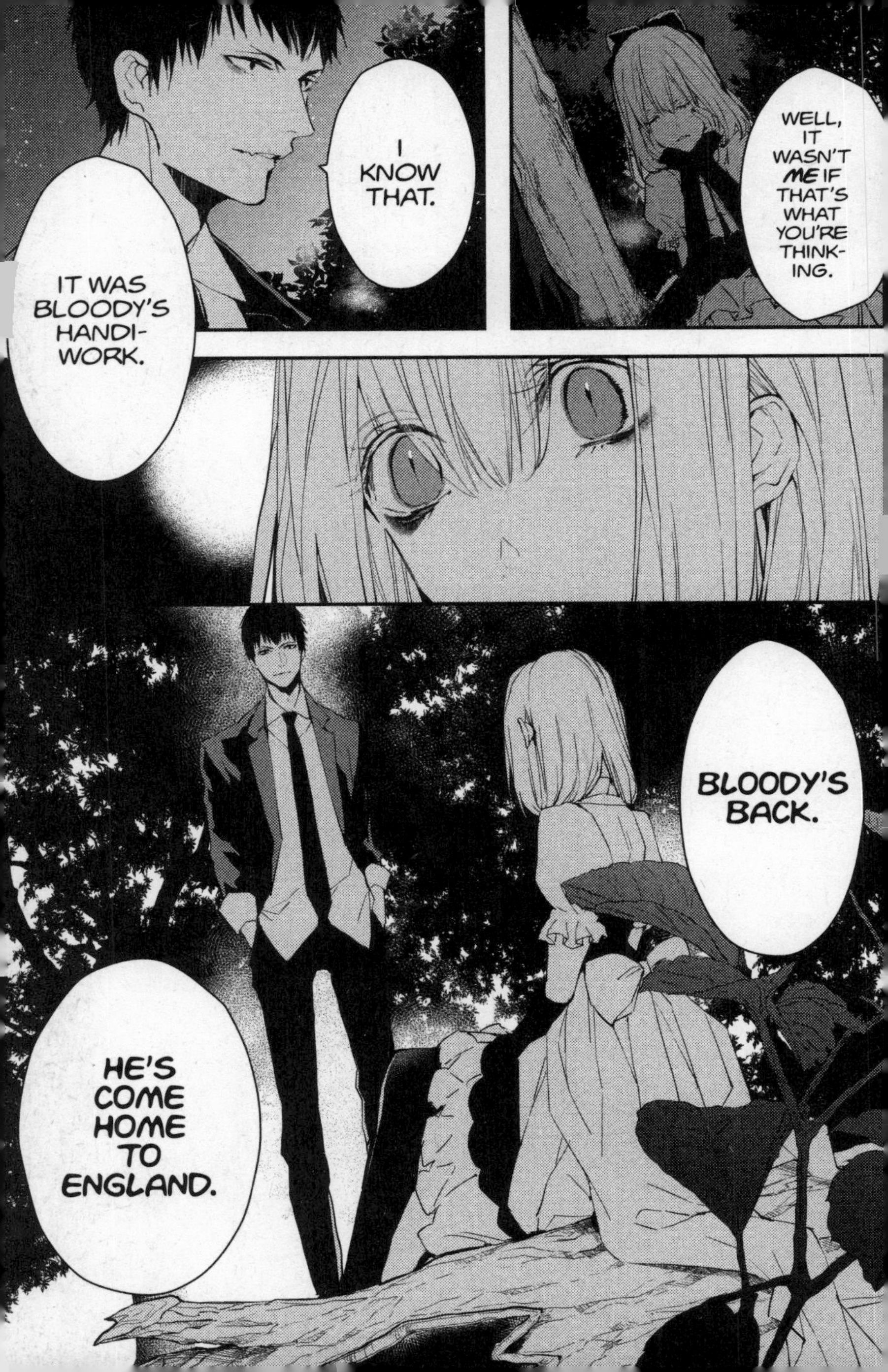
WELL, IT WASN'T *ME* IF THAT'S WHAT YOU'RE THINKING.
I KNOW THAT.
IT WAS BLOODY'S HANDIWORK.
BLOODY'S BACK.
HE'S COME HOME TO ENGLAND.

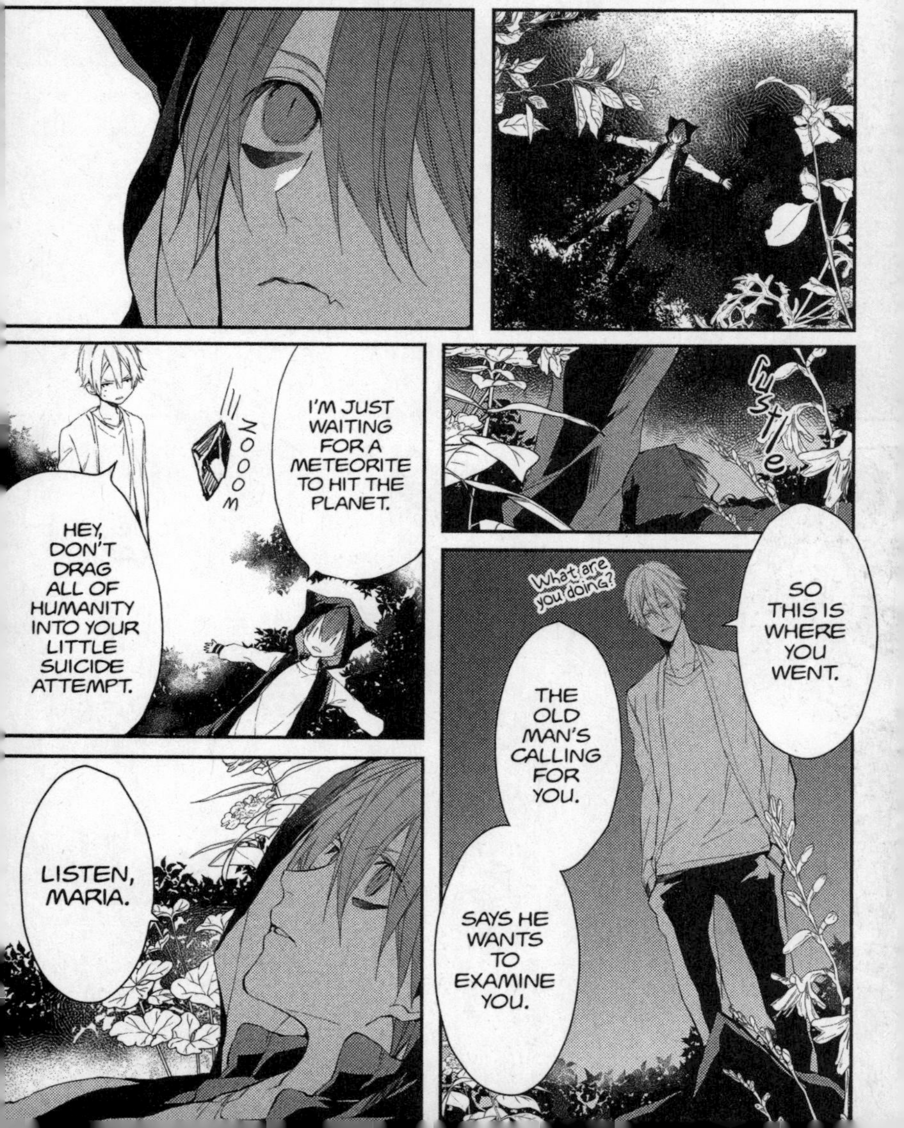
rustle
SO THIS IS WHERE YOU WENT.
What are you doing?
THE OLD MAN'S CALLING FOR YOU.
SAYS HE WANTS TO EXAMINE YOU.
I'M JUST WAITING FOR A METEORITE TO HIT THE PLANET.
ZOOOM
HEY, DON'T DRAG ALL OF HUMANITY INTO YOUR LITTLE SUICIDE ATTEMPT.
LISTEN, MARIA.

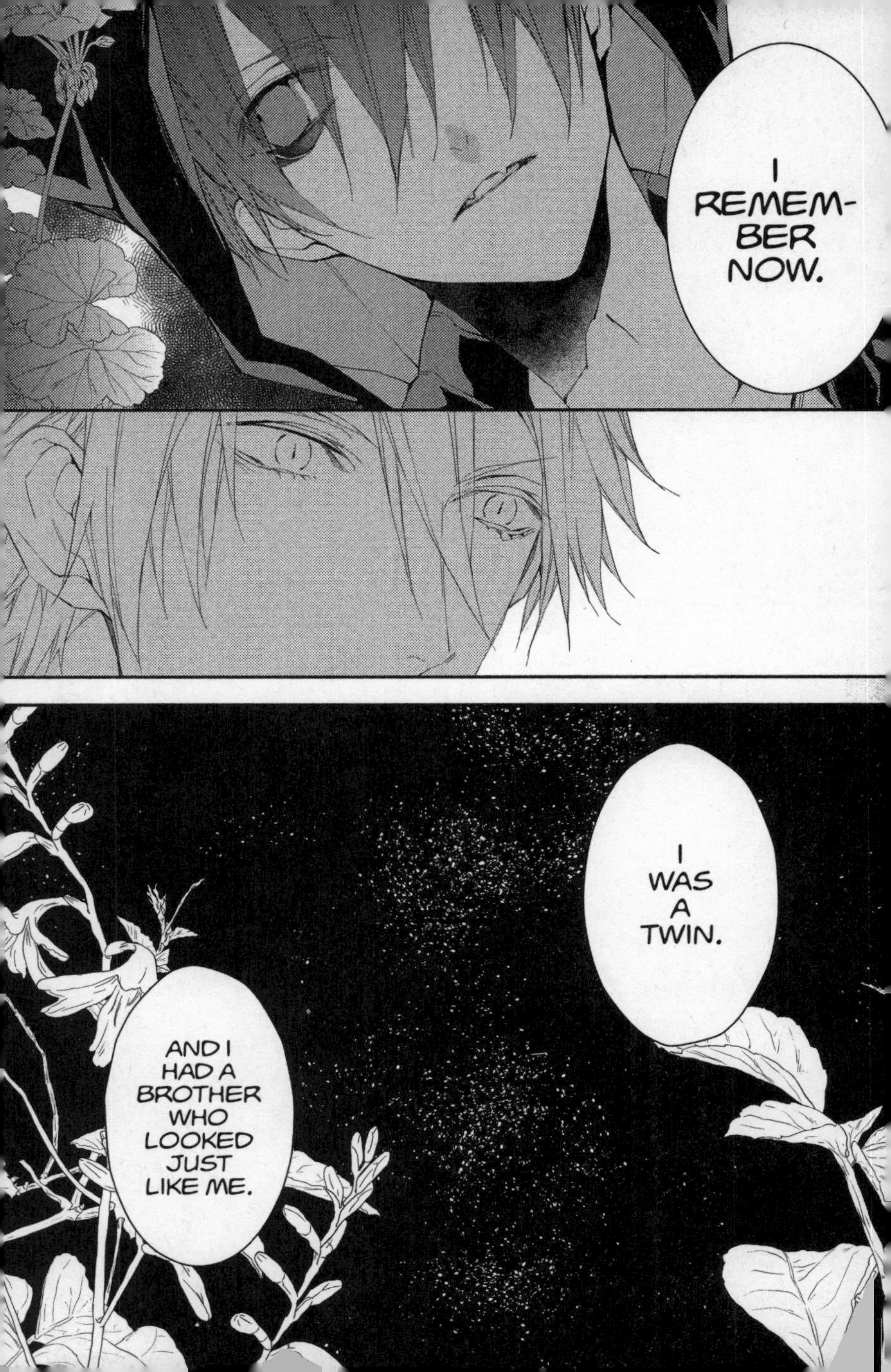
I REMEMBER NOW.
I WAS A TWIN.
AND I HAD A BROTHER WHO LOOKED JUST LIKE ME.

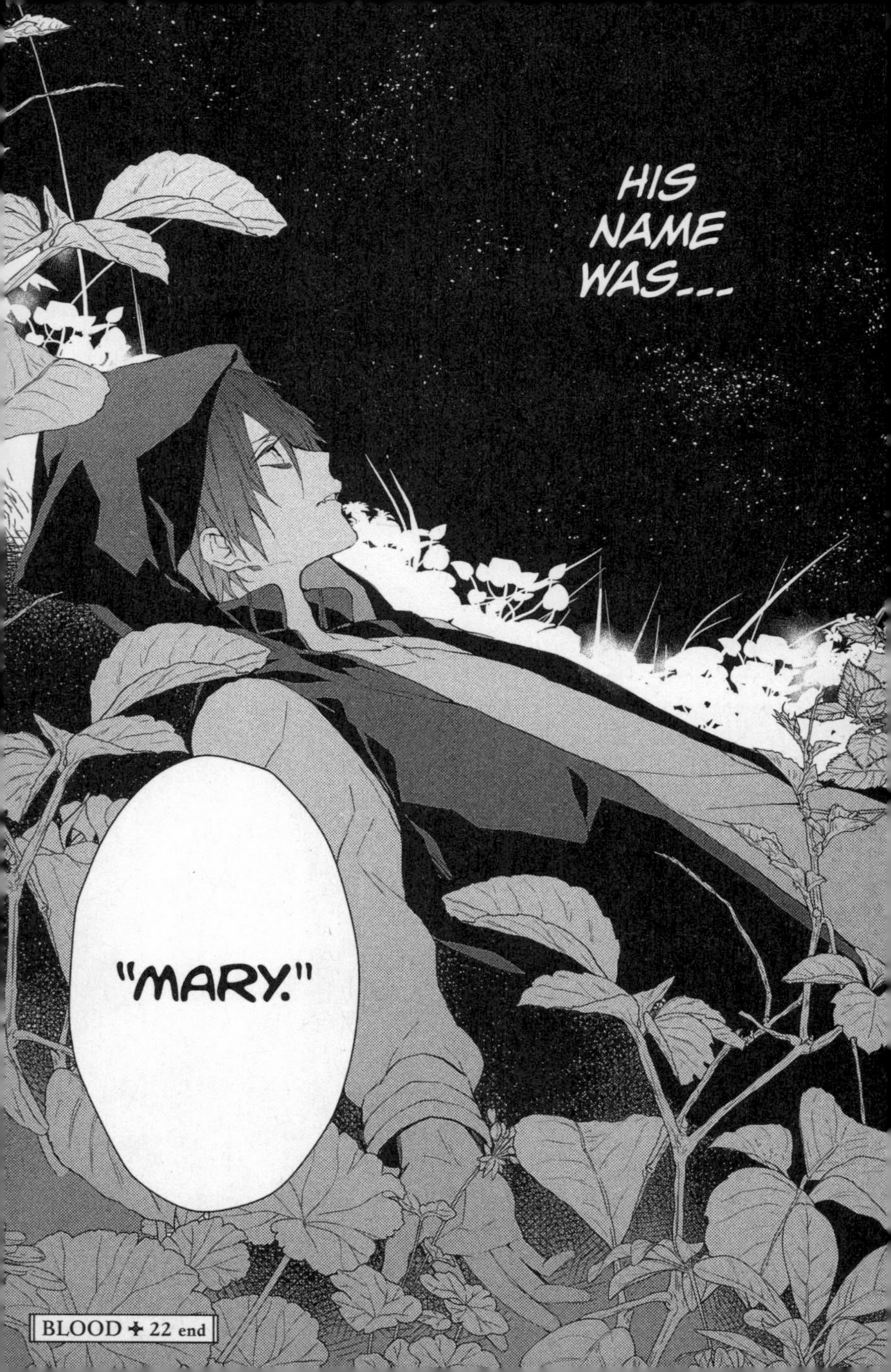
HIS NAME WAS...
"MARY."

BLOOD ✢ 22 end

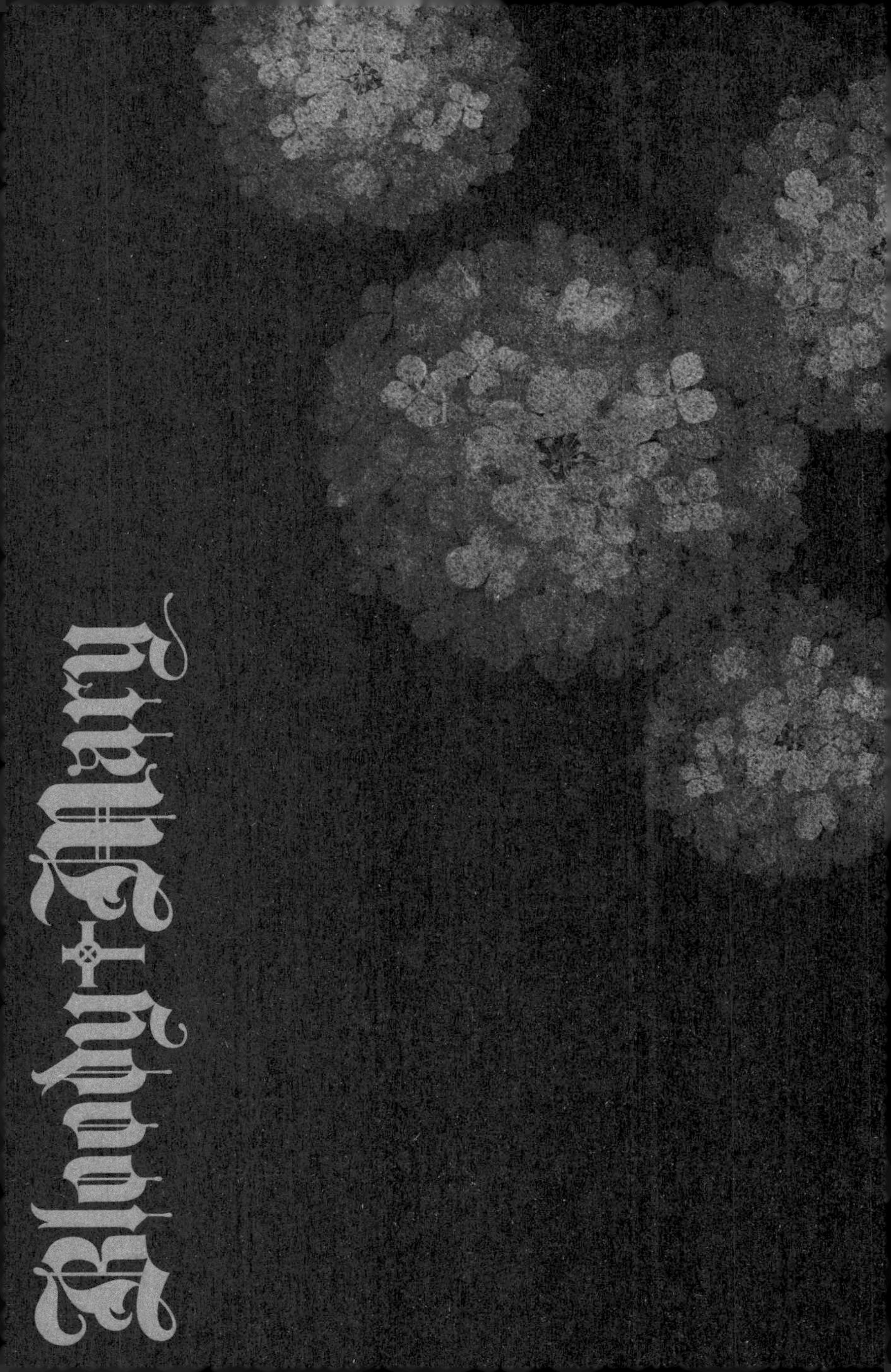
Bloody+Mary

Bloody✝Mary

YOU'RE JUST YOUNG PUPS COMPARED TO ME.

AND, UNLIKE YOU, I'M A LADY.

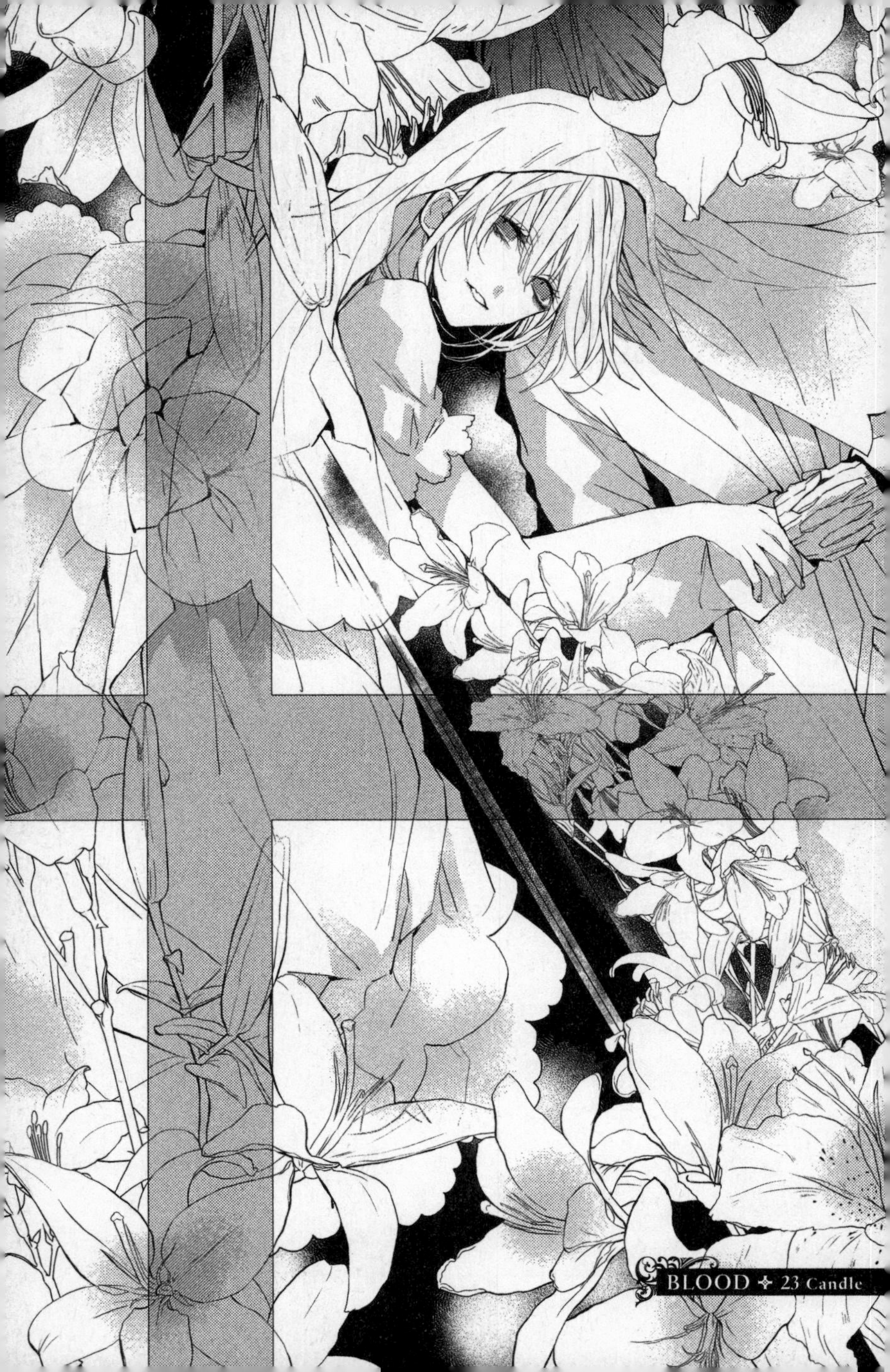
BLOOD ✧ 23 Candle

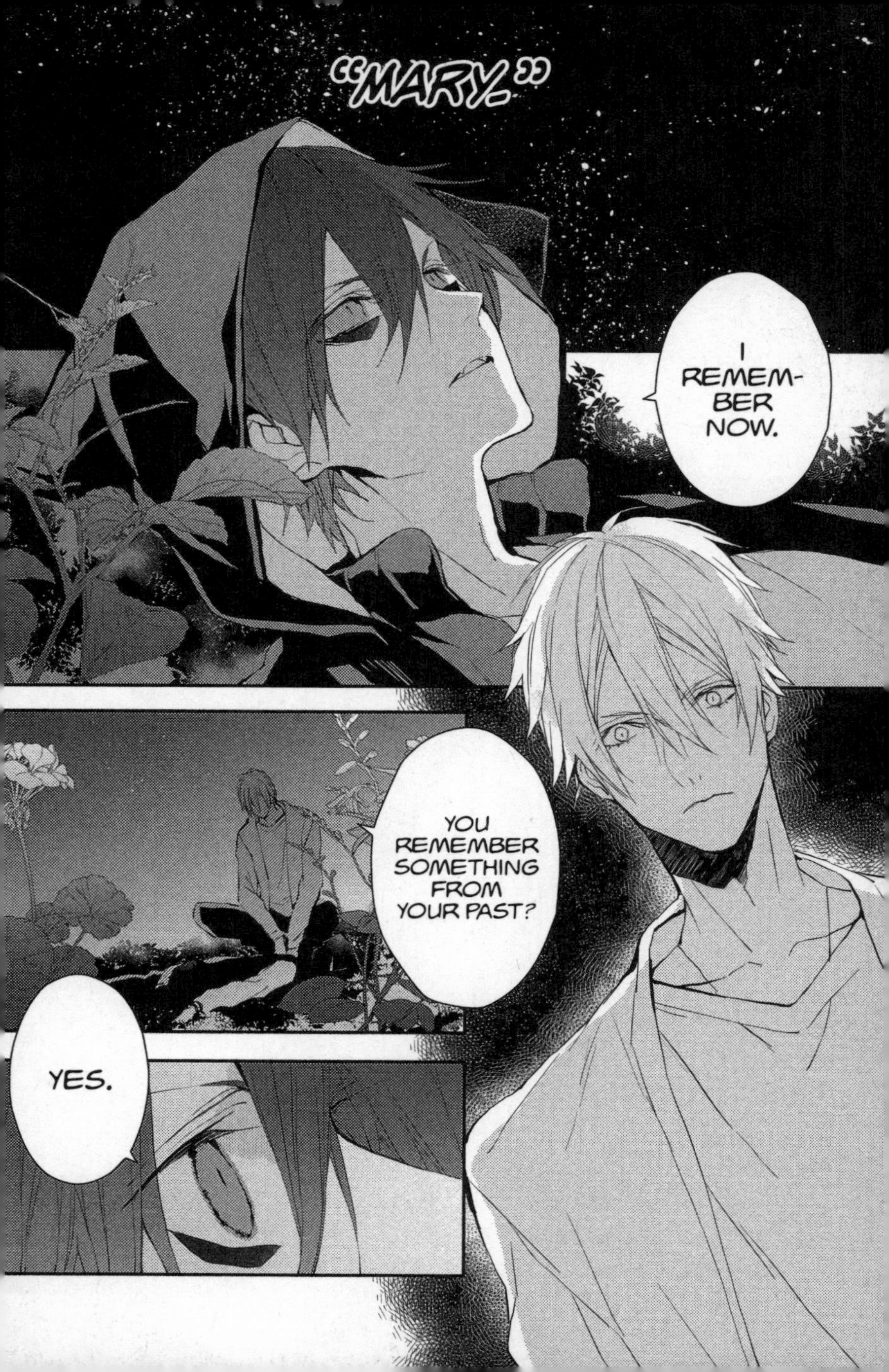
"MARY."
I REMEM-BER NOW.
YOU REMEMBER SOMETHING FROM YOUR PAST?
YES.

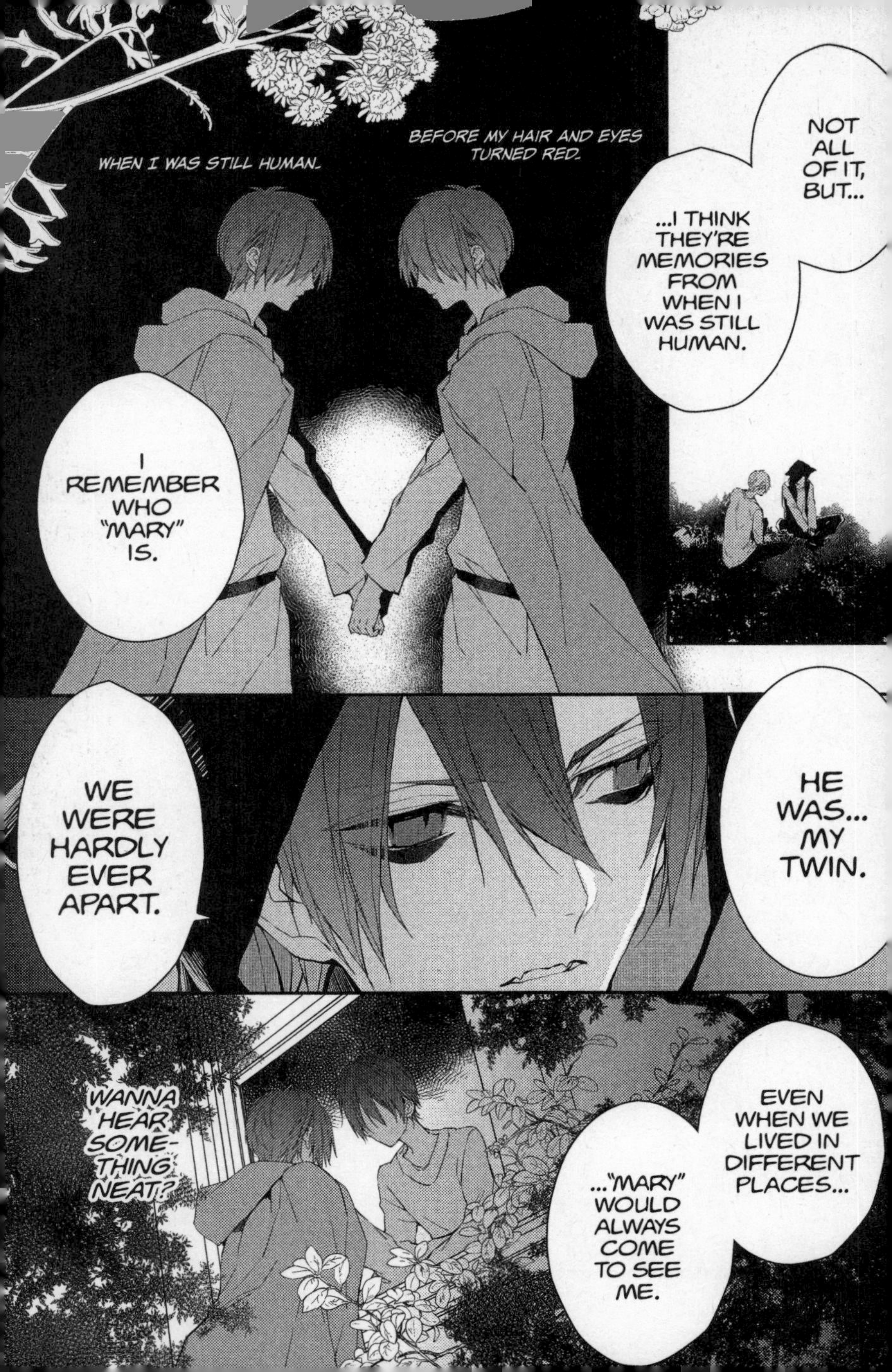
NOT ALL OF IT, BUT...
...I THINK THEY'RE MEMORIES FROM WHEN I WAS STILL HUMAN.
BEFORE MY HAIR AND EYES TURNED RED.
WHEN I WAS STILL HUMAN.
I REMEMBER WHO "MARY" IS.
HE WAS... MY TWIN.
WE WERE HARDLY EVER APART.
EVEN WHEN WE LIVED IN DIFFERENT PLACES...
..."MARY" WOULD ALWAYS COME TO SEE ME.
WANNA HEAR SOME-THING NEAT?

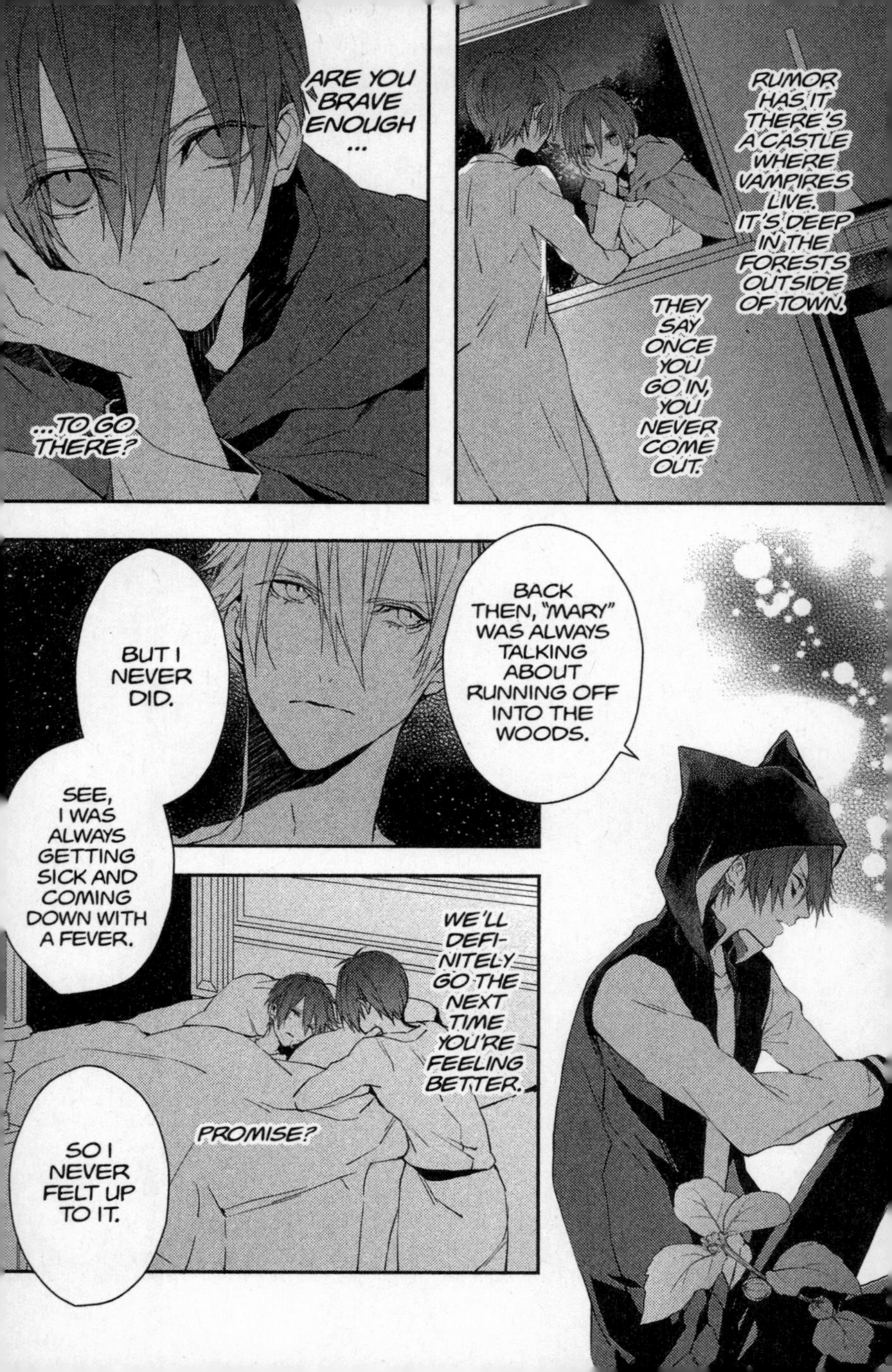
RUMOR HAS IT THERE'S A CASTLE WHERE VAMPIRES LIVE. IT'S DEEP IN THE FORESTS OUTSIDE OF TOWN.
THEY SAY ONCE YOU GO IN, YOU NEVER COME OUT.
ARE YOU BRAVE ENOUGH ...
...TO GO THERE?
BACK THEN, "MARY" WAS ALWAYS TALKING ABOUT RUNNING OFF INTO THE WOODS.
BUT I NEVER DID.
SEE, I WAS ALWAYS GETTING SICK AND COMING DOWN WITH A FEVER.
WE'LL DEFI-NITELY GO THE NEXT TIME YOU'RE FEELING BETTER.
PROMISE?
SO I NEVER FELT UP TO IT.

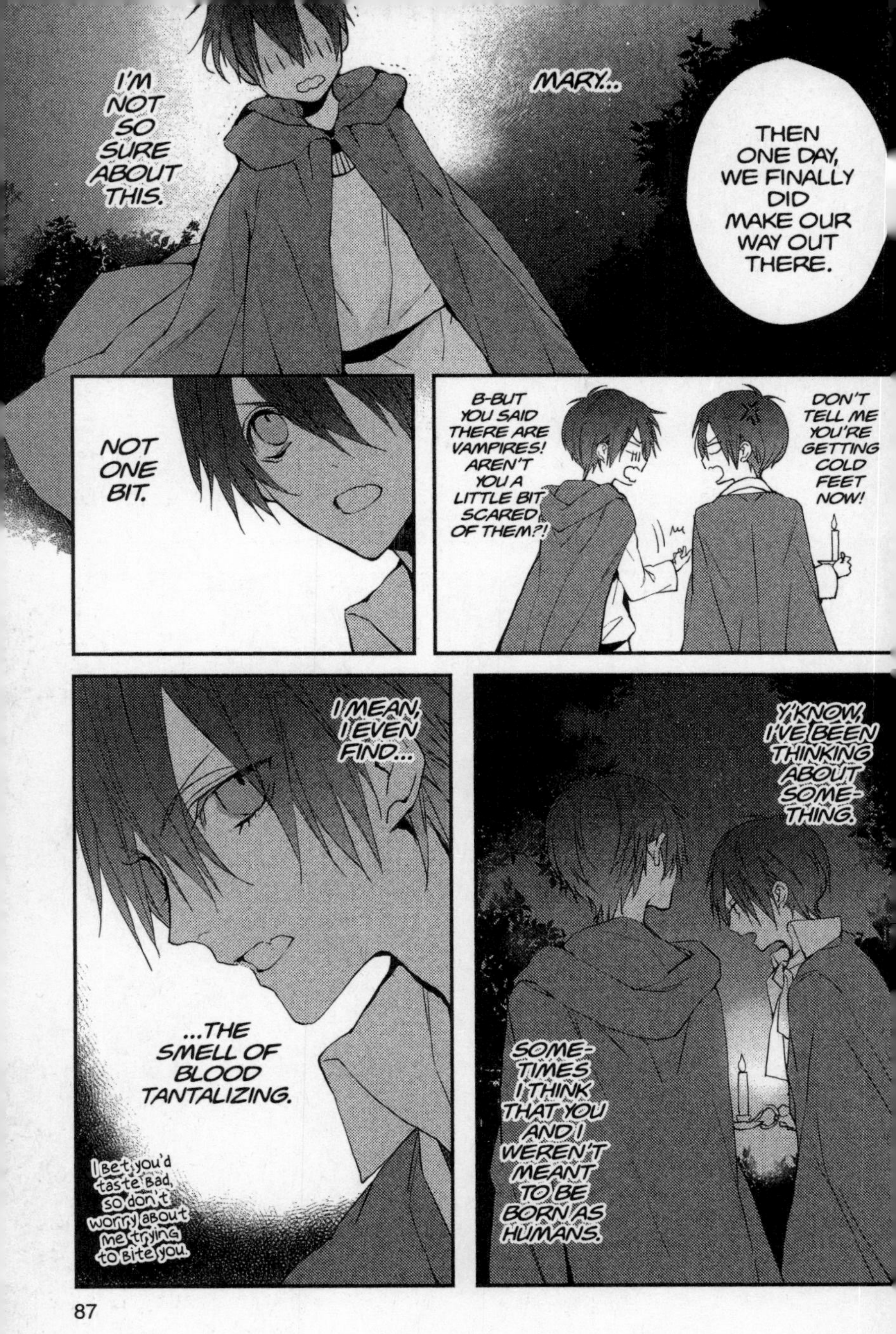
THEN ONE DAY, WE FINALLY DID MAKE OUR WAY OUT THERE.
MARY...
I'M NOT SO SURE ABOUT THIS.
DON'T TELL ME YOU'RE GETTING COLD FEET NOW!
B-BUT YOU SAID THERE ARE VAMPIRES! AREN'T YOU A LITTLE BIT SCARED OF THEM?!
NOT ONE BIT.
Y'KNOW, I'VE BEEN THINKING ABOUT SOME-THING.
SOME-TIMES I THINK THAT YOU AND I WEREN'T MEANT TO BE BORN AS HUMANS.
I MEAN, I EVEN FIND...
...THE SMELL OF BLOOD TANTALIZING.
I bet you'd taste bad, so don't worry about me trying to bite you.

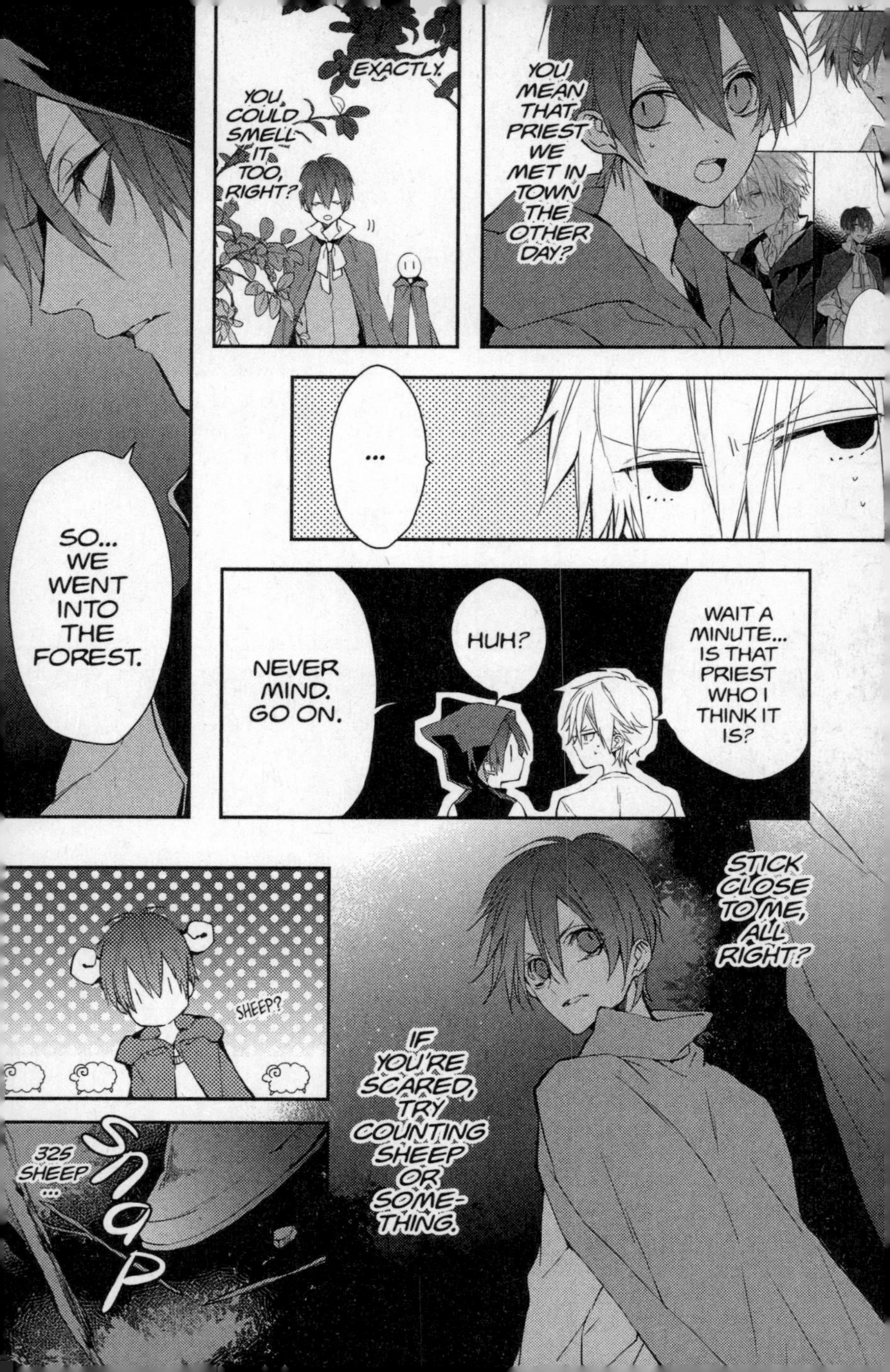
YOU MEAN THAT PRIEST WE MET IN TOWN THE OTHER DAY?
EXACTLY.
YOU COULD SMELL IT, TOO, RIGHT?
...
WAIT A MINUTE... IS THAT PRIEST WHO I THINK IT IS?
HUH?
NEVER MIND. GO ON.
SO... WE WENT INTO THE FOREST.
STICK CLOSE TO ME, ALL RIGHT?
IF YOU'RE SCARED, TRY COUNTING SHEEP OR SOMETHING.
SHEEP?
325 SHEEP...
SNAP

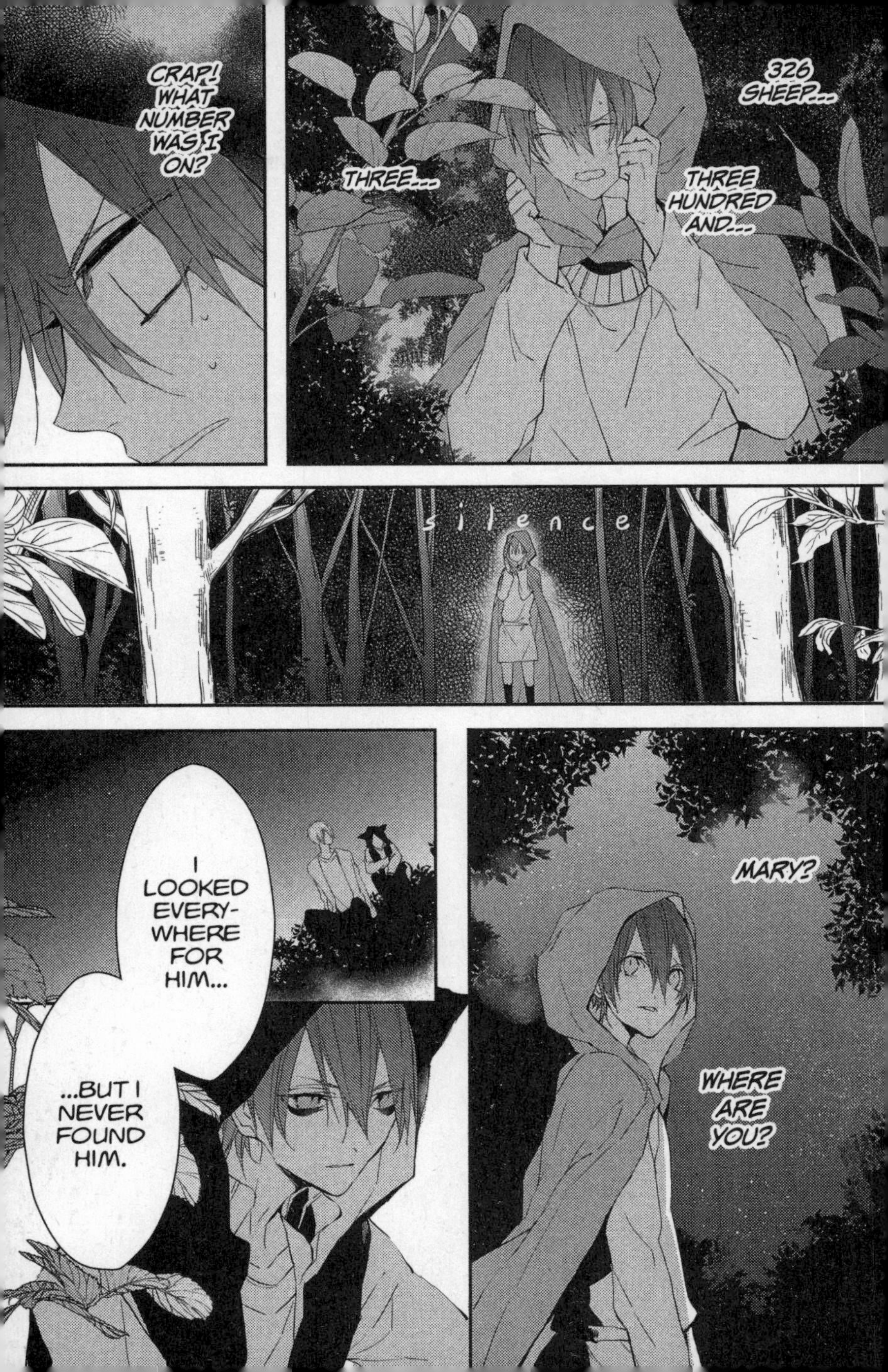
326 SHEEP...
THREE HUNDRED AND...
THREE...
CRAP! WHAT NUMBER WAS I ON?
silence
MARY?
WHERE ARE YOU?
I LOOKED EVERY-WHERE FOR HIM...
...BUT I NEVER FOUND HIM.

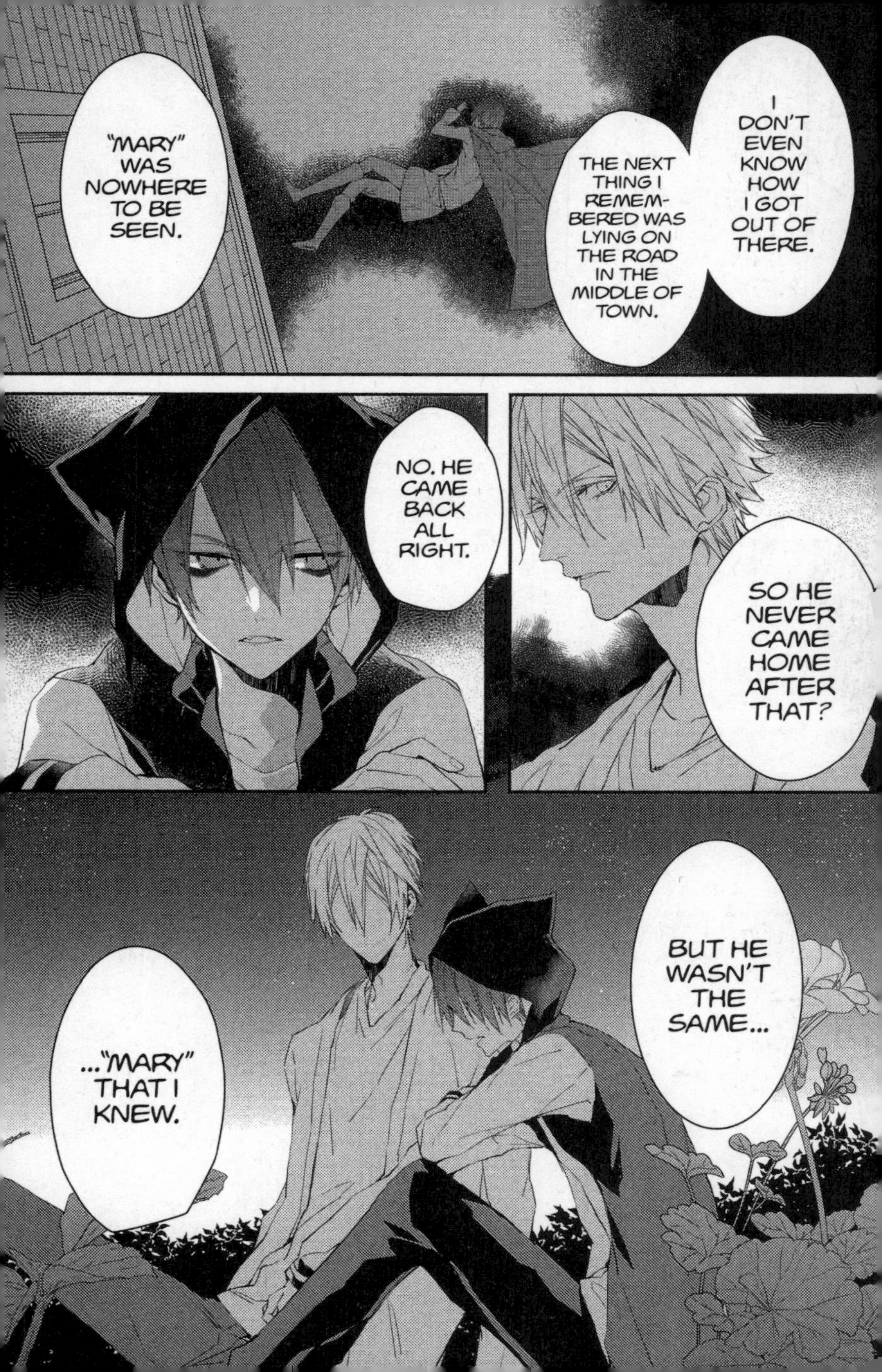
I DON'T EVEN KNOW HOW I GOT OUT OF THERE.
THE NEXT THING I REMEMBERED WAS LYING ON THE ROAD IN THE MIDDLE OF TOWN.
"MARY" WAS NOWHERE TO BE SEEN.
SO HE NEVER CAME HOME AFTER THAT?
NO. HE CAME BACK ALL RIGHT.
BUT HE WASN'T THE SAME...
..."MARY" THAT I KNEW.

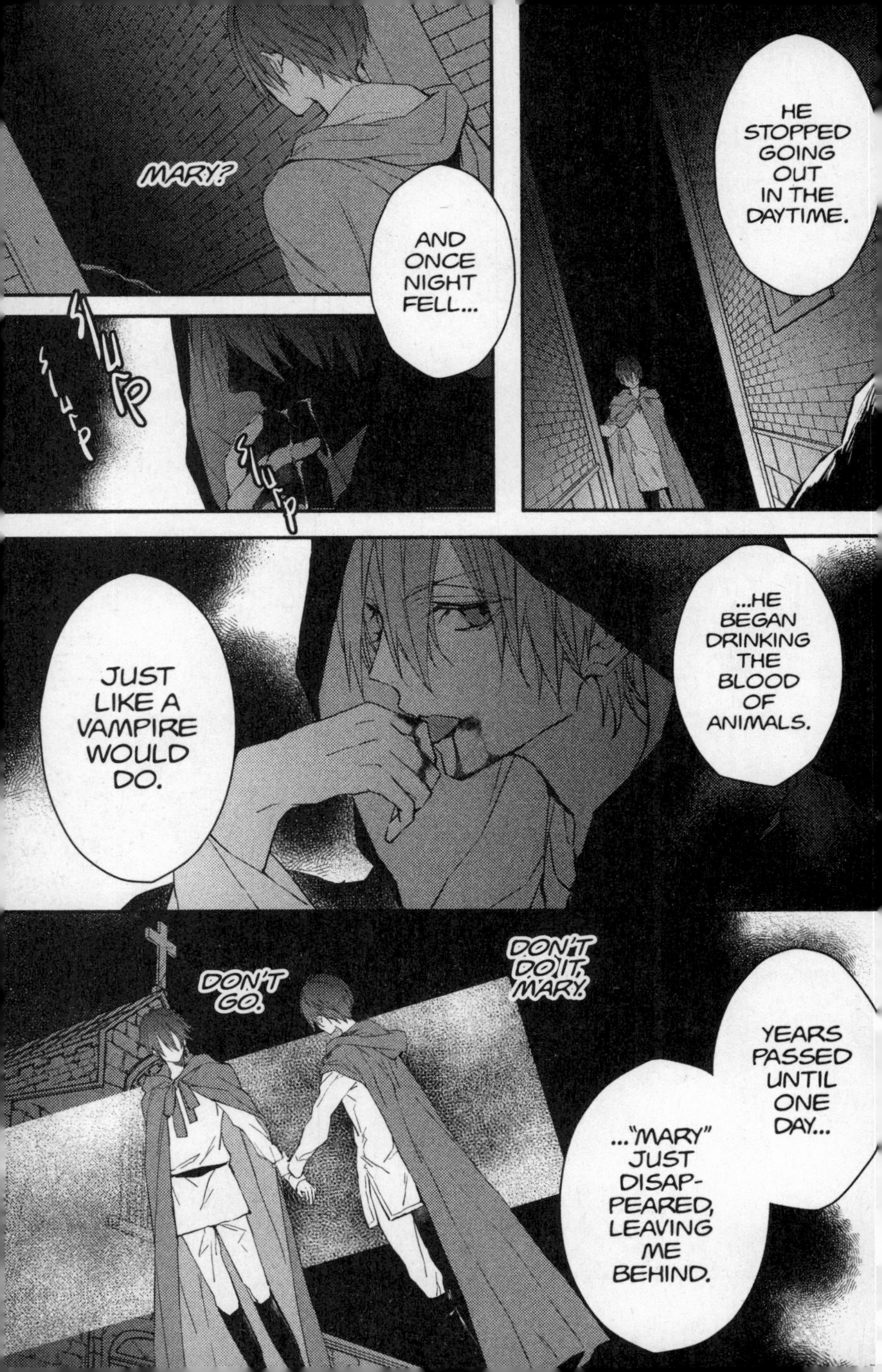
HE STOPPED GOING OUT IN THE DAYTIME.
AND ONCE NIGHT FELL...
MARY?
SLURP
SLURP
SLURP
...HE BEGAN DRINKING THE BLOOD OF ANIMALS.
JUST LIKE A VAMPIRE WOULD DO.
YEARS PASSED UNTIL ONE DAY...
..."MARY" JUST DISAPPEARED, LEAVING ME BEHIND.
DON'T DO IT, MARY.
DON'T GO.

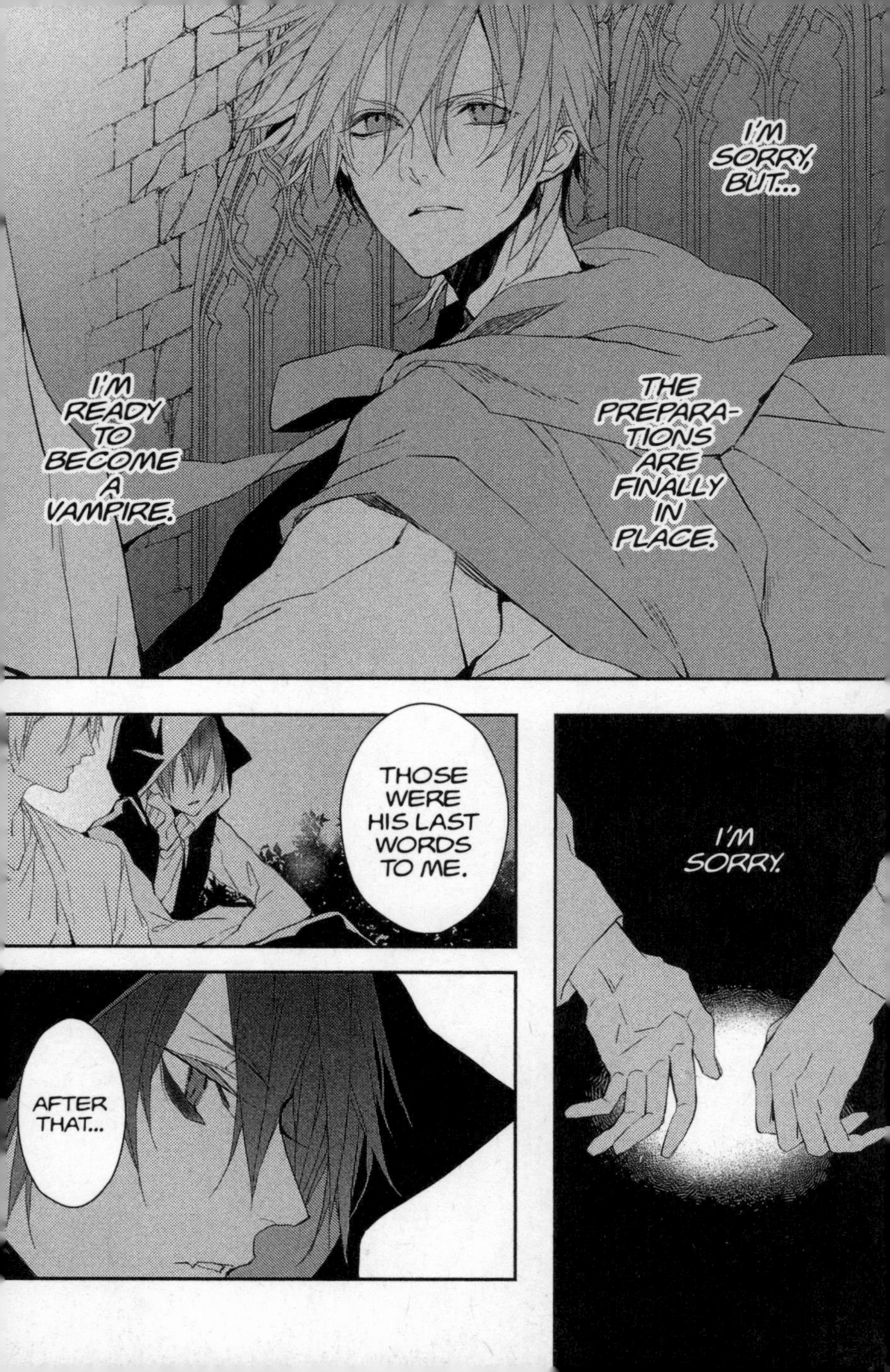
I'M SORRY, BUT...
THE PREPARATIONS ARE FINALLY IN PLACE.
I'M READY TO BECOME A VAMPIRE.
I'M SORRY.
THOSE WERE HIS LAST WORDS TO ME.
AFTER THAT...

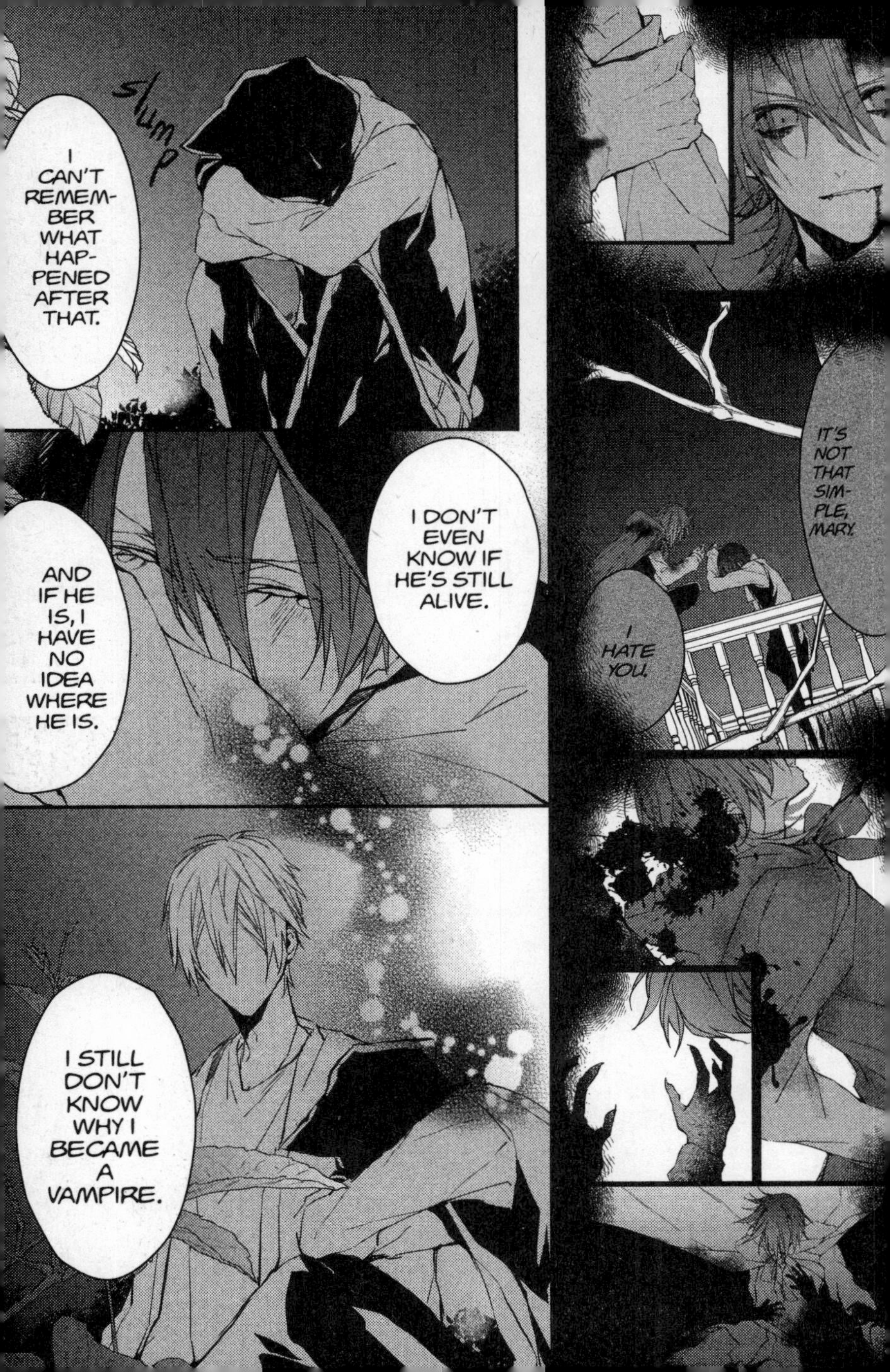
IT'S NOT THAT SIMPLE, MARY.
I HATE YOU.
slump
I CAN'T REMEMBER WHAT HAPPENED AFTER THAT.
I DON'T EVEN KNOW IF HE'S STILL ALIVE.
AND IF HE IS, I HAVE NO IDEA WHERE HE IS.
I STILL DON'T KNOW WHY I BECAME A VAMPIRE.

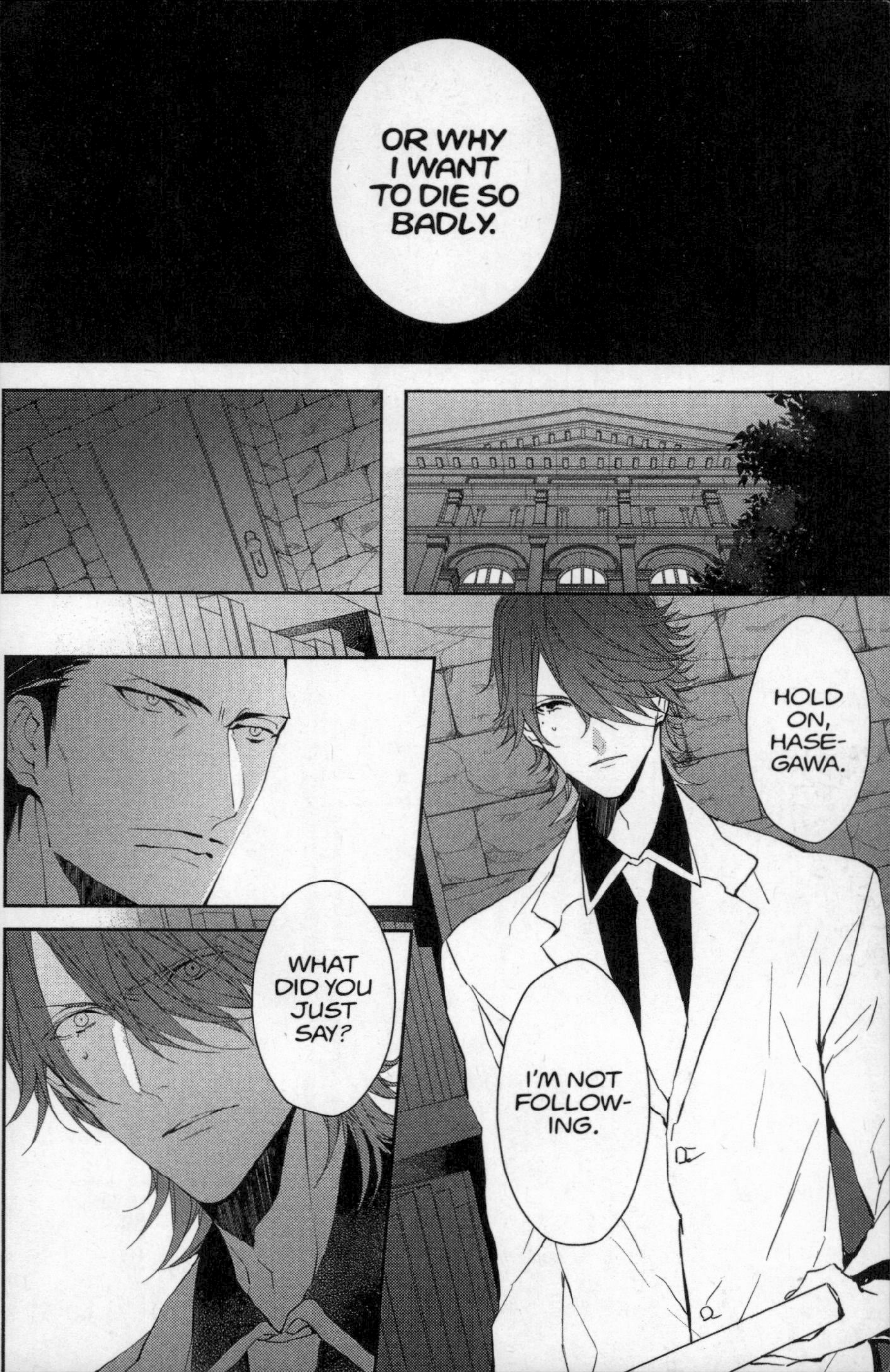
OR WHY I WANT TO DIE SO BADLY.
HOLD ON, HASE-GAWA.
WHAT DID YOU JUST SAY?
I'M NOT FOLLOW-ING.

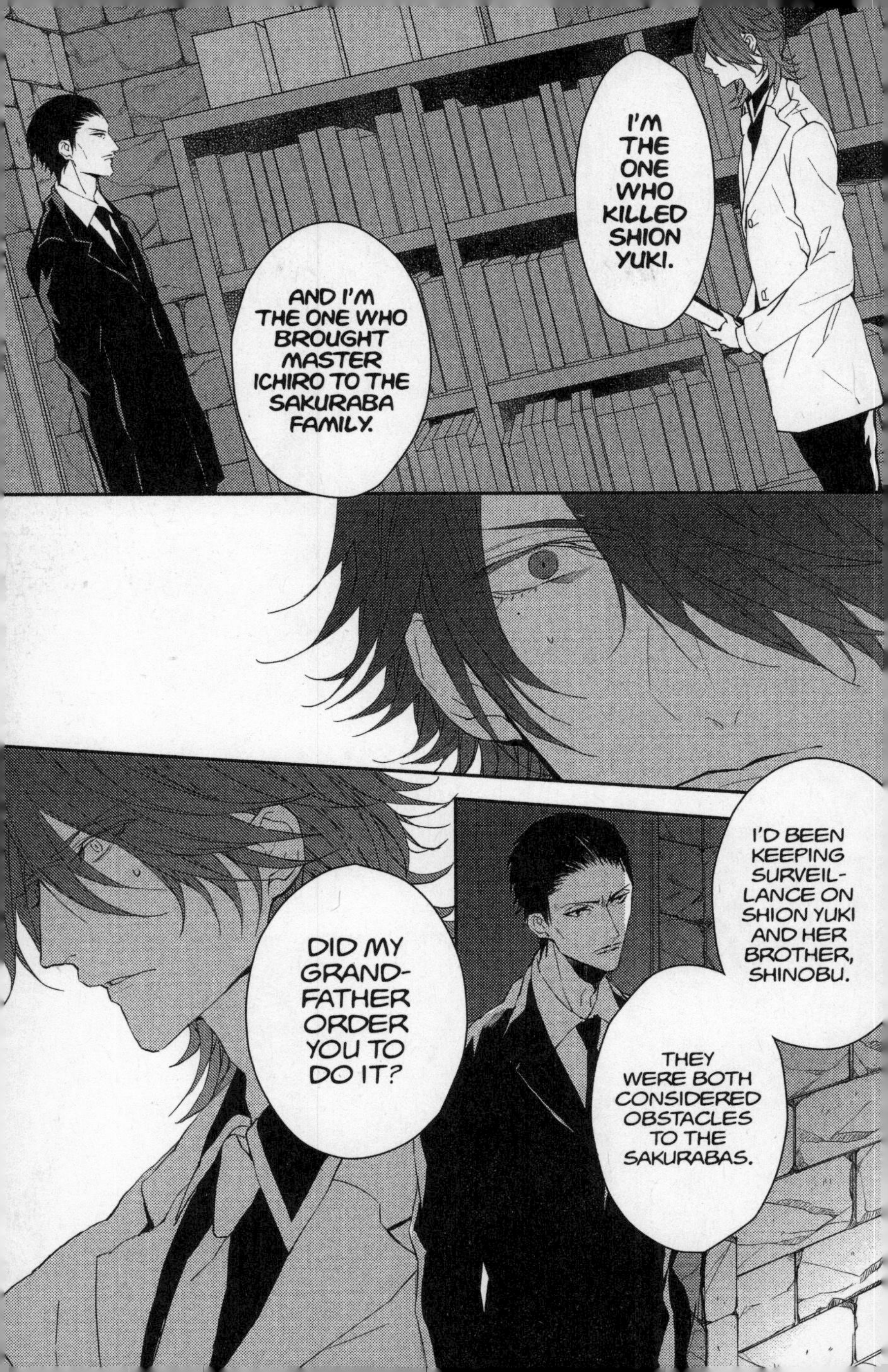
I'M THE ONE WHO KILLED SHION YUKI.
AND I'M THE ONE WHO BROUGHT MASTER ICHIRO TO THE SAKURABA FAMILY.
I'D BEEN KEEPING SURVEIL-LANCE ON SHION YUKI AND HER BROTHER, SHINOBU.
THEY WERE BOTH CONSIDERED OBSTACLES TO THE SAKURABAS.
DID MY GRAND-FATHER ORDER YOU TO DO IT?

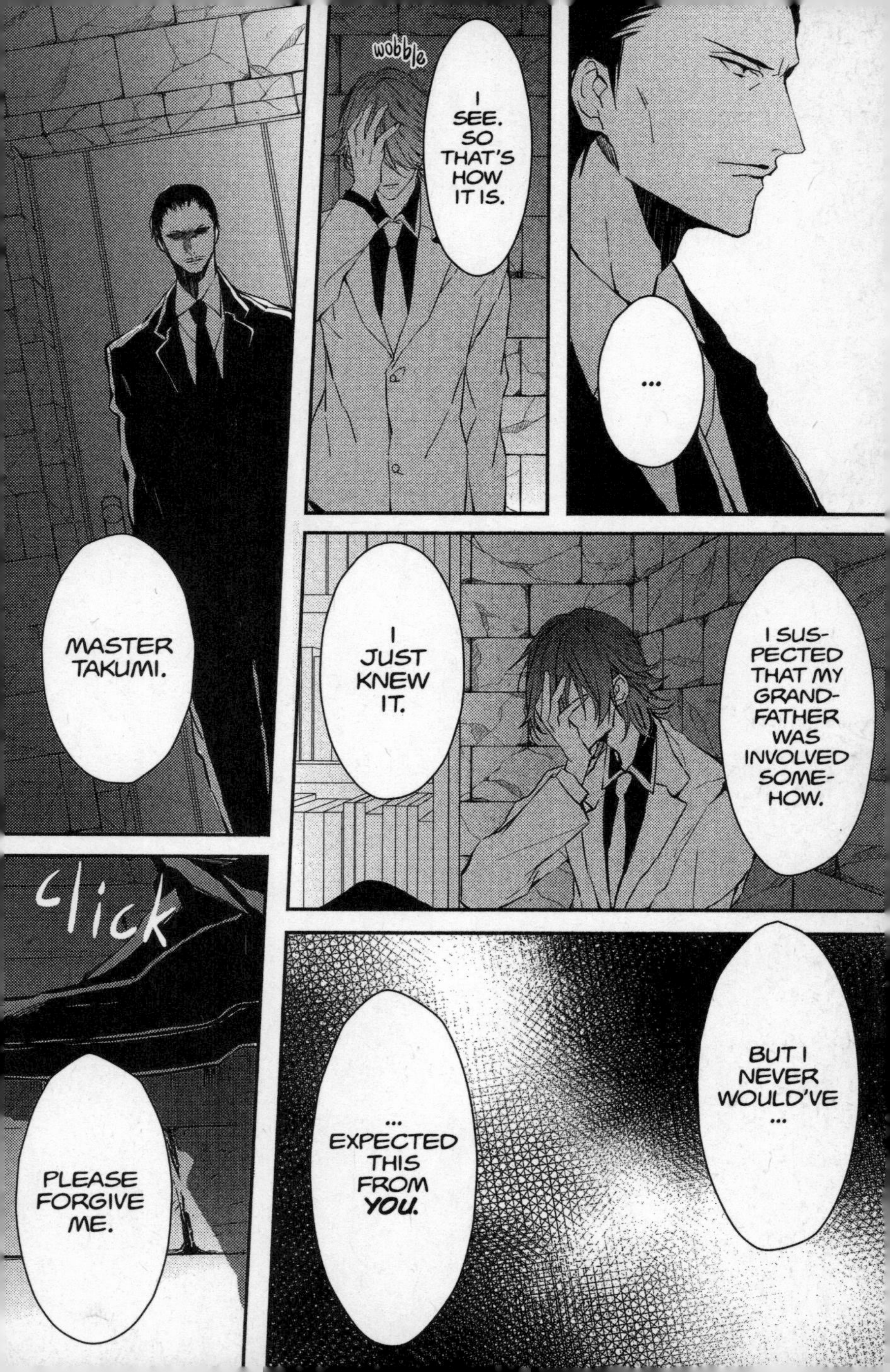
...
wobble
I SEE. SO THAT'S HOW IT IS.
I SUSPECTED THAT MY GRANDFATHER WAS INVOLVED SOMEHOW.
I JUST KNEW IT.
MASTER TAKUMI.
BUT I NEVER WOULD'VE ...
... EXPECTED THIS FROM *YOU*.
click
PLEASE FORGIVE ME.

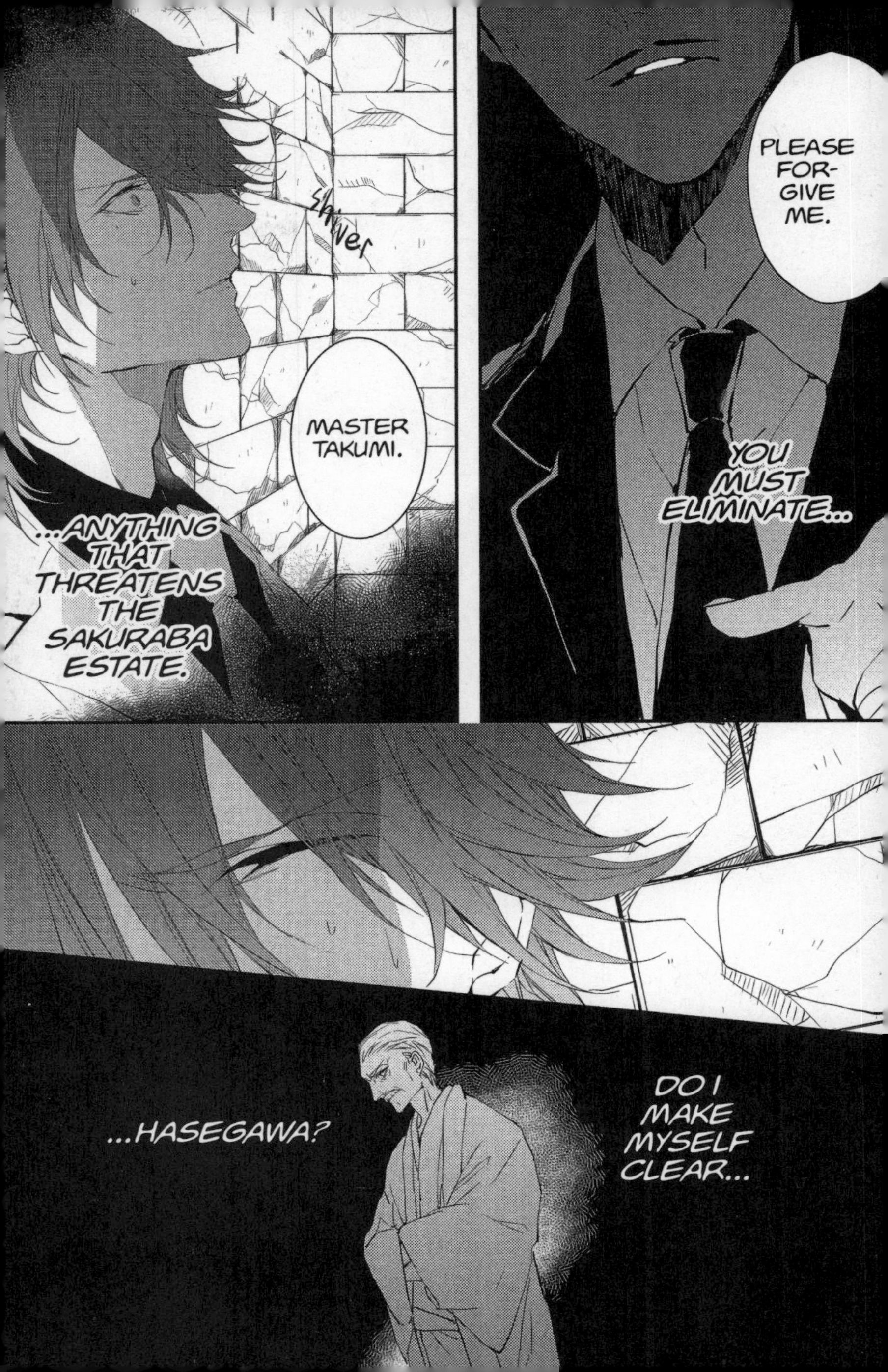
PLEASE FOR-GIVE ME.
YOU MUST ELIMINATE...
shiver
MASTER TAKUMI.
...ANYTHING THAT THREATENS THE SAKURABA ESTATE.
DO I MAKE MYSELF CLEAR...
...HASEGAWA?

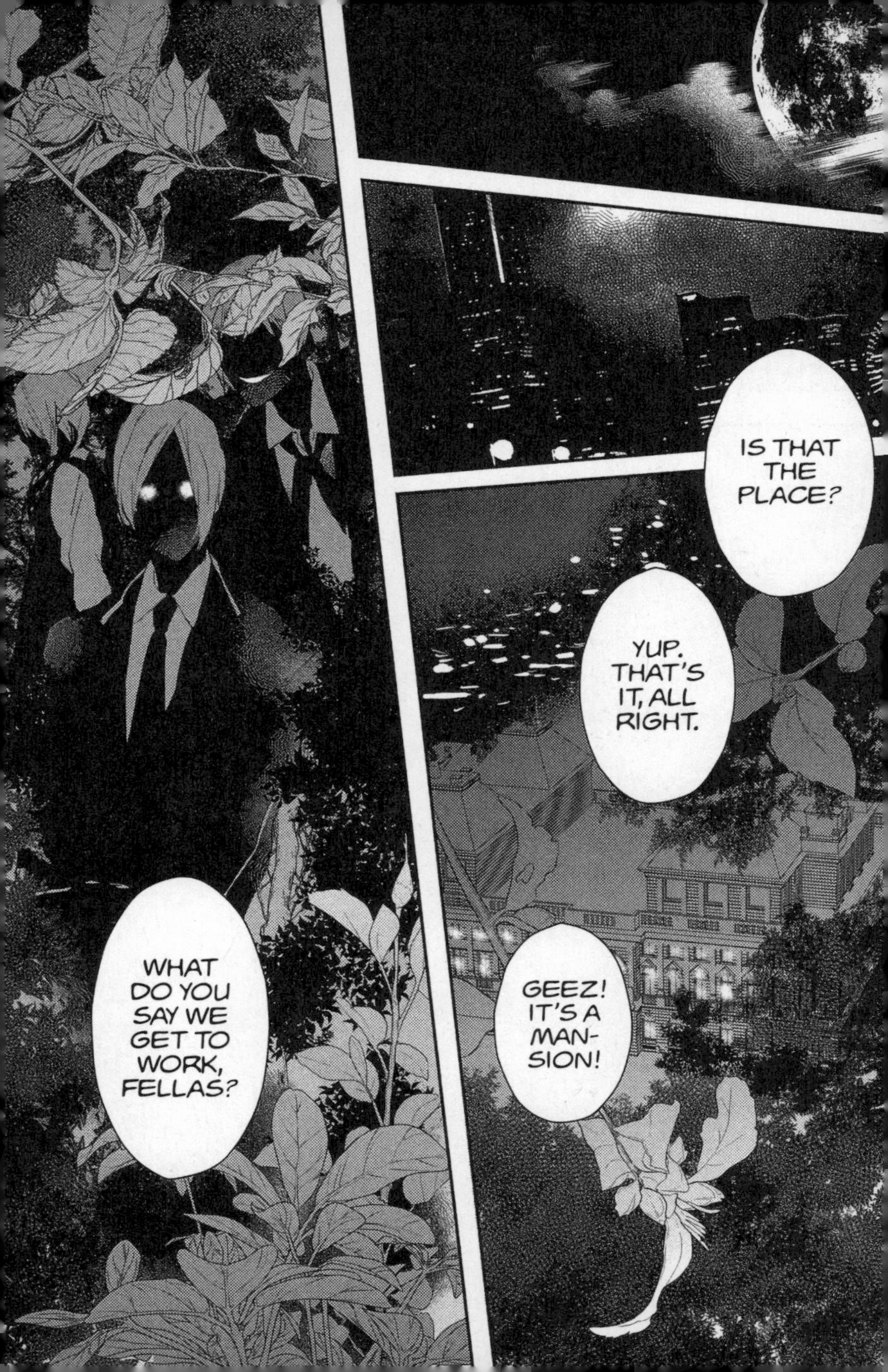
IS THAT THE PLACE?
YUP. THAT'S IT, ALL RIGHT.
GEEZ! IT'S A MAN-SION!
WHAT DO YOU SAY WE GET TO WORK, FELLAS?

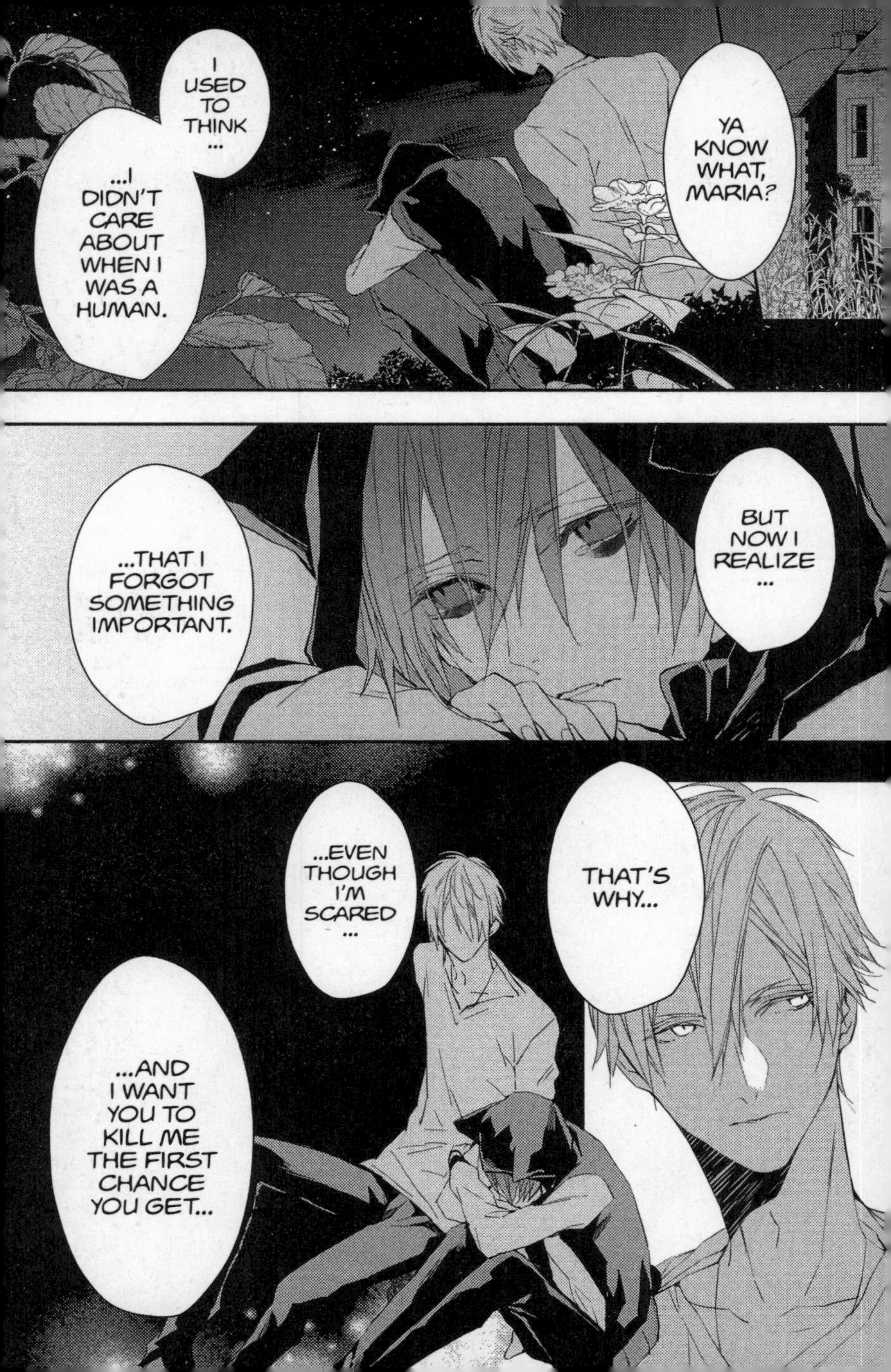
YA KNOW WHAT, MARIA?
I USED TO THINK...
...I DIDN'T CARE ABOUT WHEN I WAS A HUMAN.
BUT NOW I REALIZE...
...THAT I FORGOT SOMETHING IMPORTANT.
THAT'S WHY...
...EVEN THOUGH I'M SCARED...
...AND I WANT YOU TO KILL ME THE FIRST CHANCE YOU GET...

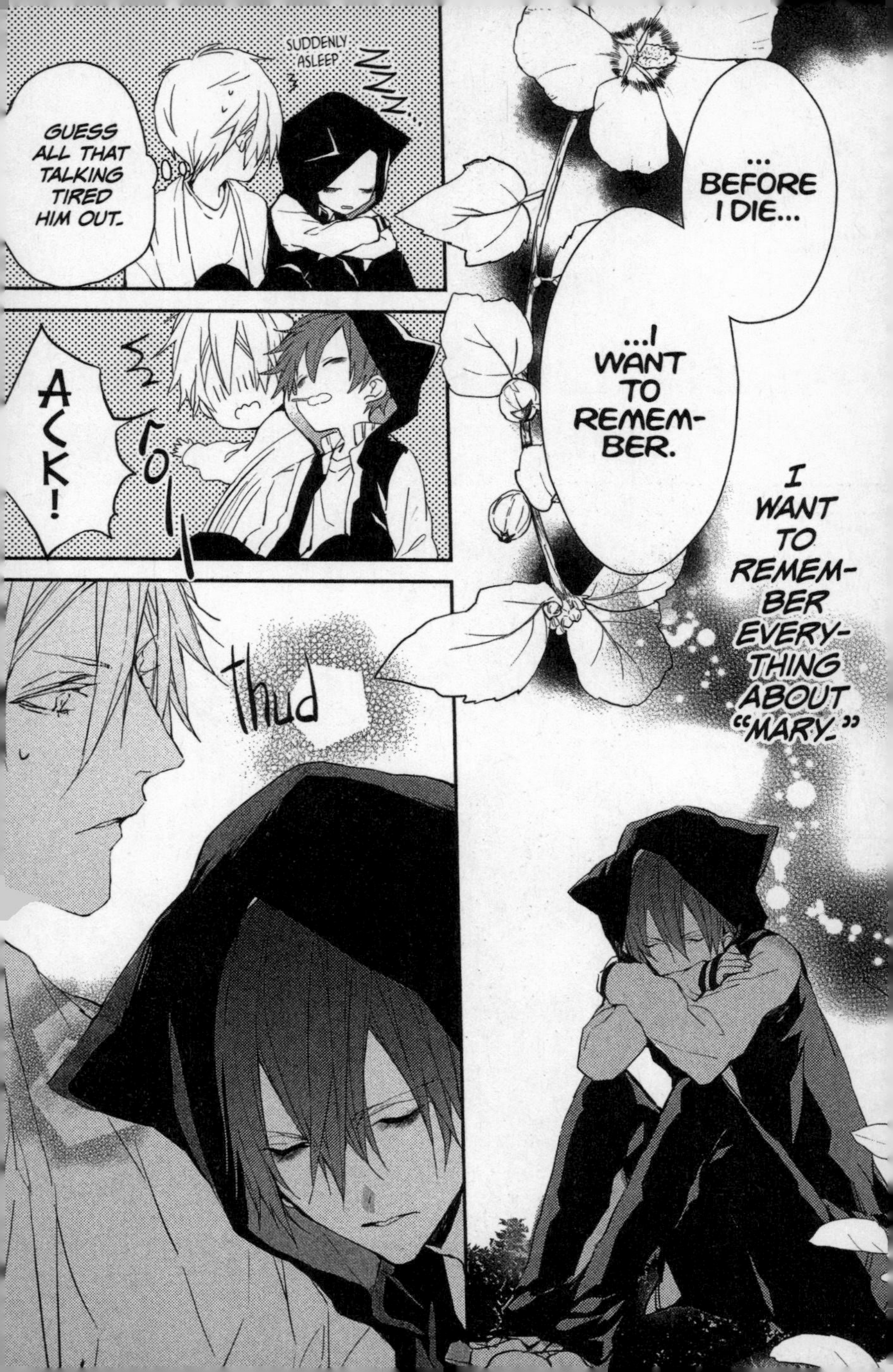
... BEFORE I DIE...
...I WANT TO REMEMBER.
I WANT TO REMEMBER EVERYTHING ABOUT "MARY."
SUDDENLY ASLEEP
ZZZ...
GUESS ALL THAT TALKING TIRED HIM OUT.
ACK!
thud

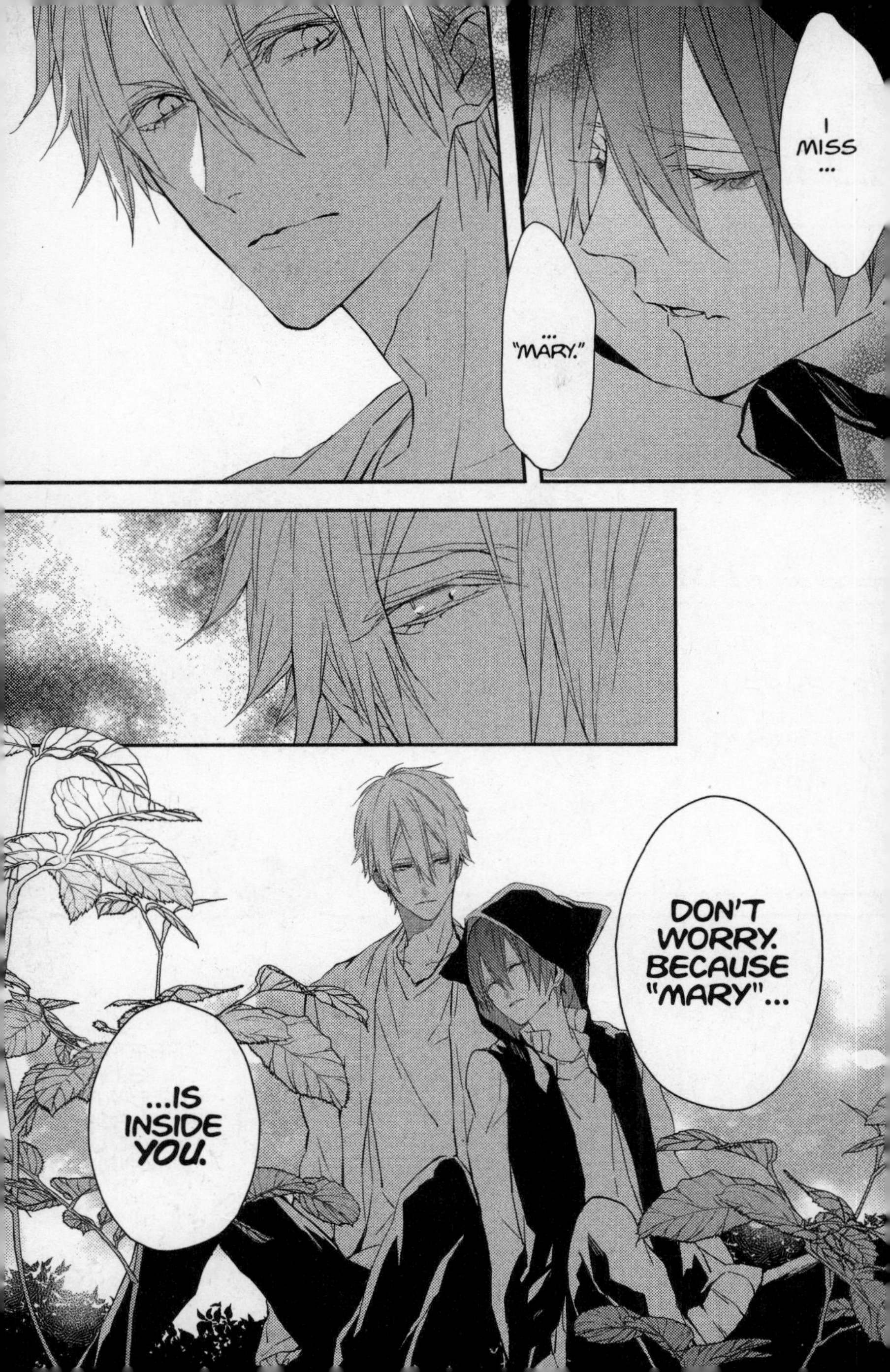
I MISS ...
... "MARY."
DON'T WORRY. BECAUSE "MARY"...
...IS INSIDE YOU.

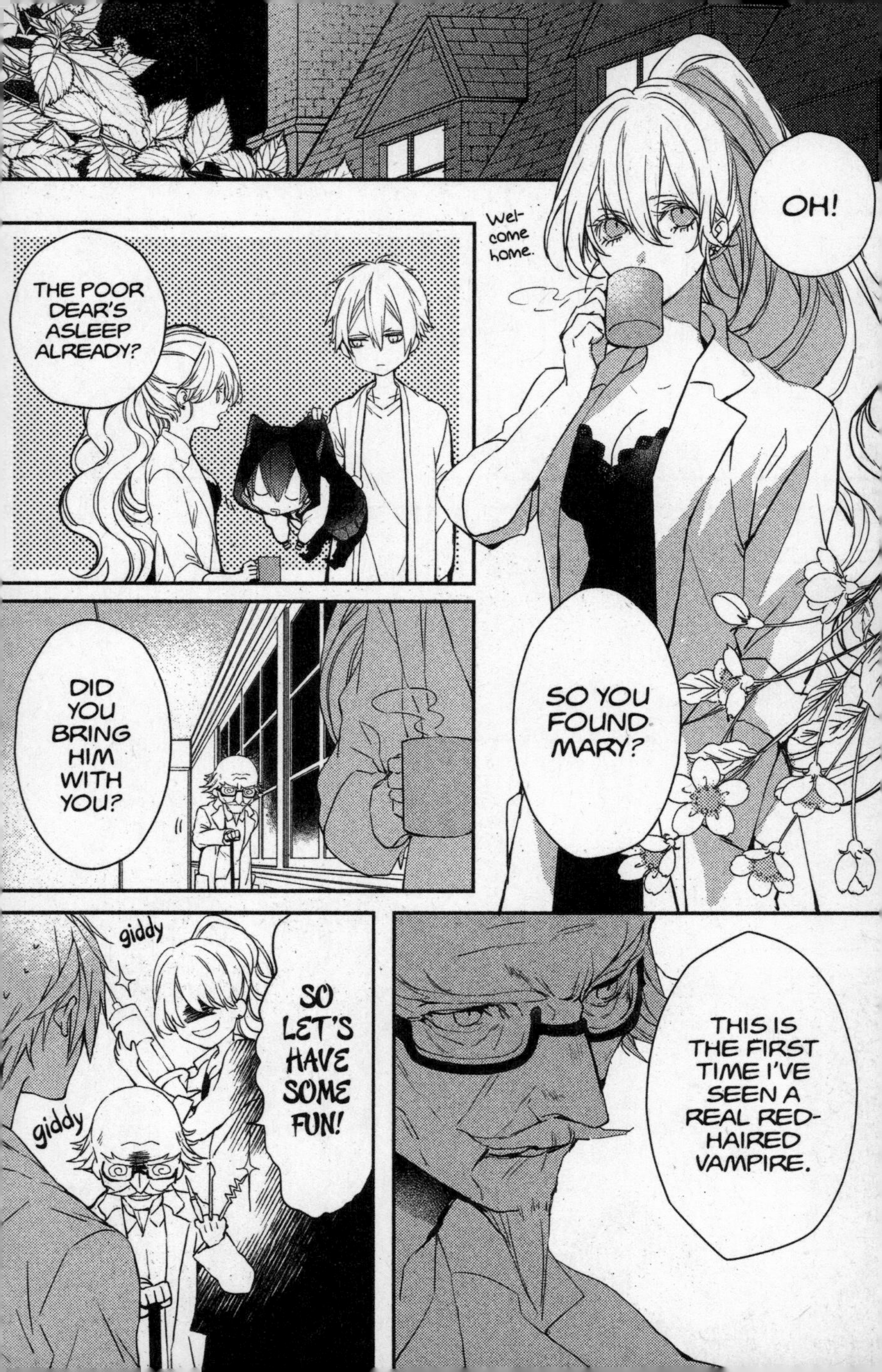
OH!
Wel-come home.
SO YOU FOUND MARY?
THE POOR DEAR'S ASLEEP ALREADY?
DID YOU BRING HIM WITH YOU?
THIS IS THE FIRST TIME I'VE SEEN A REAL RED-HAIRED VAMPIRE.
giddy
giddy
SO LET'S HAVE SOME FUN!

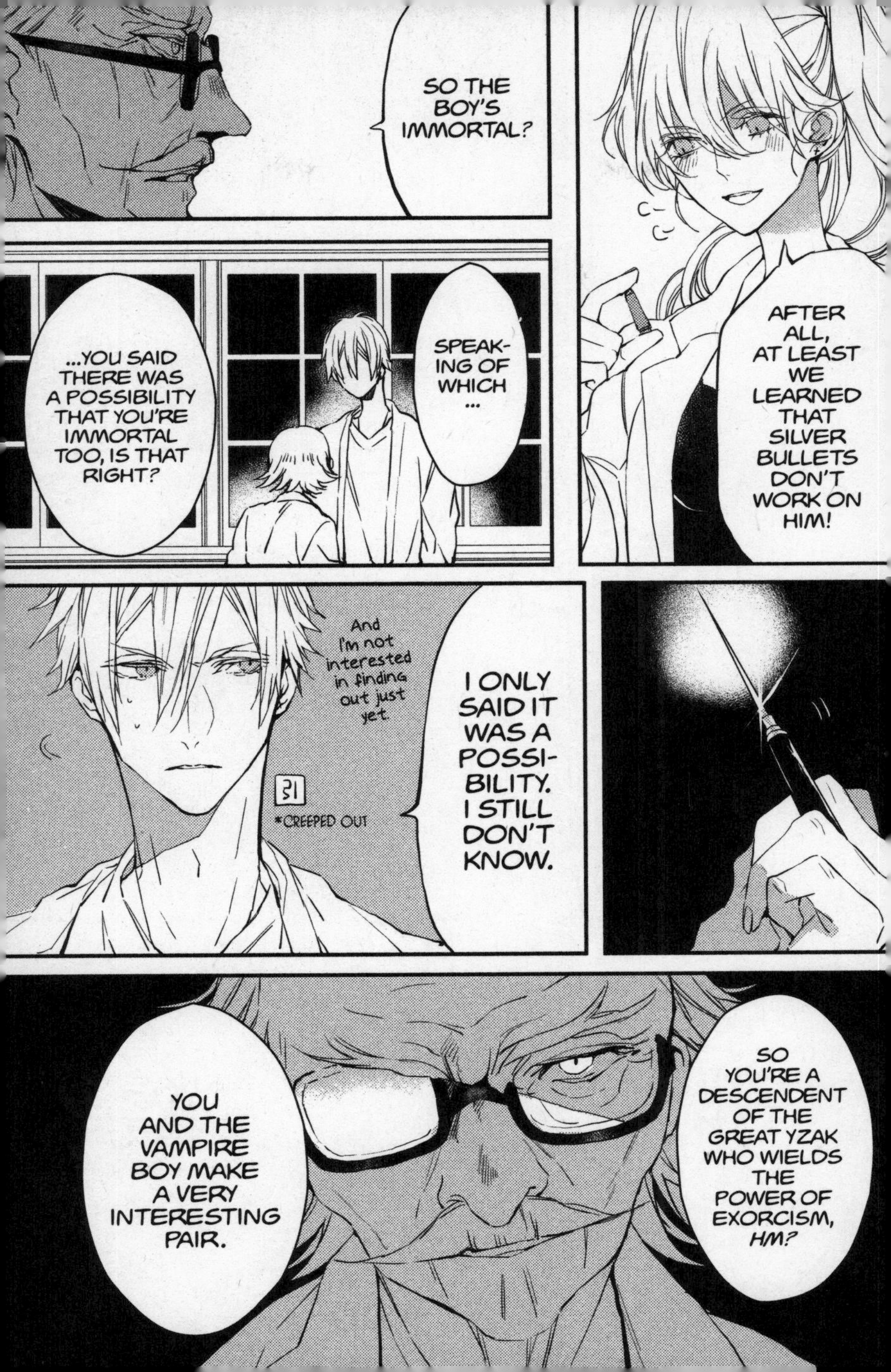
AFTER ALL, AT LEAST WE LEARNED THAT SILVER BULLETS DON'T WORK ON HIM!
SO THE BOY'S IMMORTAL?
SPEAK-ING OF WHICH ...
...YOU SAID THERE WAS A POSSIBILITY THAT YOU'RE IMMORTAL TOO, IS THAT RIGHT?
I ONLY SAID IT WAS A POSSI-BILITY. I STILL DON'T KNOW.
And I'm not interested in finding out just yet.
*CREEPED OUT
SO YOU'RE A DESCENDENT OF THE GREAT YZAK WHO WIELDS THE POWER OF EXORCISM, HM?
YOU AND THE VAMPIRE BOY MAKE A VERY INTERESTING PAIR.

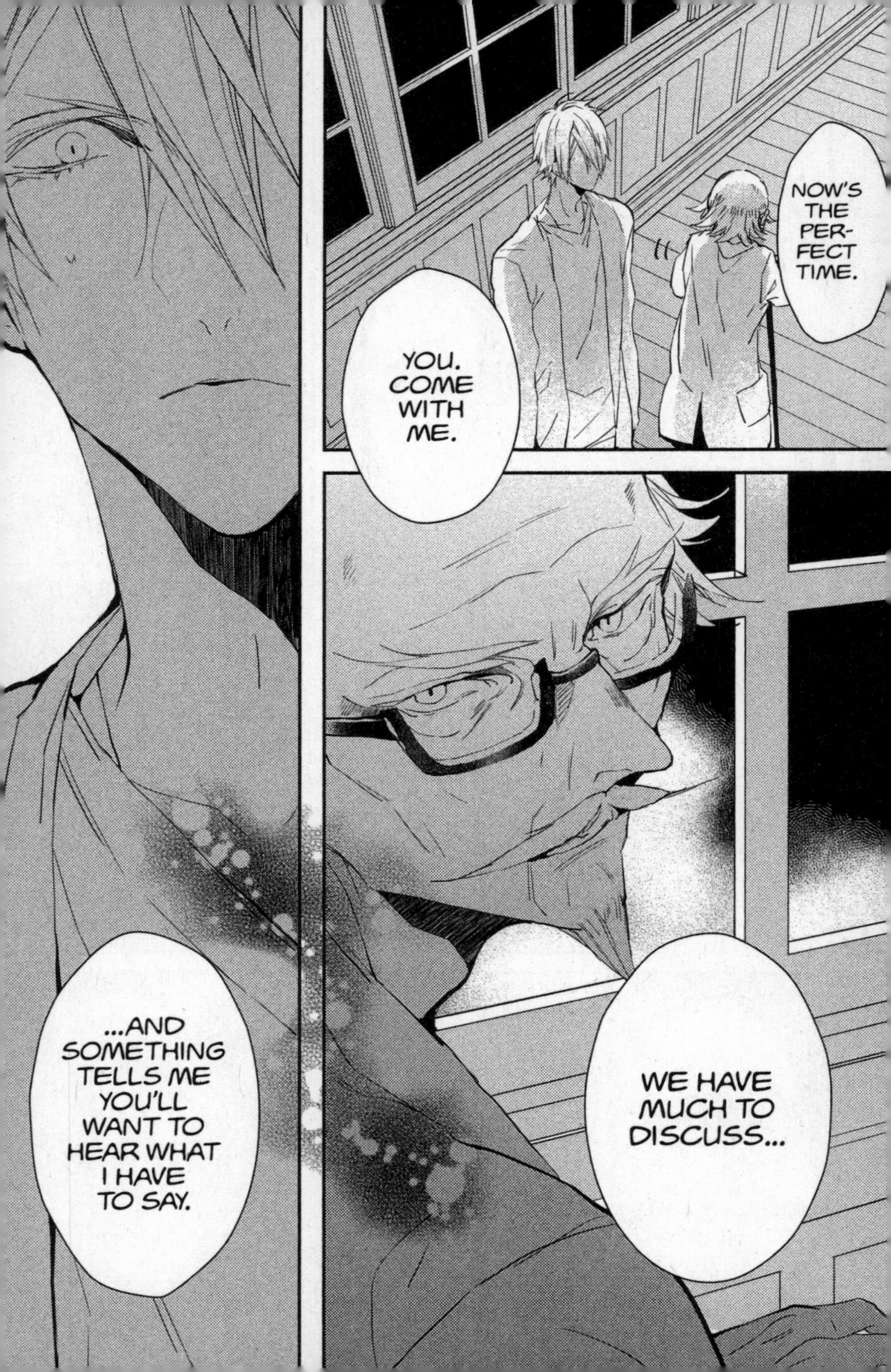
NOW'S THE PER-FECT TIME.
YOU. COME WITH ME.
WE HAVE MUCH TO DISCUSS...
...AND SOMETHING TELLS ME YOU'LL WANT TO HEAR WHAT I HAVE TO SAY.

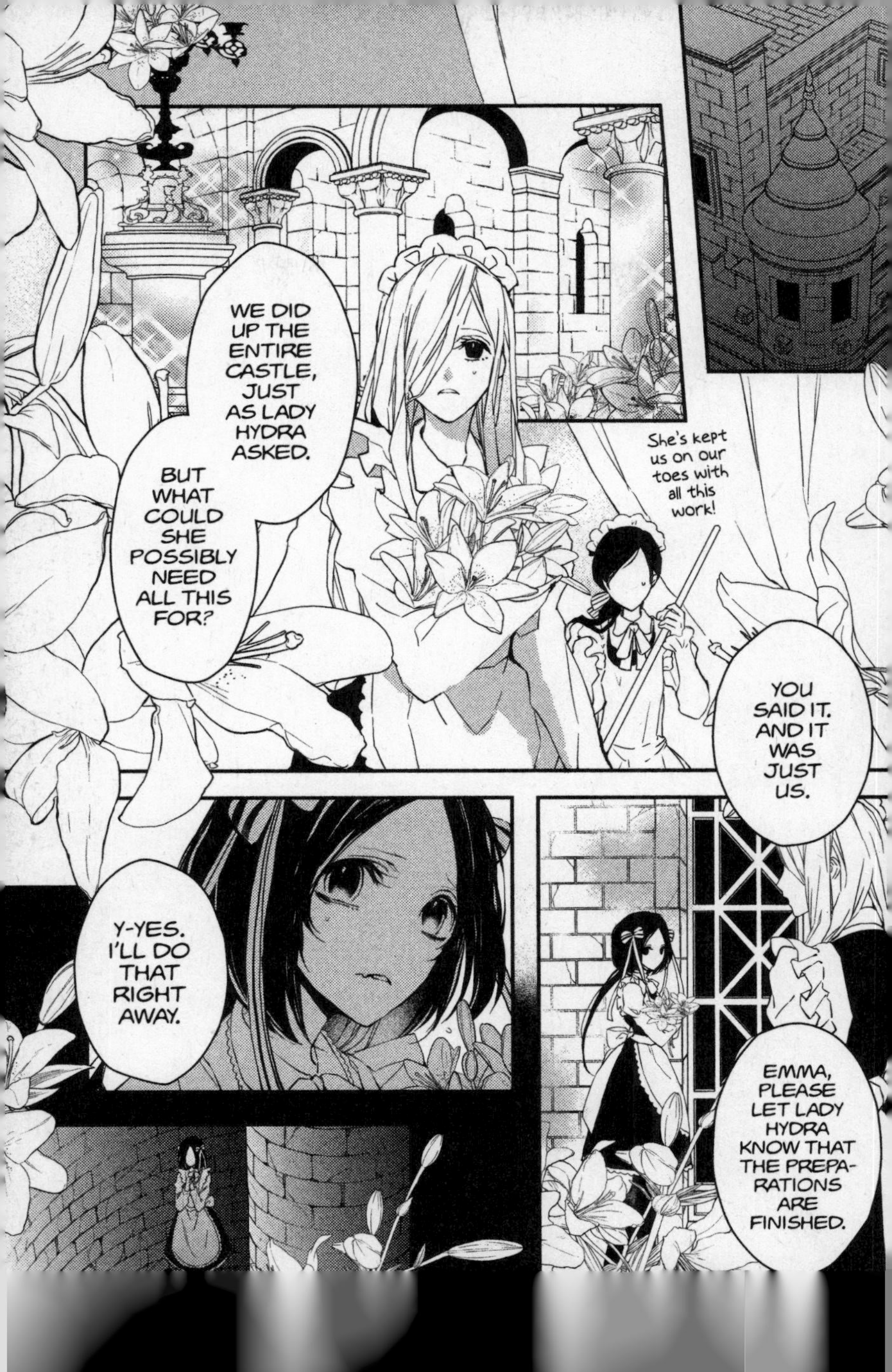
WE DID UP THE ENTIRE CASTLE, JUST AS LADY HYDRA ASKED.
BUT WHAT COULD SHE POSSIBLY NEED ALL THIS FOR?
She's kept us on our toes with all this work!
YOU SAID IT. AND IT WAS JUST US.
EMMA, PLEASE LET LADY HYDRA KNOW THAT THE PREPARATIONS ARE FINISHED.
Y-YES. I'LL DO THAT RIGHT AWAY.

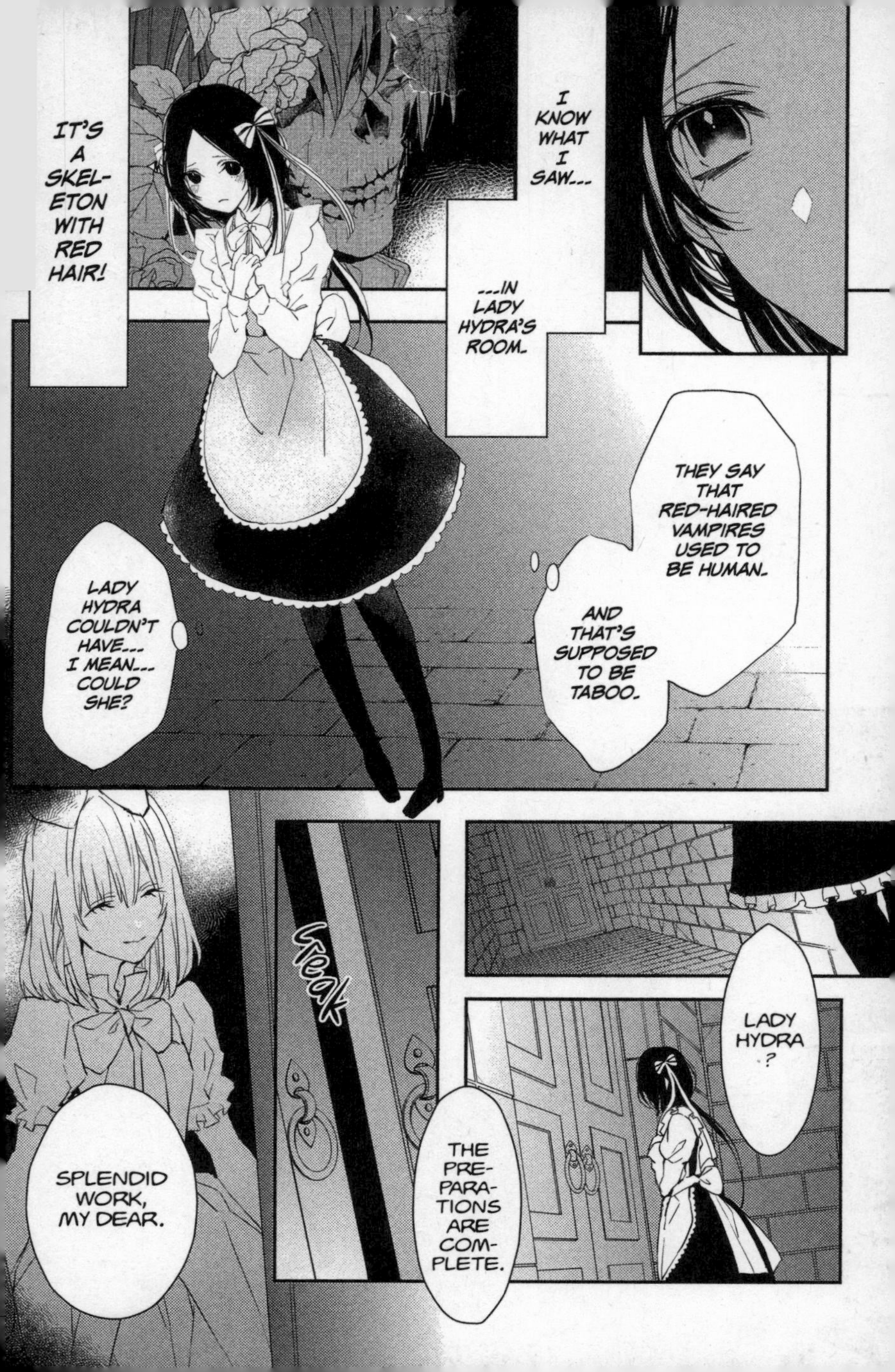
I KNOW WHAT I SAW...
...IN LADY HYDRA'S ROOM.
IT'S A SKELETON WITH RED HAIR!
THEY SAY THAT RED-HAIRED VAMPIRES USED TO BE HUMAN.
AND THAT'S SUPPOSED TO BE TABOO.
LADY HYDRA COULDN'T HAVE... I MEAN... COULD SHE?
LADY HYDRA?
creak
THE PREPARATIONS ARE COMPLETE.
SPLENDID WORK, MY DEAR.

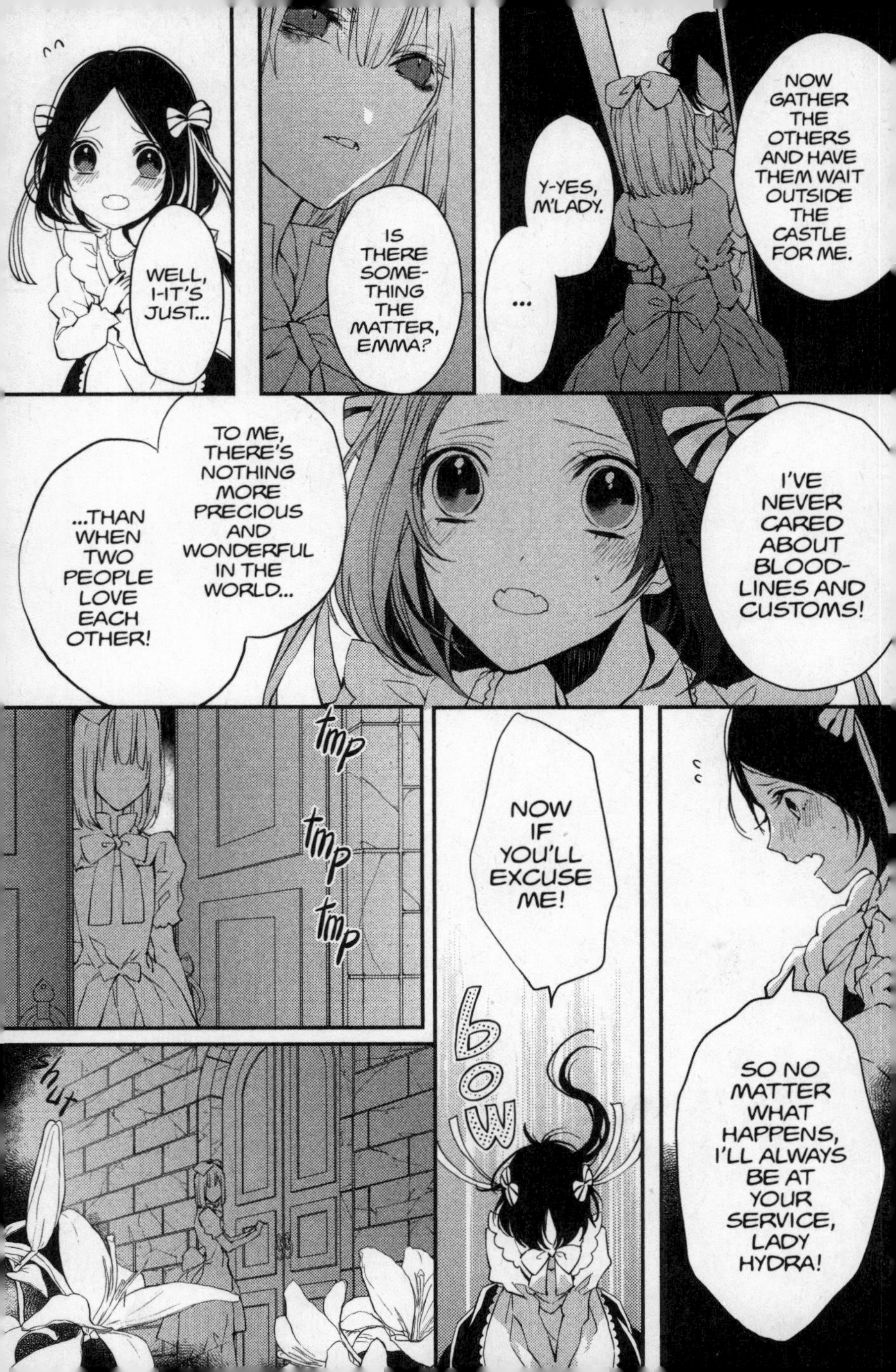
NOW GATHER THE OTHERS AND HAVE THEM WAIT OUTSIDE THE CASTLE FOR ME.
Y-YES, M'LADY.
...
IS THERE SOMETHING THE MATTER, EMMA?
WELL, I-IT'S JUST...
I'VE NEVER CARED ABOUT BLOODLINES AND CUSTOMS!
TO ME, THERE'S NOTHING MORE PRECIOUS AND WONDERFUL IN THE WORLD...
...THAN WHEN TWO PEOPLE LOVE EACH OTHER!
SO NO MATTER WHAT HAPPENS, I'LL ALWAYS BE AT YOUR SERVICE, LADY HYDRA!
NOW IF YOU'LL EXCUSE ME!
BOW
tmp
tmp
tmp
shut

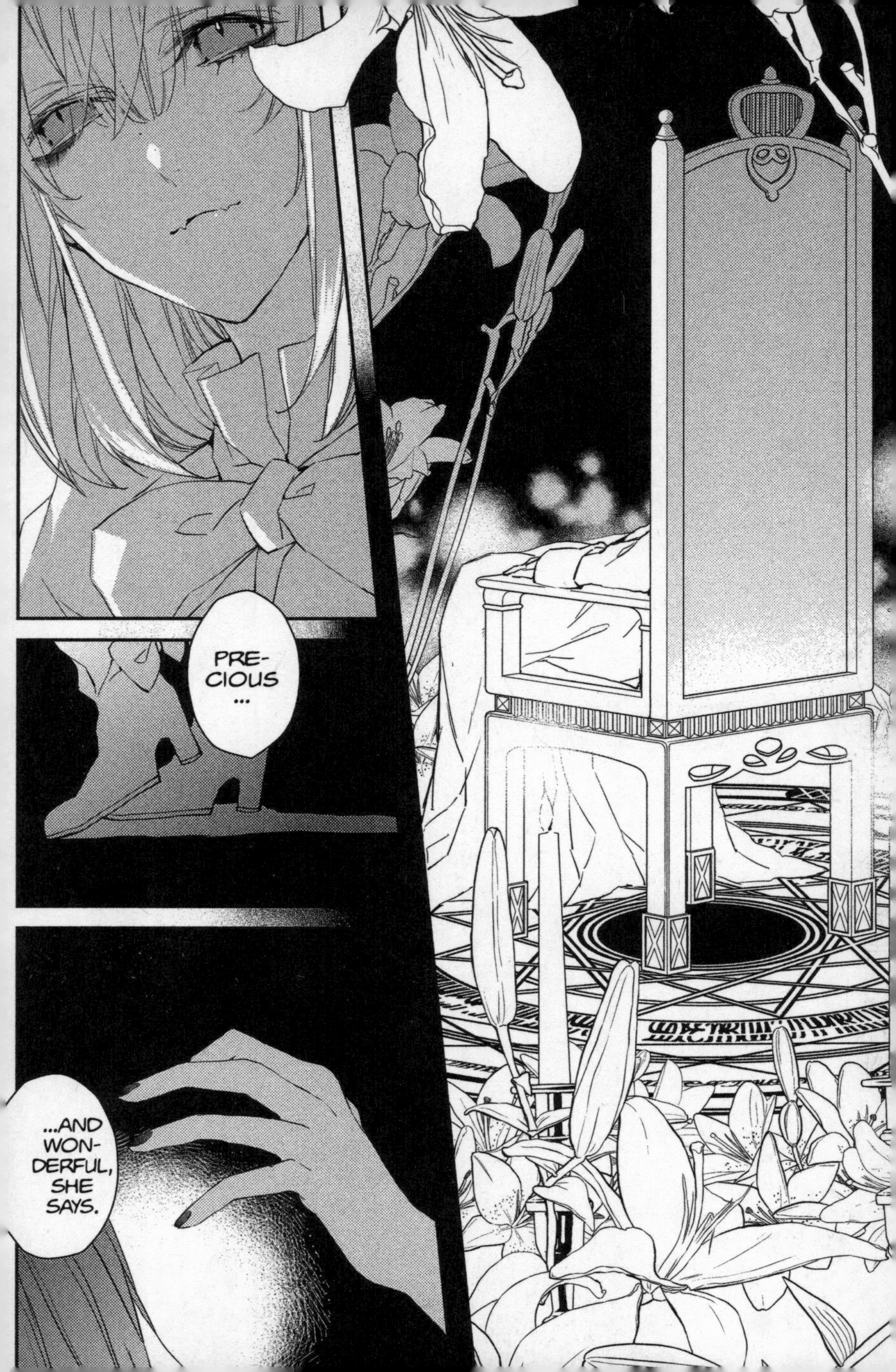
PRE-CIOUS...
...AND WON-DERFUL, SHE SAYS.

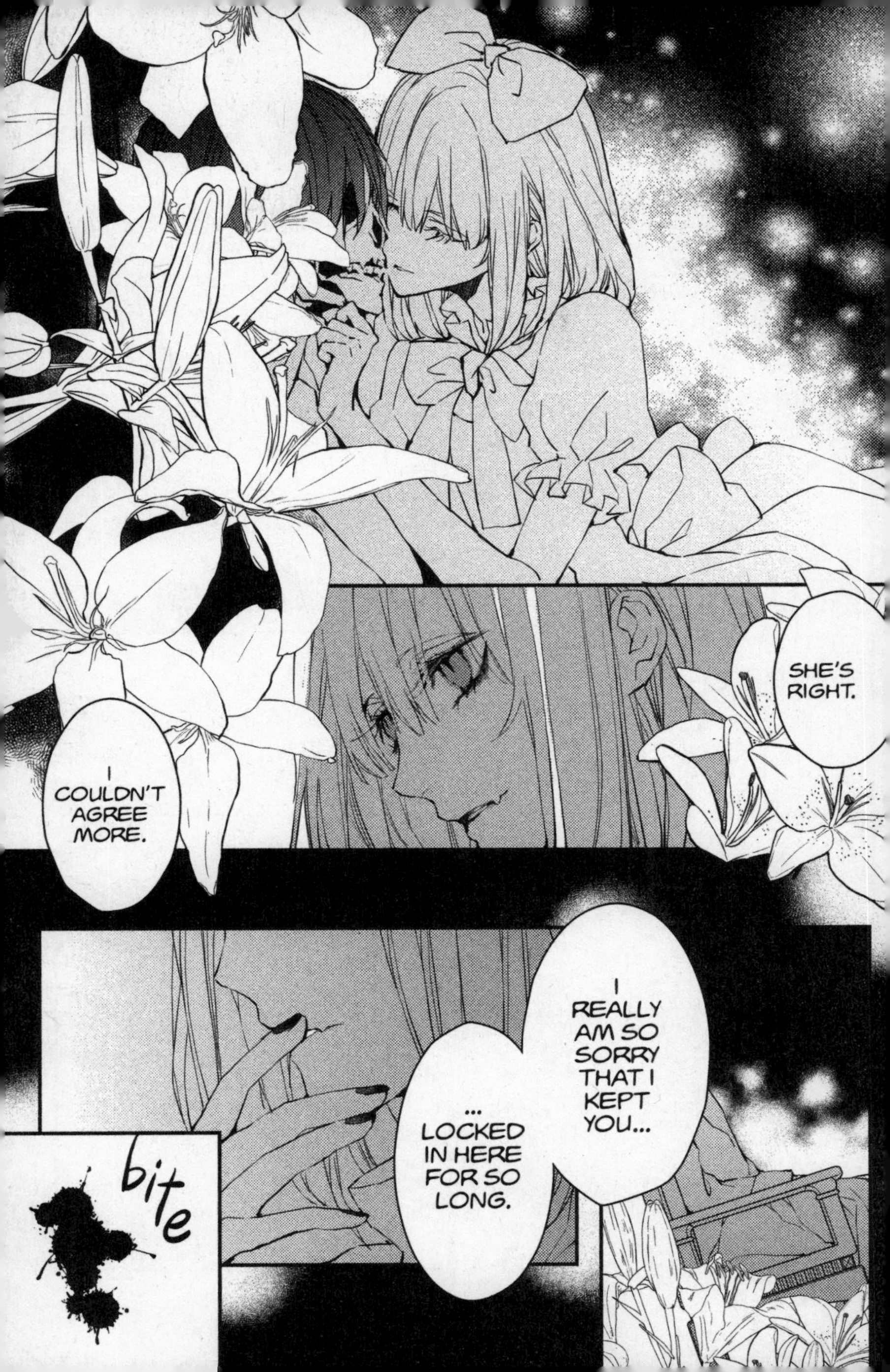
SHE'S RIGHT.
I COULDN'T AGREE MORE.
I REALLY AM SO SORRY THAT I KEPT YOU...
...LOCKED IN HERE FOR SO LONG.
bite

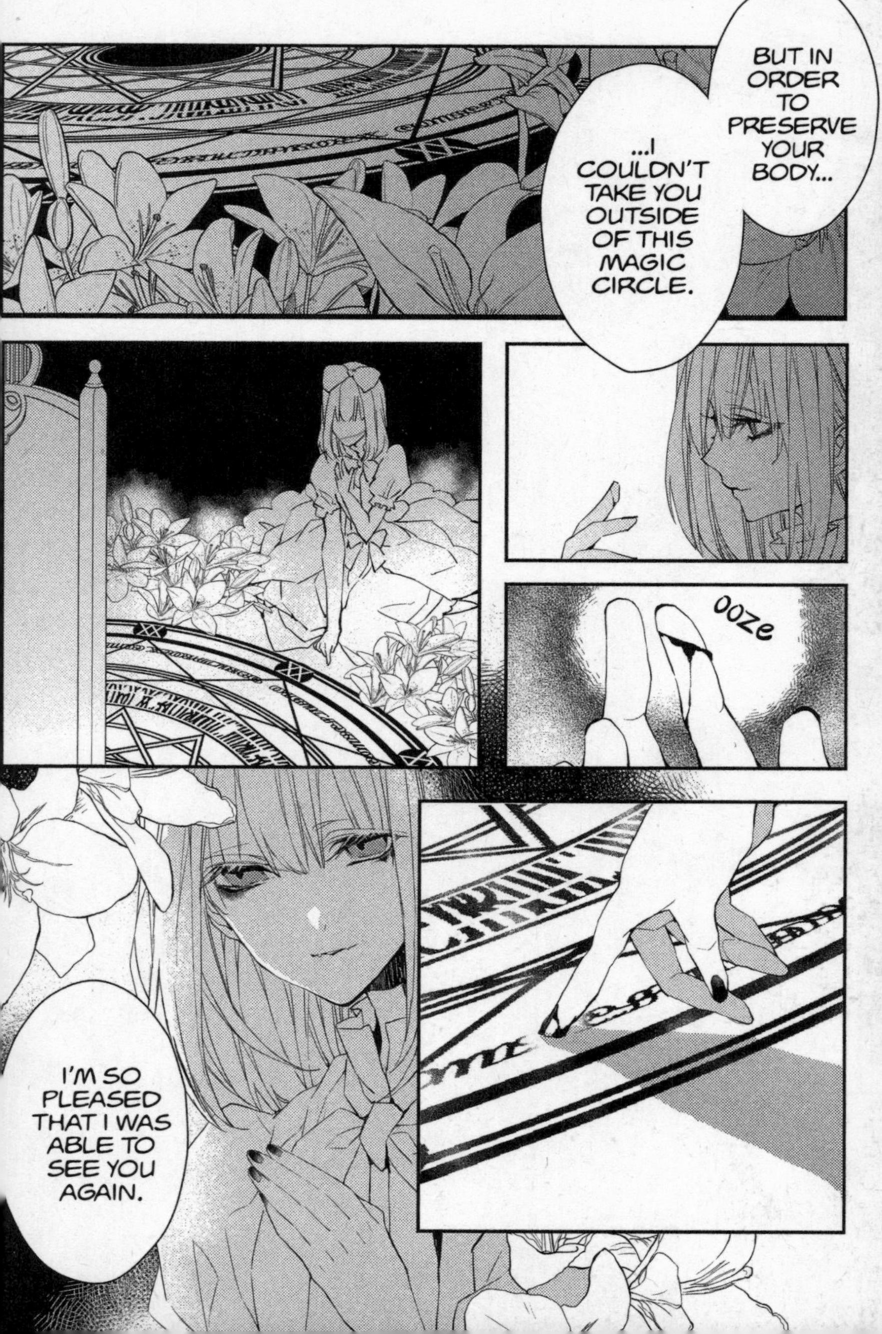
BUT IN ORDER TO PRESERVE YOUR BODY...
...I COULDN'T TAKE YOU OUTSIDE OF THIS MAGIC CIRCLE.
ooze
I'M SO PLEASED THAT I WAS ABLE TO SEE YOU AGAIN.

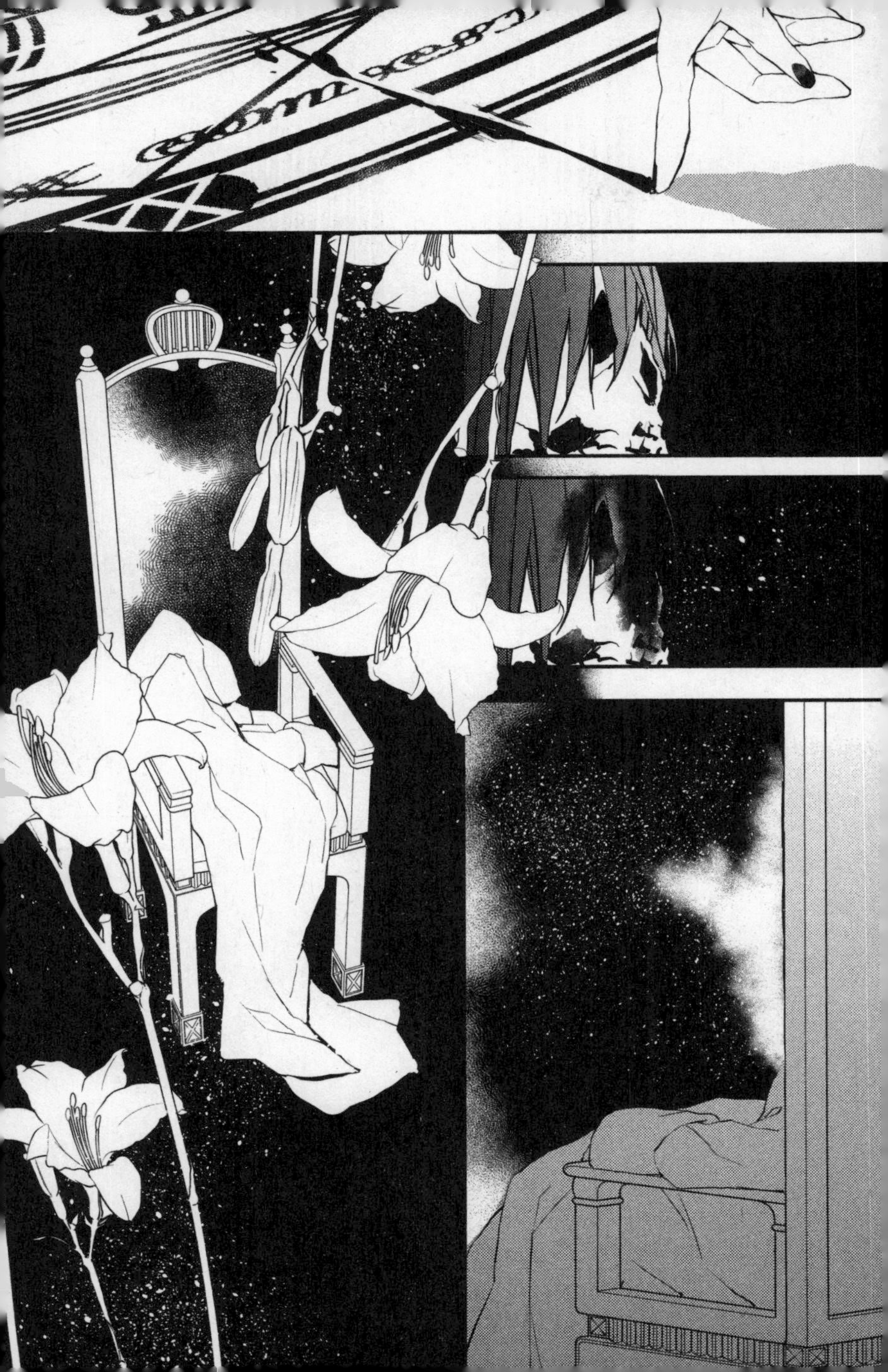

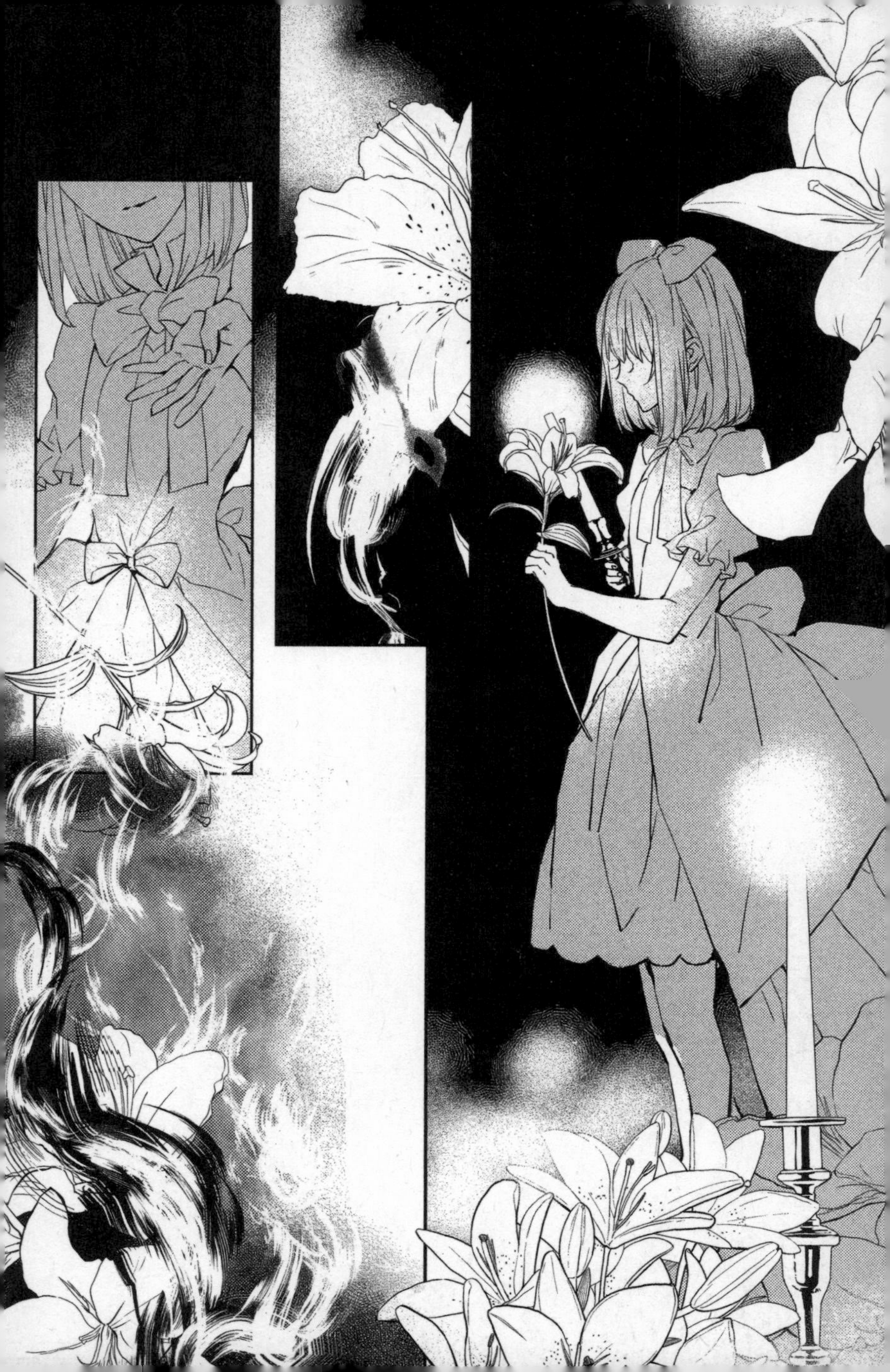

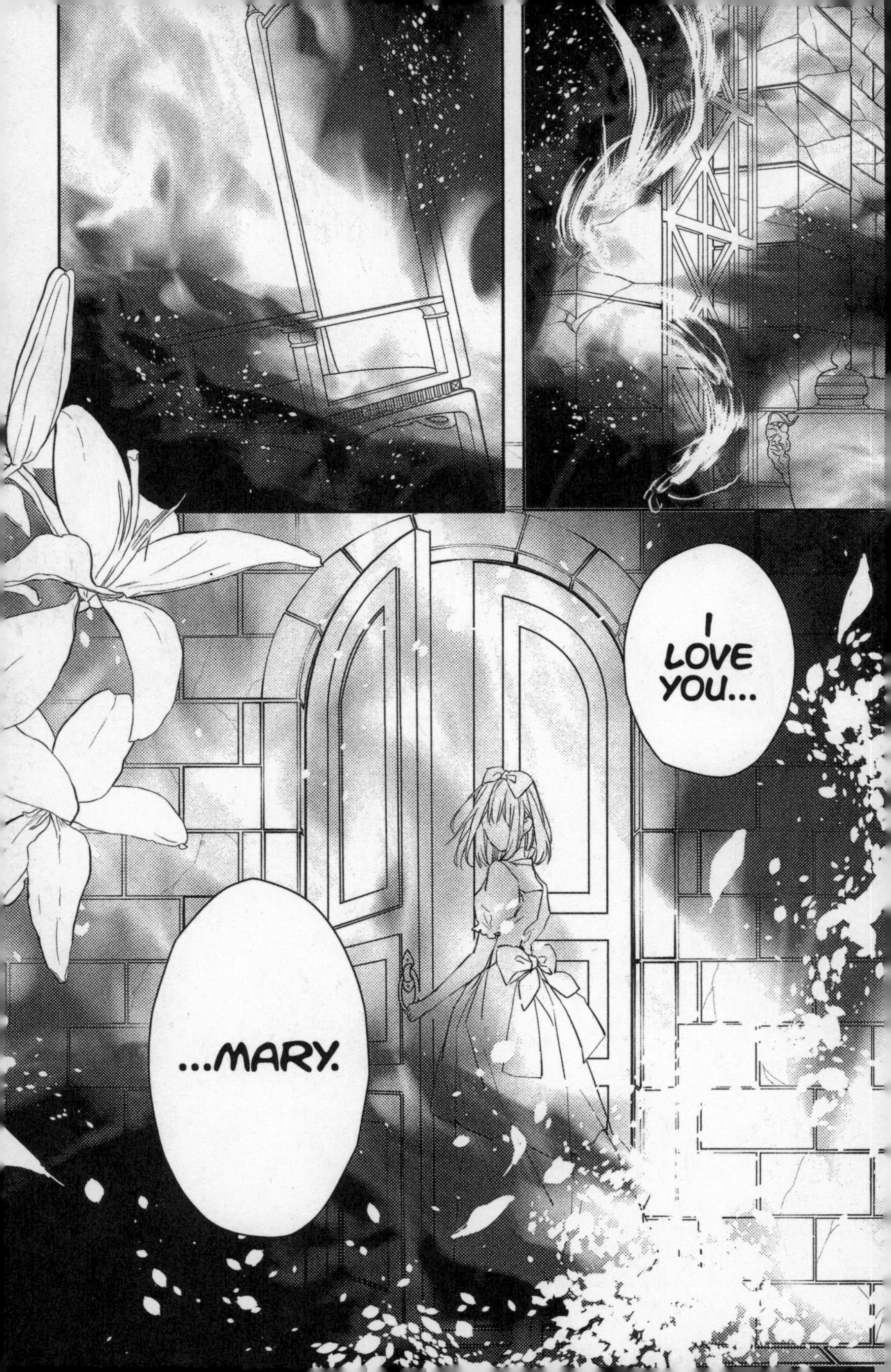
I LOVE YOU...
...MARY.

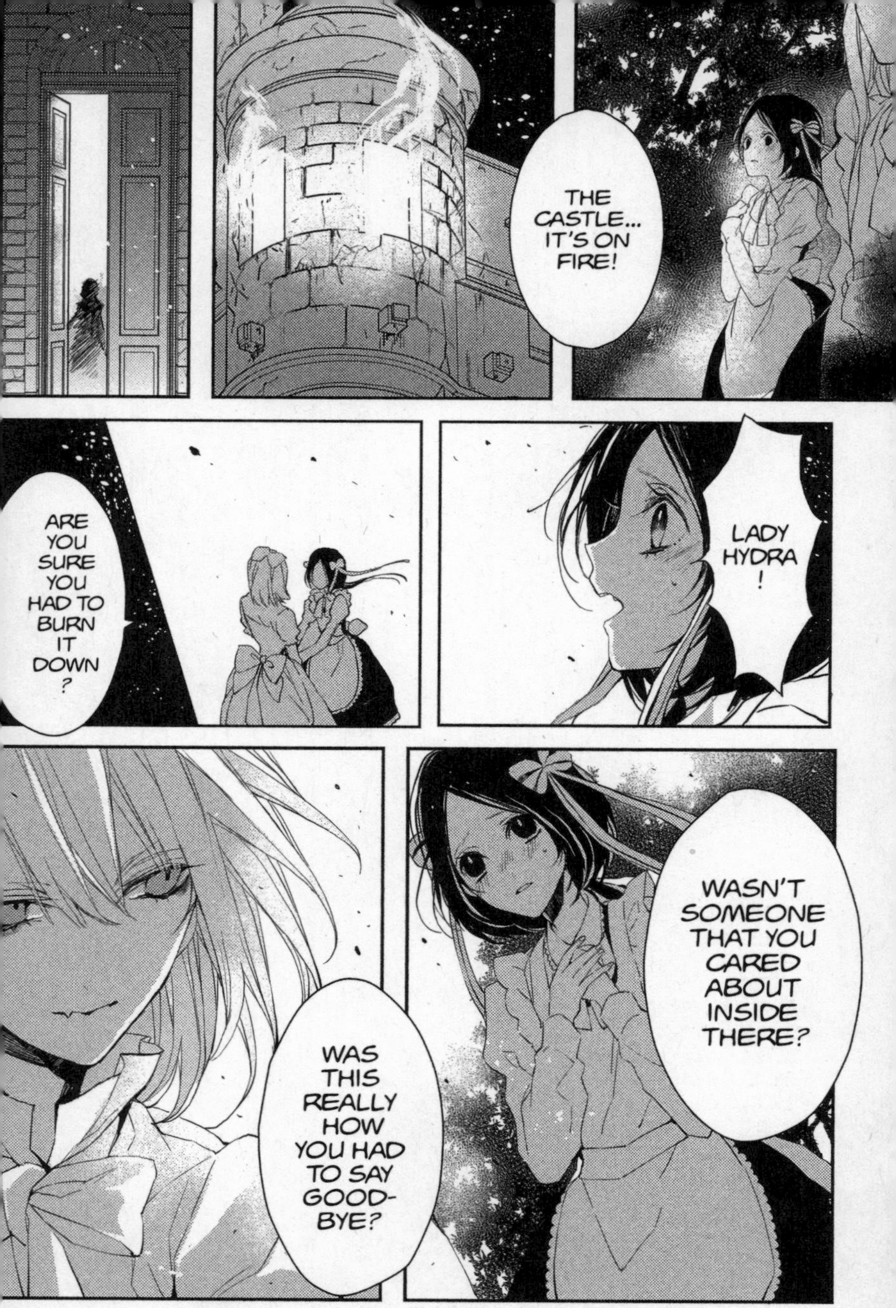
THE CASTLE... IT'S ON FIRE!
LADY HYDRA!
ARE YOU SURE YOU HAD TO BURN IT DOWN?
WASN'T SOMEONE THAT YOU CARED ABOUT INSIDE THERE?
WAS THIS REALLY HOW YOU HAD TO SAY GOOD-BYE?

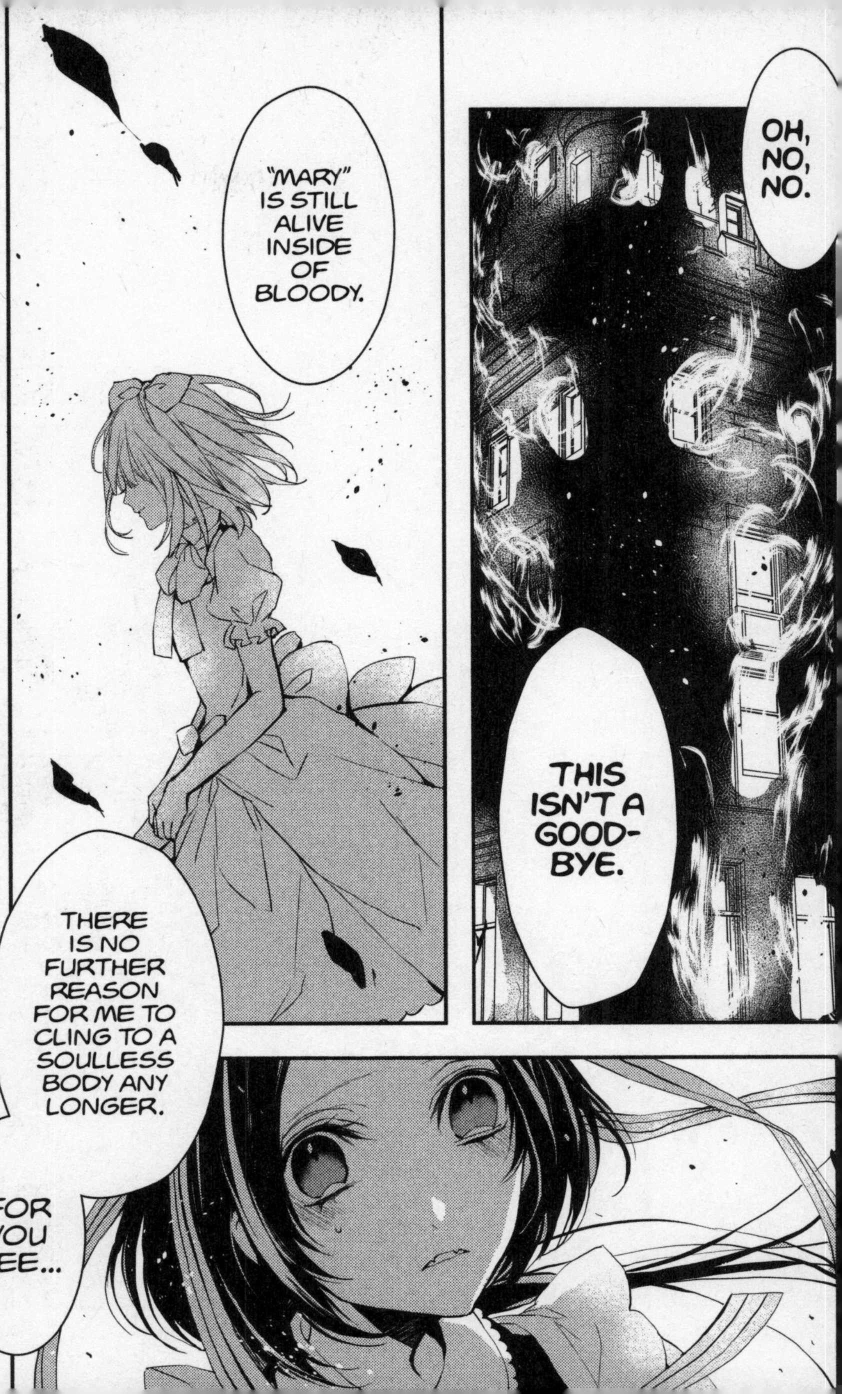
OH, NO, NO.
THIS ISN'T A GOOD-BYE.
"MARY" IS STILL ALIVE INSIDE OF BLOODY.
THERE IS NO FURTHER REASON FOR ME TO CLING TO A SOULLESS BODY ANY LONGER.
FOR YOU SEE...

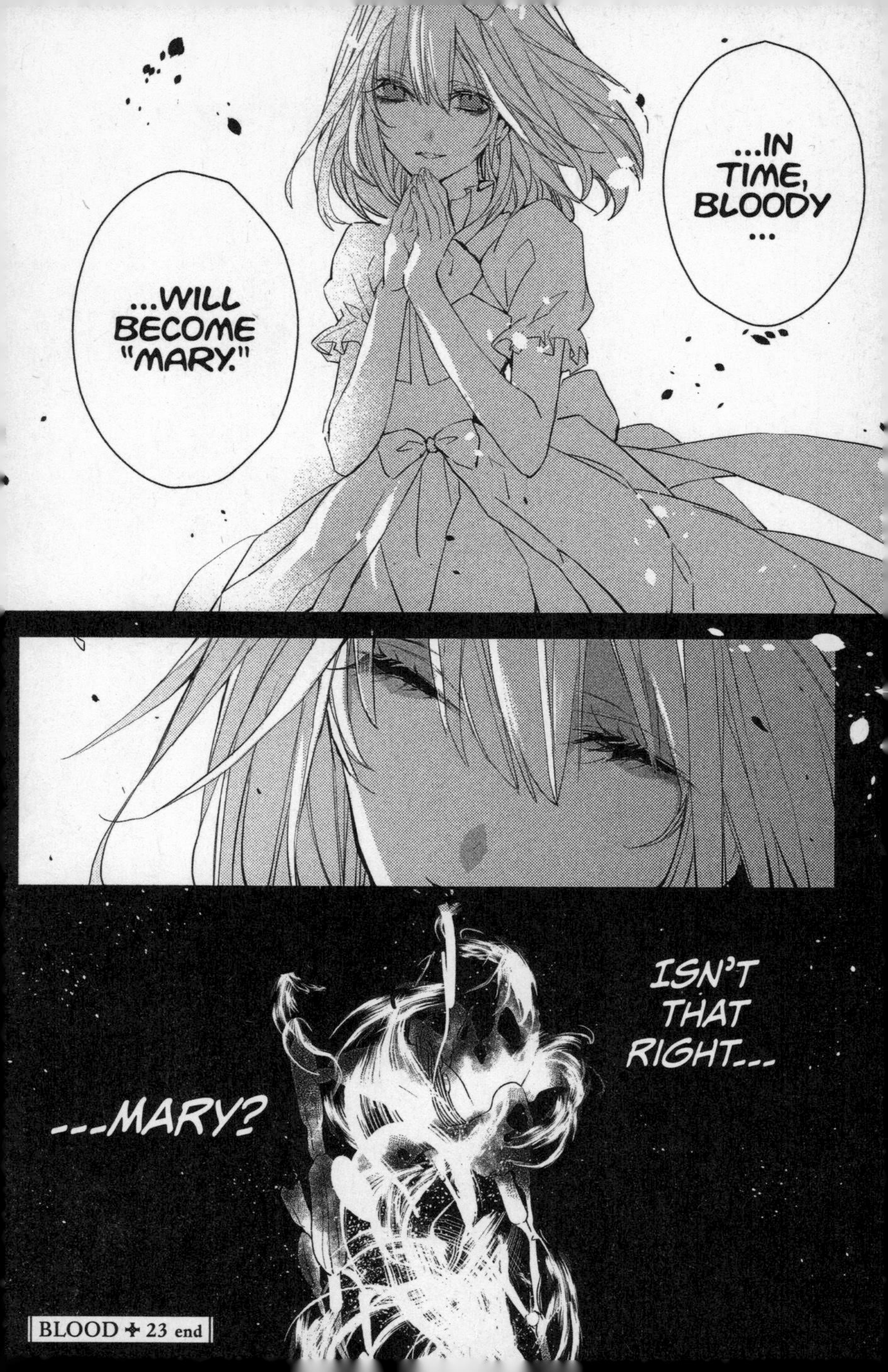
...IN TIME, BLOODY ...
...WILL BECOME "MARY."
ISN'T THAT RIGHT...
...MARY?
BLOOD ✤ 23 end

Bloody+Mary

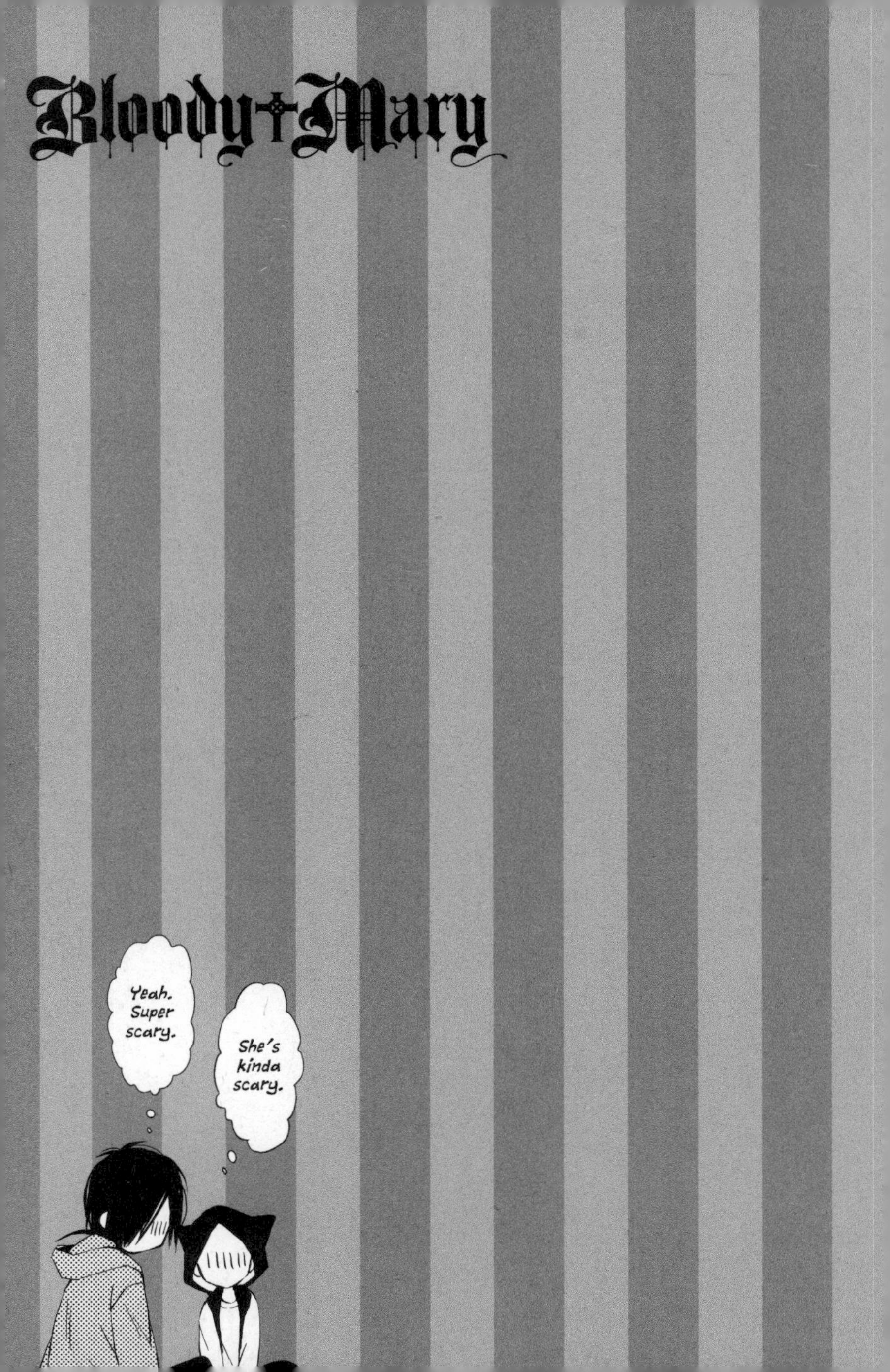
She's kinda scary.
Yeah. Super scary.

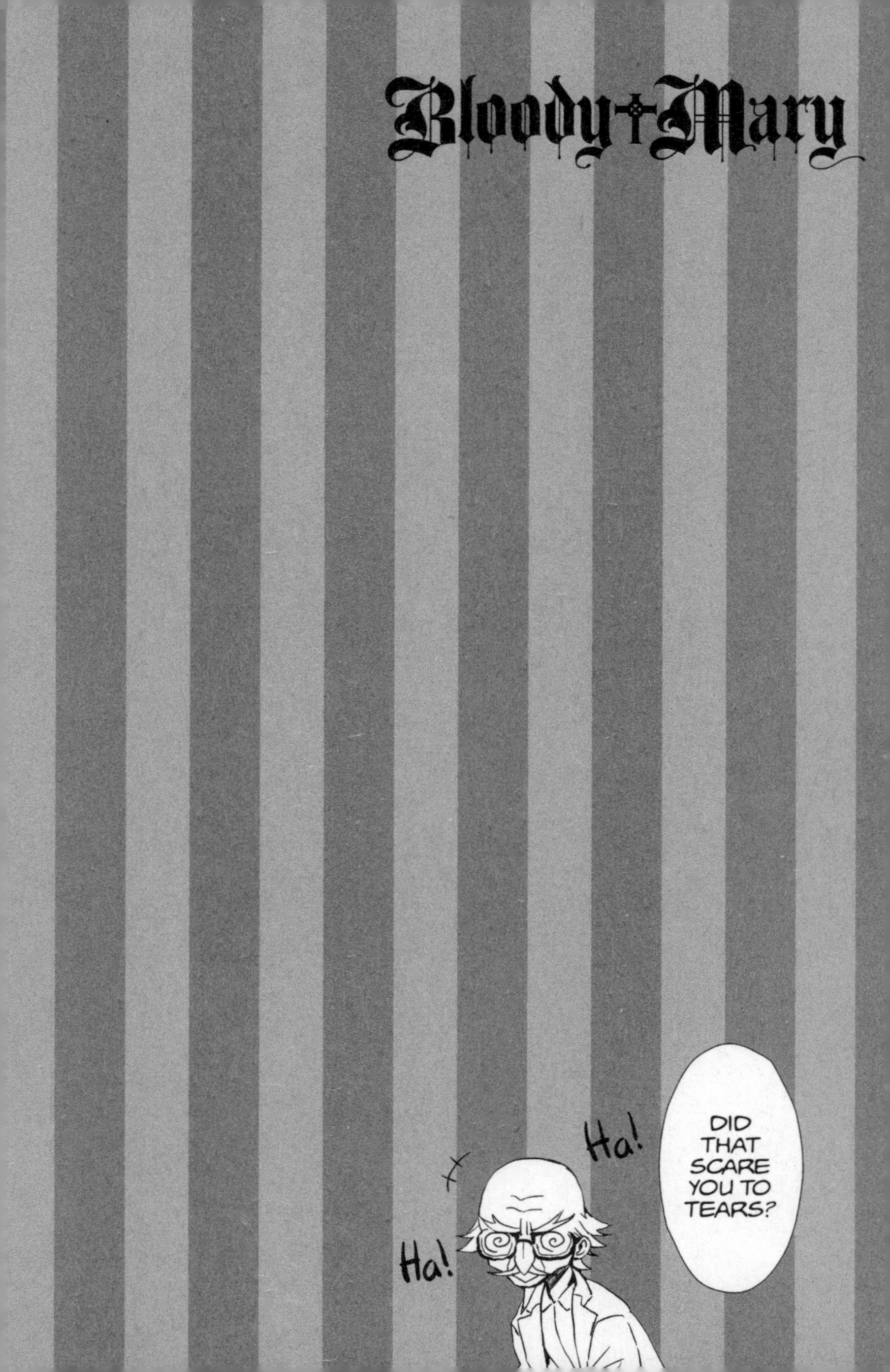
Bloody+Mary
DID THAT SCARE YOU TO TEARS?
Ha!
Ha!

BLOOD ✧ 24 Then Alone

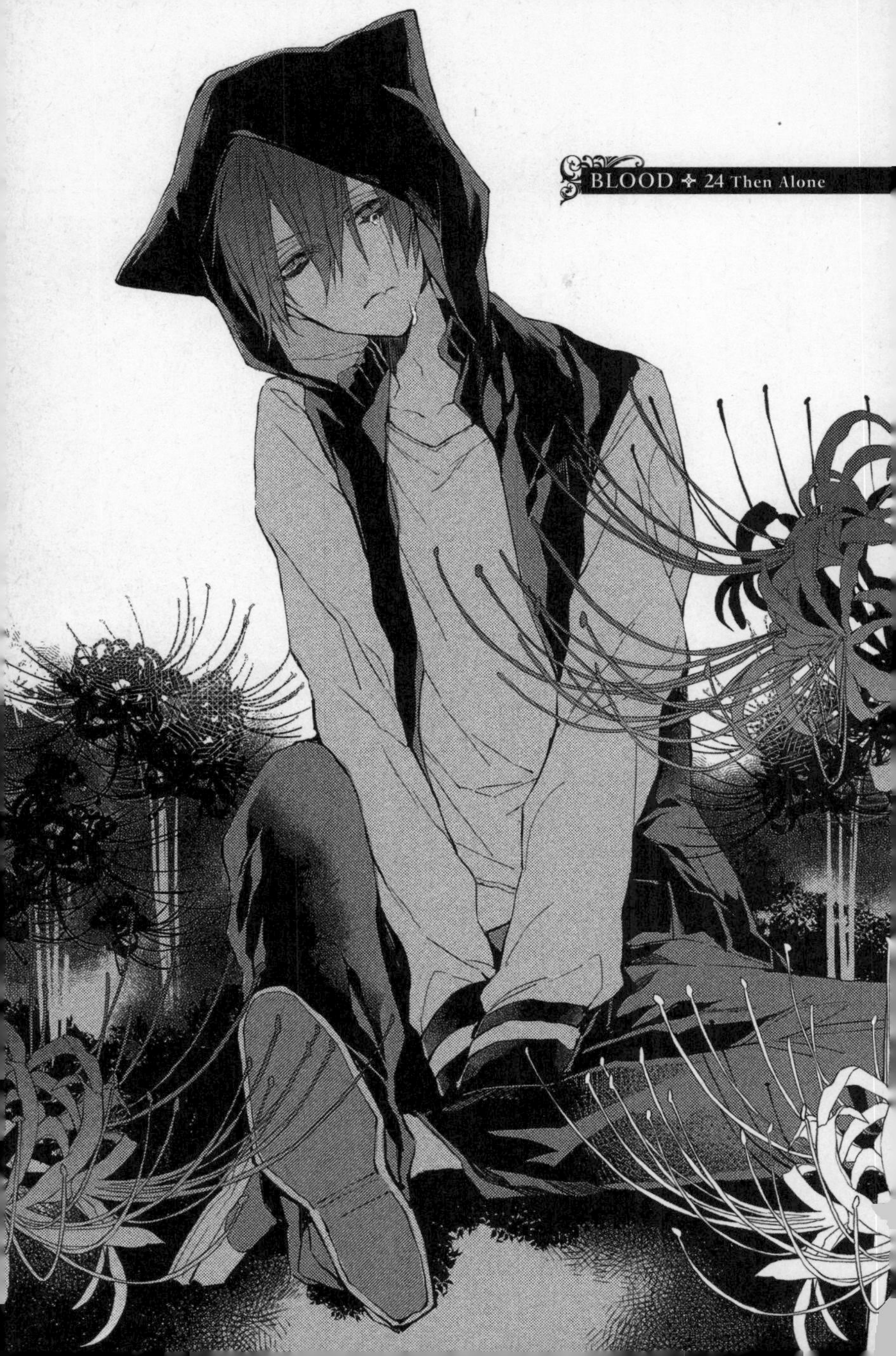

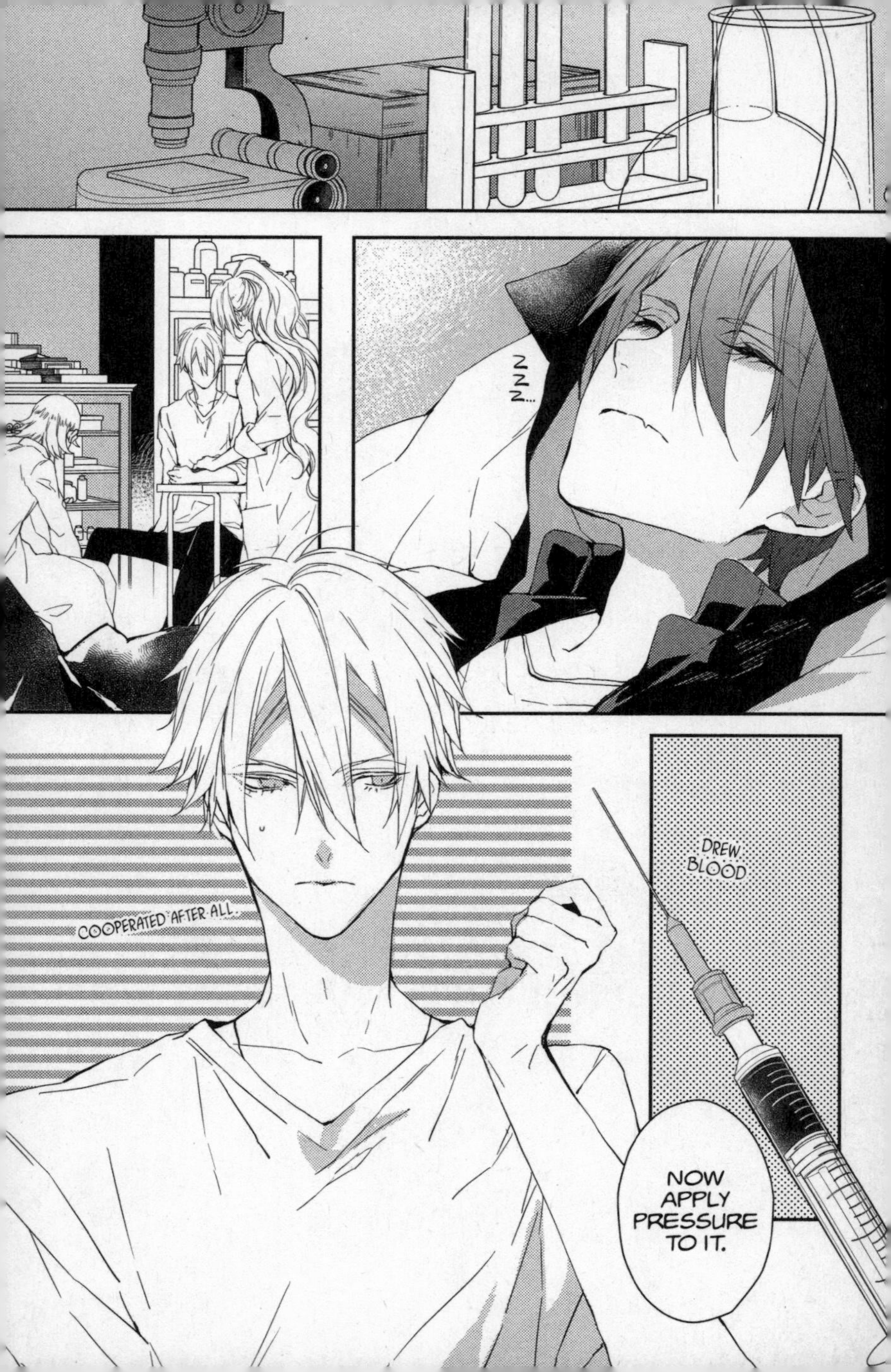
ZZZ...
DREW BLOOD
NOW APPLY PRESSURE TO IT.
COOPERATED AFTER ALL.

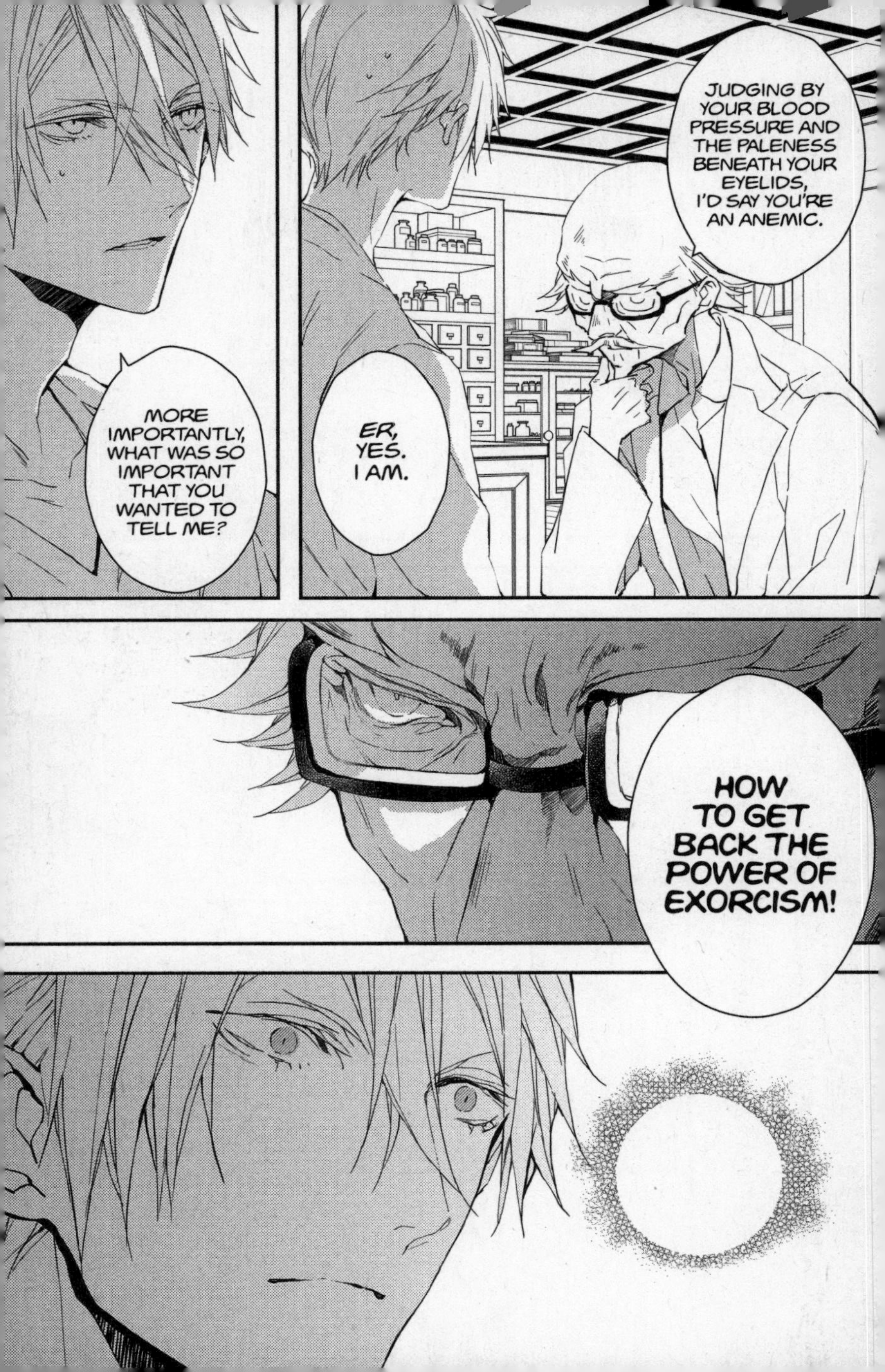
JUDGING BY YOUR BLOOD PRESSURE AND THE PALENESS BENEATH YOUR EYELIDS, I'D SAY YOU'RE AN ANEMIC.
ER, YES. I AM.
MORE IMPORTANTLY, WHAT WAS SO IMPORTANT THAT YOU WANTED TO TELL ME?
HOW TO GET BACK THE POWER OF EXORCISM!

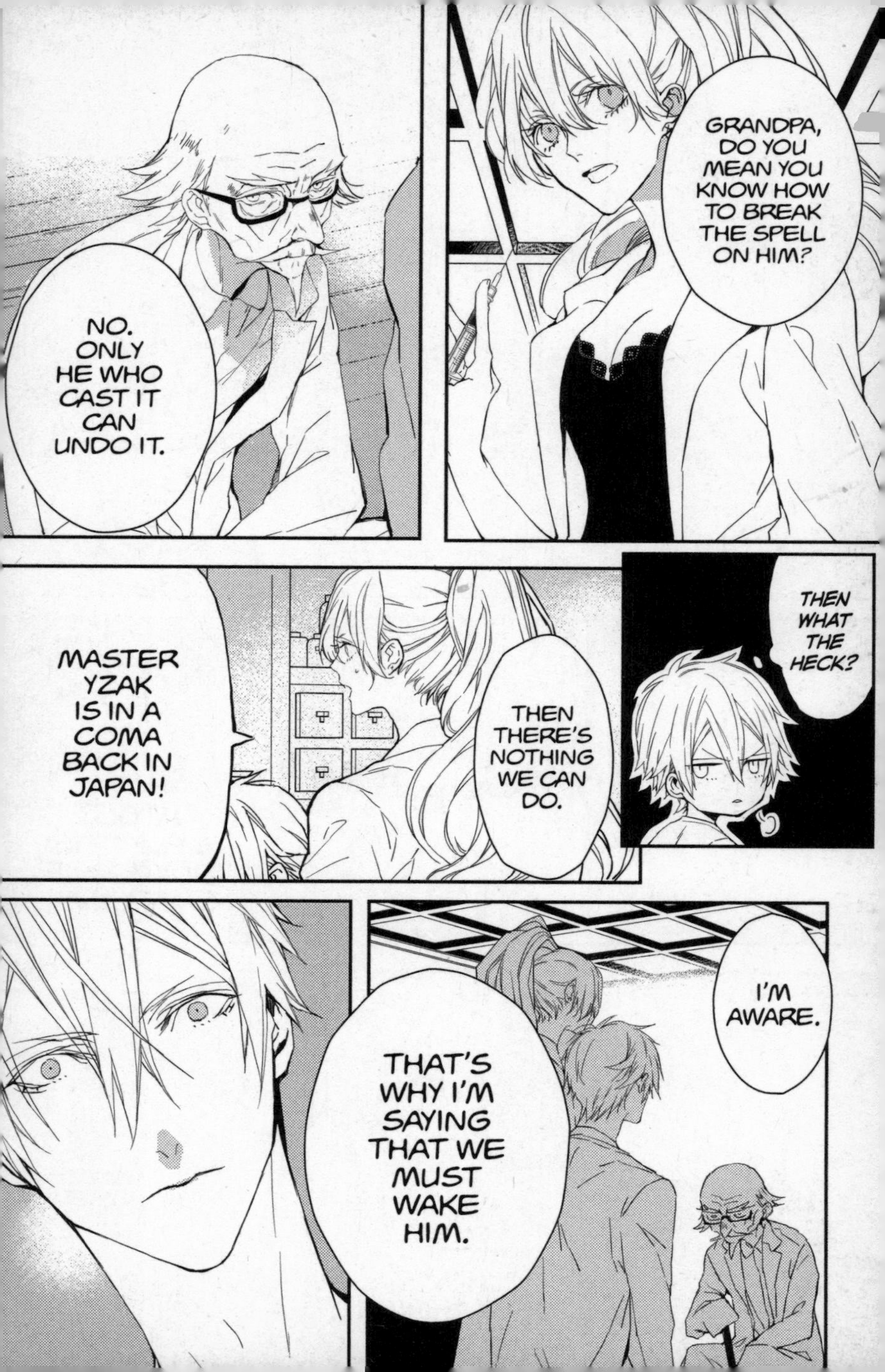
GRANDPA, DO YOU MEAN YOU KNOW HOW TO BREAK THE SPELL ON HIM?
NO. ONLY HE WHO CAST IT CAN UNDO IT.
THEN WHAT THE HECK?
THEN THERE'S NOTHING WE CAN DO.
MASTER YZAK IS IN A COMA BACK IN JAPAN!
I'M AWARE.
THAT'S WHY I'M SAYING THAT WE MUST WAKE HIM.

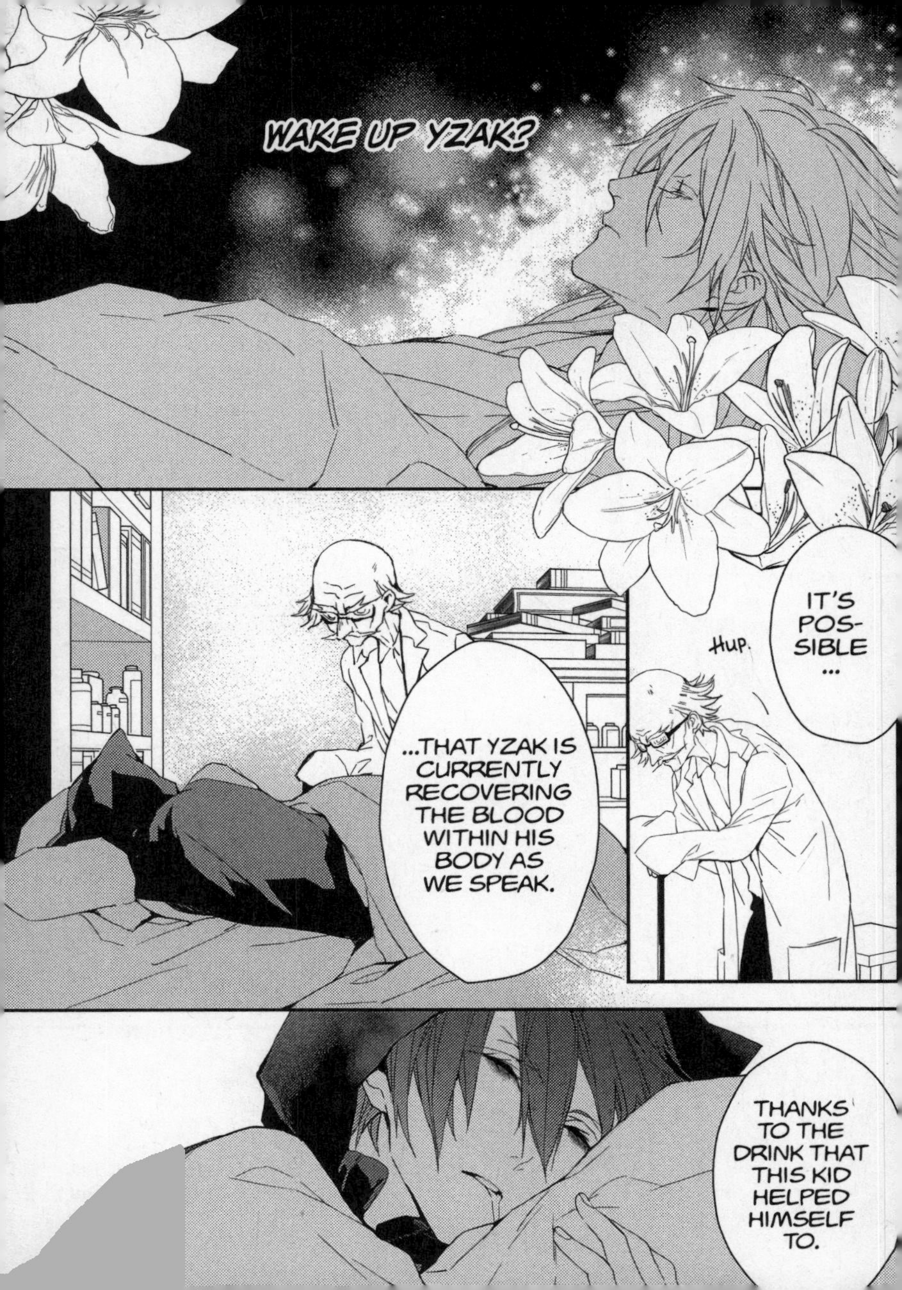
WAKE UP YZAK?
IT'S POS-SIBLE...
Hup.
...THAT YZAK IS CURRENTLY RECOVERING THE BLOOD WITHIN HIS BODY AS WE SPEAK.
THANKS TO THE DRINK THAT THIS KID HELPED HIMSELF TO.

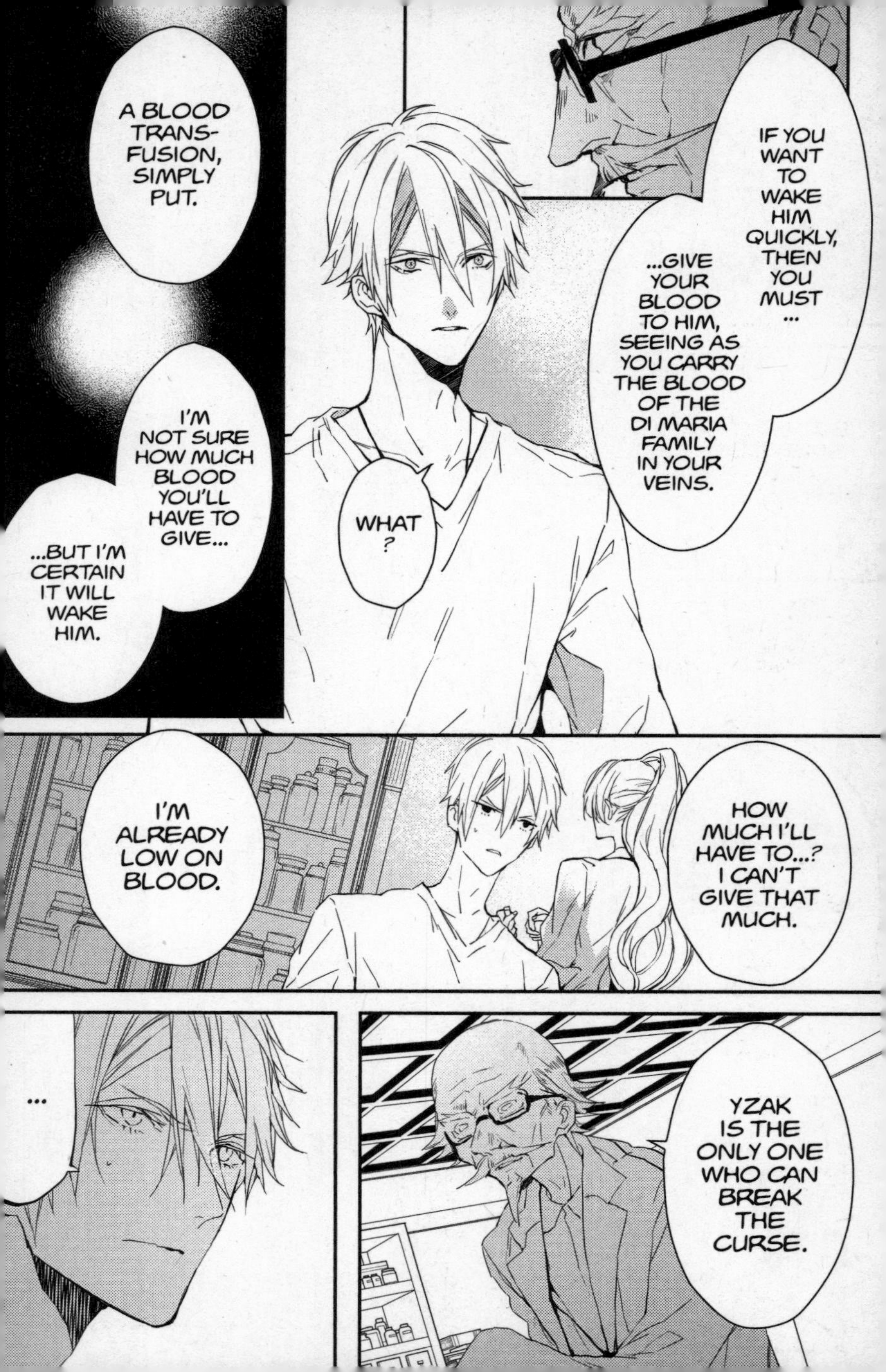
IF YOU WANT TO WAKE HIM QUICKLY, THEN YOU MUST...
...GIVE YOUR BLOOD TO HIM, SEEING AS YOU CARRY THE BLOOD OF THE DI MARIA FAMILY IN YOUR VEINS.
WHAT?
A BLOOD TRANS-FUSION, SIMPLY PUT.
I'M NOT SURE HOW MUCH BLOOD YOU'LL HAVE TO GIVE...
...BUT I'M CERTAIN IT WILL WAKE HIM.
HOW MUCH I'LL HAVE TO...? I CAN'T GIVE THAT MUCH.
I'M ALREADY LOW ON BLOOD.
YZAK IS THE ONLY ONE WHO CAN BREAK THE CURSE.
...

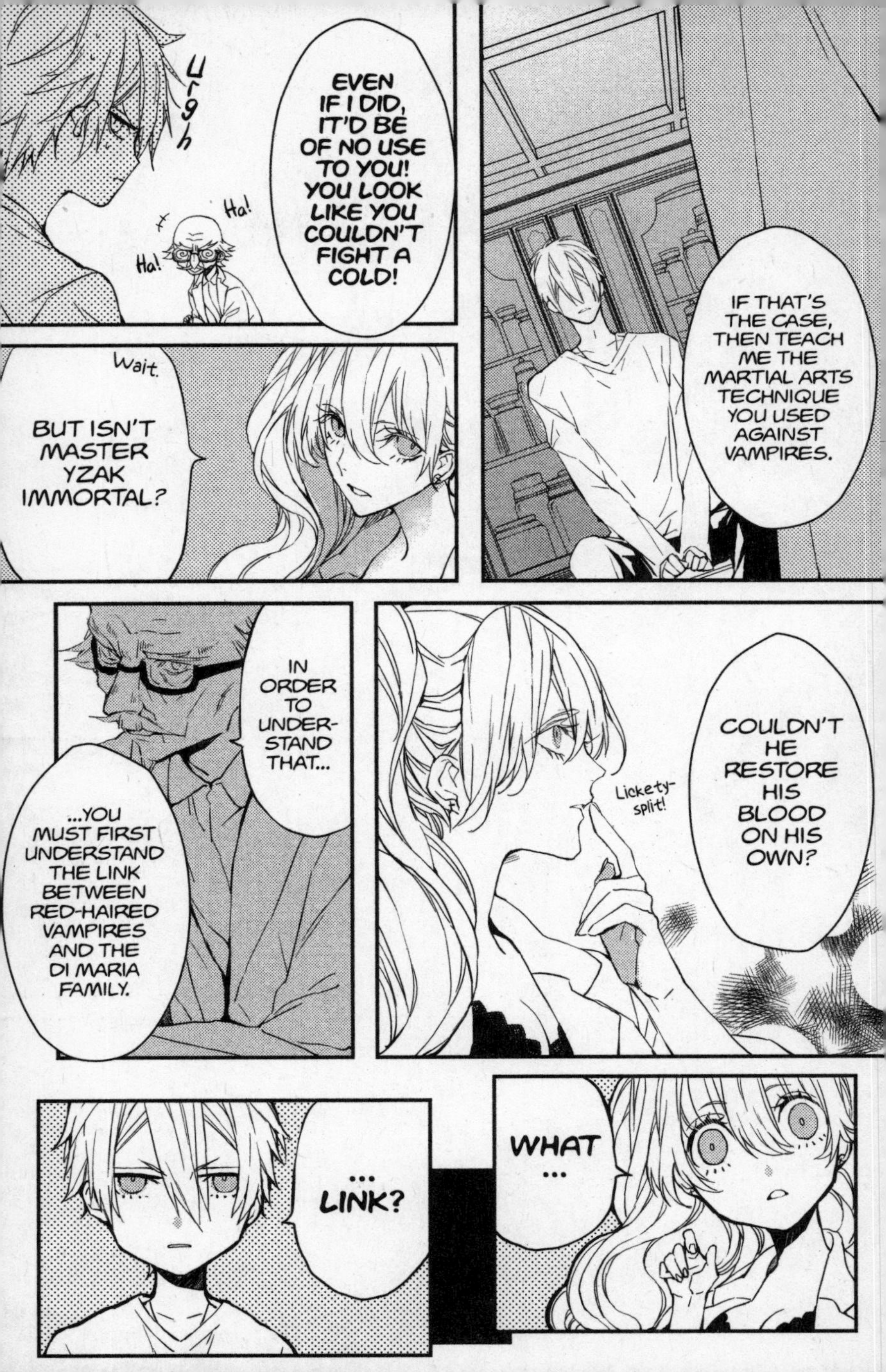
IF THAT'S THE CASE, THEN TEACH ME THE MARTIAL ARTS TECHNIQUE YOU USED AGAINST VAMPIRES.
EVEN IF I DID, IT'D BE OF NO USE TO YOU! YOU LOOK LIKE YOU COULDN'T FIGHT A COLD!
Urgh
Ha!
Ha!
Wait.
BUT ISN'T MASTER YZAK IMMORTAL?
COULDN'T HE RESTORE HIS BLOOD ON HIS OWN?
Lickety-split!
IN ORDER TO UNDER-STAND THAT...
...YOU MUST FIRST UNDERSTAND THE LINK BETWEEN RED-HAIRED VAMPIRES AND THE DI MARIA FAMILY.
WHAT...
...LINK?

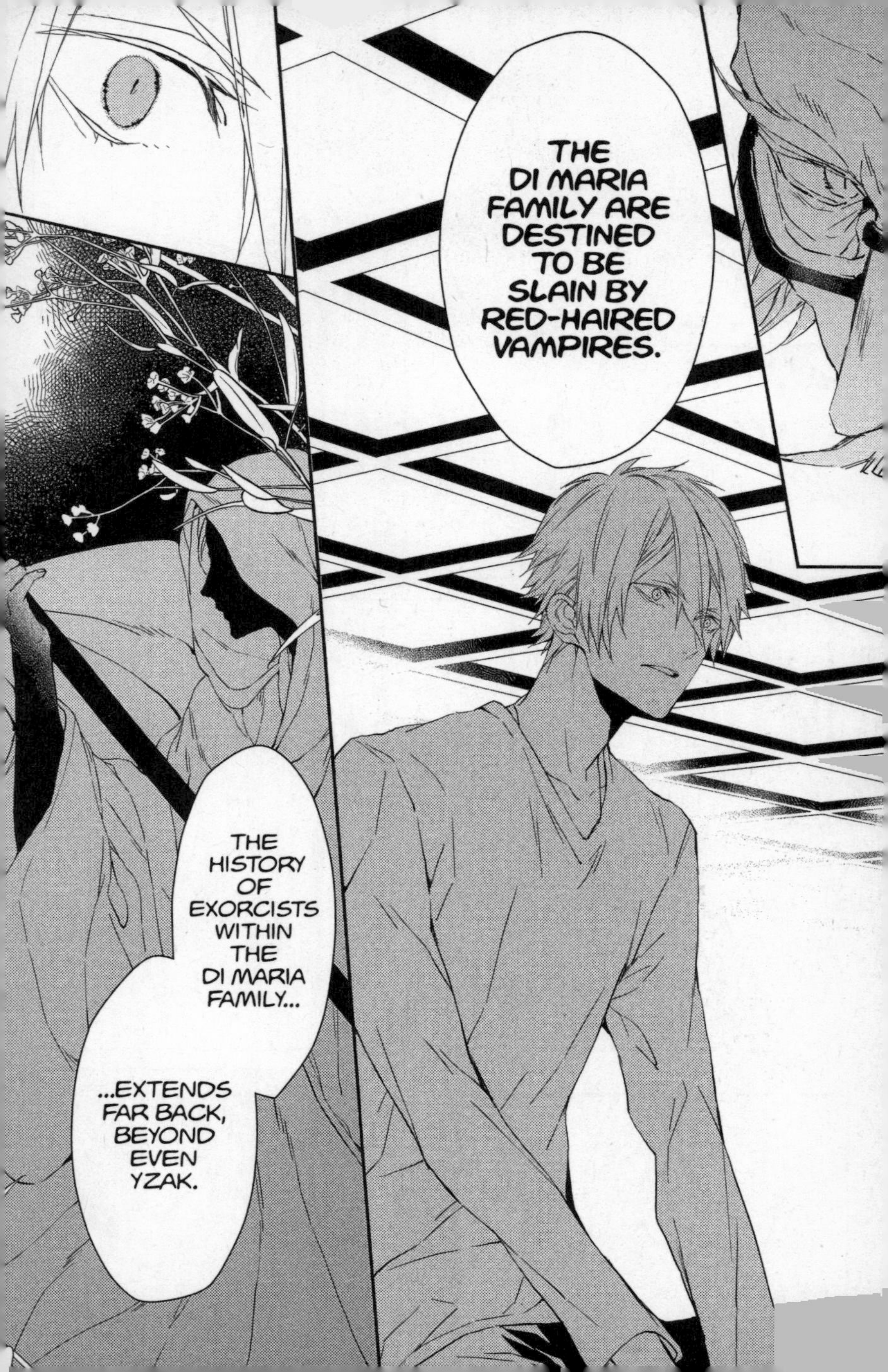
THE DI MARIA FAMILY ARE DESTINED TO BE SLAIN BY RED-HAIRED VAMPIRES.
THE HISTORY OF EXORCISTS WITHIN THE DI MARIA FAMILY...
...EXTENDS FAR BACK, BEYOND EVEN YZAK.

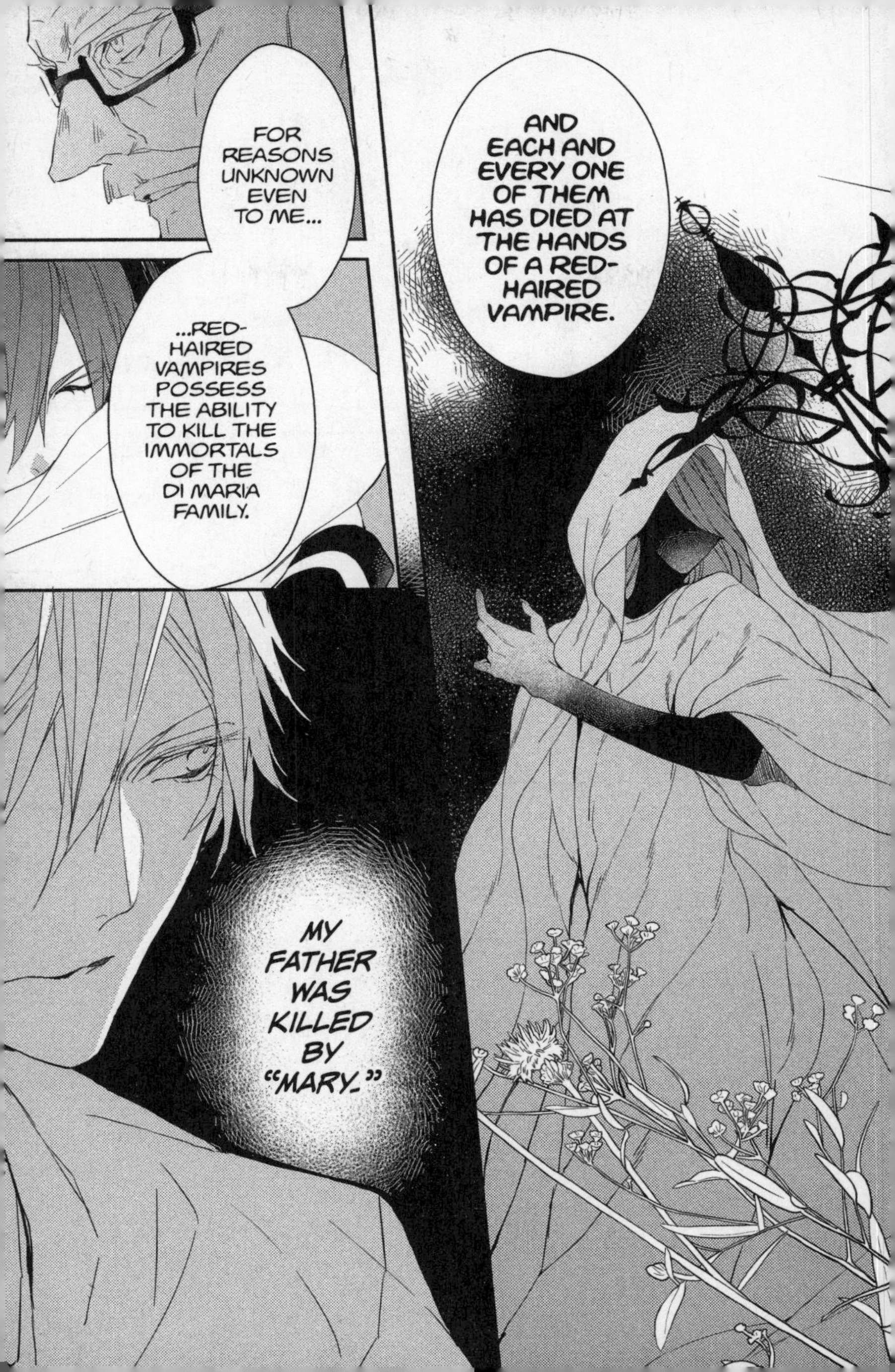
AND EACH AND EVERY ONE OF THEM HAS DIED AT THE HANDS OF A RED-HAIRED VAMPIRE.
FOR REASONS UNKNOWN EVEN TO ME...
...RED-HAIRED VAMPIRES POSSESS THE ABILITY TO KILL THE IMMORTALS OF THE DI MARIA FAMILY.
MY FATHER WAS KILLED BY "MARY."

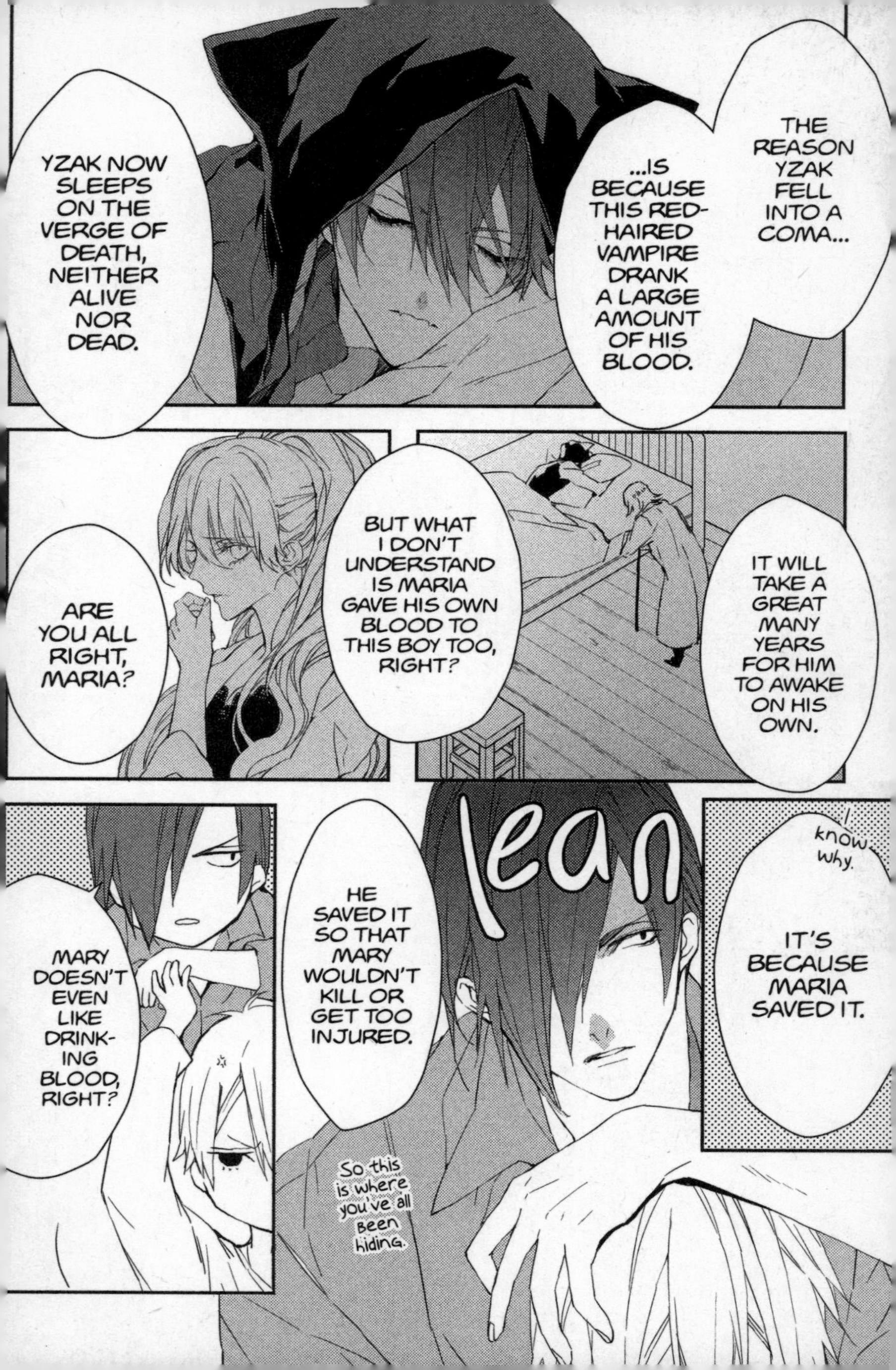
THE REASON YZAK FELL INTO A COMA...
...IS BECAUSE THIS RED-HAIRED VAMPIRE DRANK A LARGE AMOUNT OF HIS BLOOD.
YZAK NOW SLEEPS ON THE VERGE OF DEATH, NEITHER ALIVE NOR DEAD.
IT WILL TAKE A GREAT MANY YEARS FOR HIM TO AWAKE ON HIS OWN.
BUT WHAT I DON'T UNDERSTAND IS MARIA GAVE HIS OWN BLOOD TO THIS BOY TOO, RIGHT?
ARE YOU ALL RIGHT, MARIA?
I know why.
IT'S BECAUSE MARIA SAVED IT.
lean
HE SAVED IT SO THAT MARY WOULDN'T KILL OR GET TOO INJURED.
MARY DOESN'T EVEN LIKE DRINK-ING BLOOD, RIGHT?
So this is where you've all been hiding.

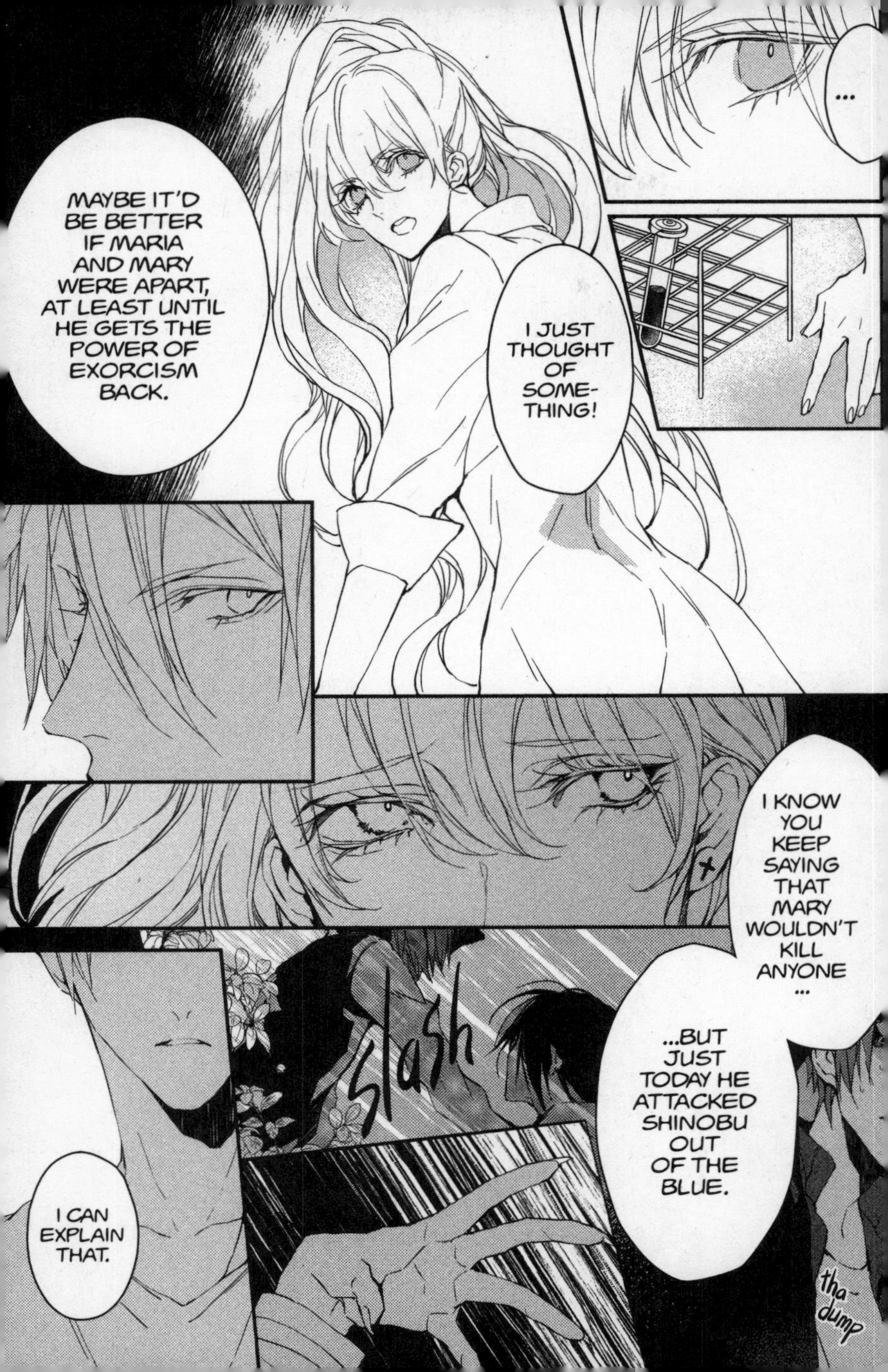
...
I JUST THOUGHT OF SOME-THING!
MAYBE IT'D BE BETTER IF MARIA AND MARY WERE APART, AT LEAST UNTIL HE GETS THE POWER OF EXORCISM BACK.
I KNOW YOU KEEP SAYING THAT MARY WOULDN'T KILL ANYONE...
...BUT JUST TODAY HE ATTACKED SHINOBU OUT OF THE BLUE.
tha-dump
slash
I CAN EXPLAIN THAT.

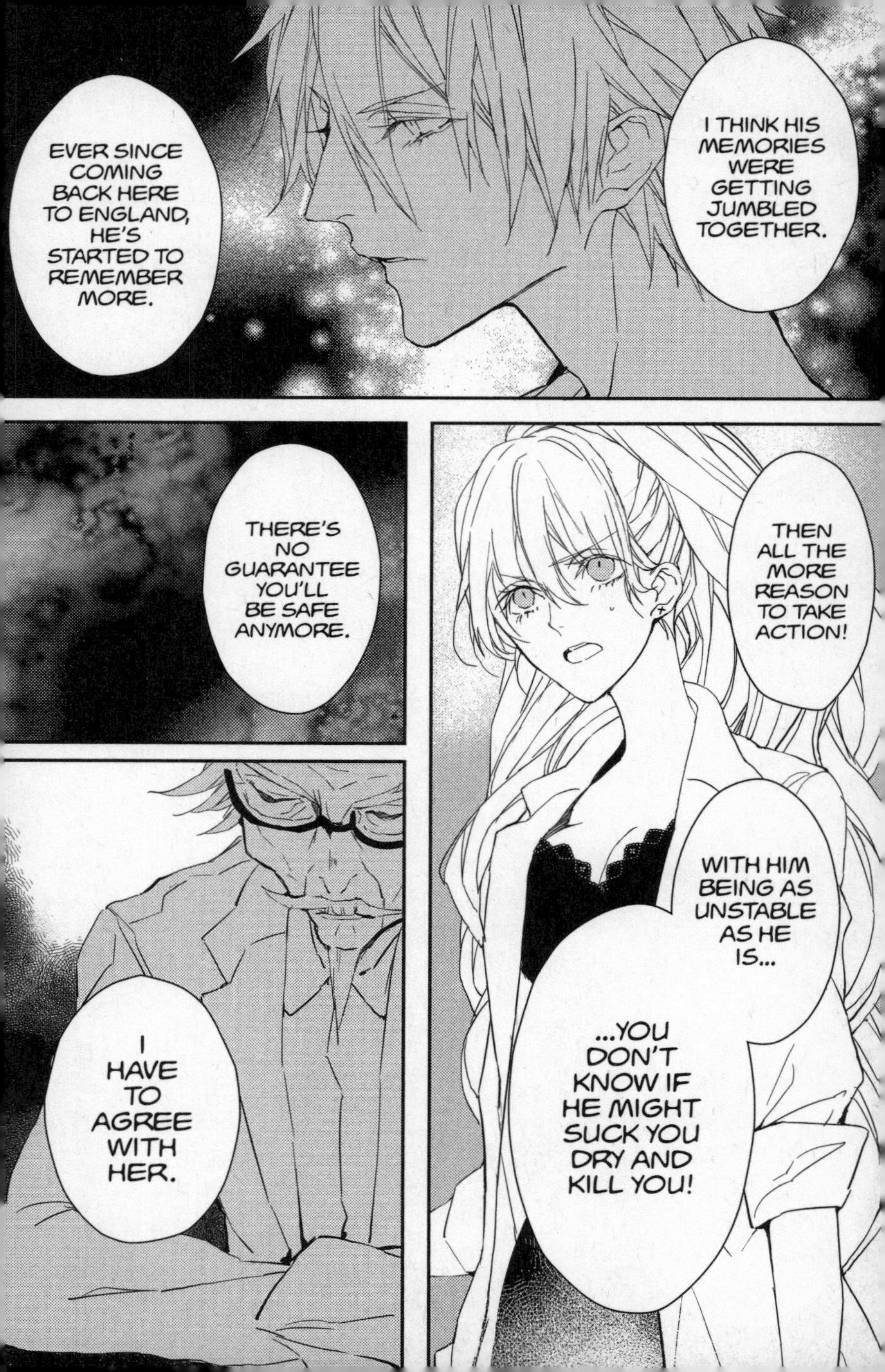
I THINK HIS MEMORIES WERE GETTING JUMBLED TOGETHER.
EVER SINCE COMING BACK HERE TO ENGLAND, HE'S STARTED TO REMEMBER MORE.
THEN ALL THE MORE REASON TO TAKE ACTION!
WITH HIM BEING AS UNSTABLE AS HE IS...
...YOU DON'T KNOW IF HE MIGHT SUCK YOU DRY AND KILL YOU!
THERE'S NO GUARANTEE YOU'LL BE SAFE ANYMORE.
I HAVE TO AGREE WITH HER.

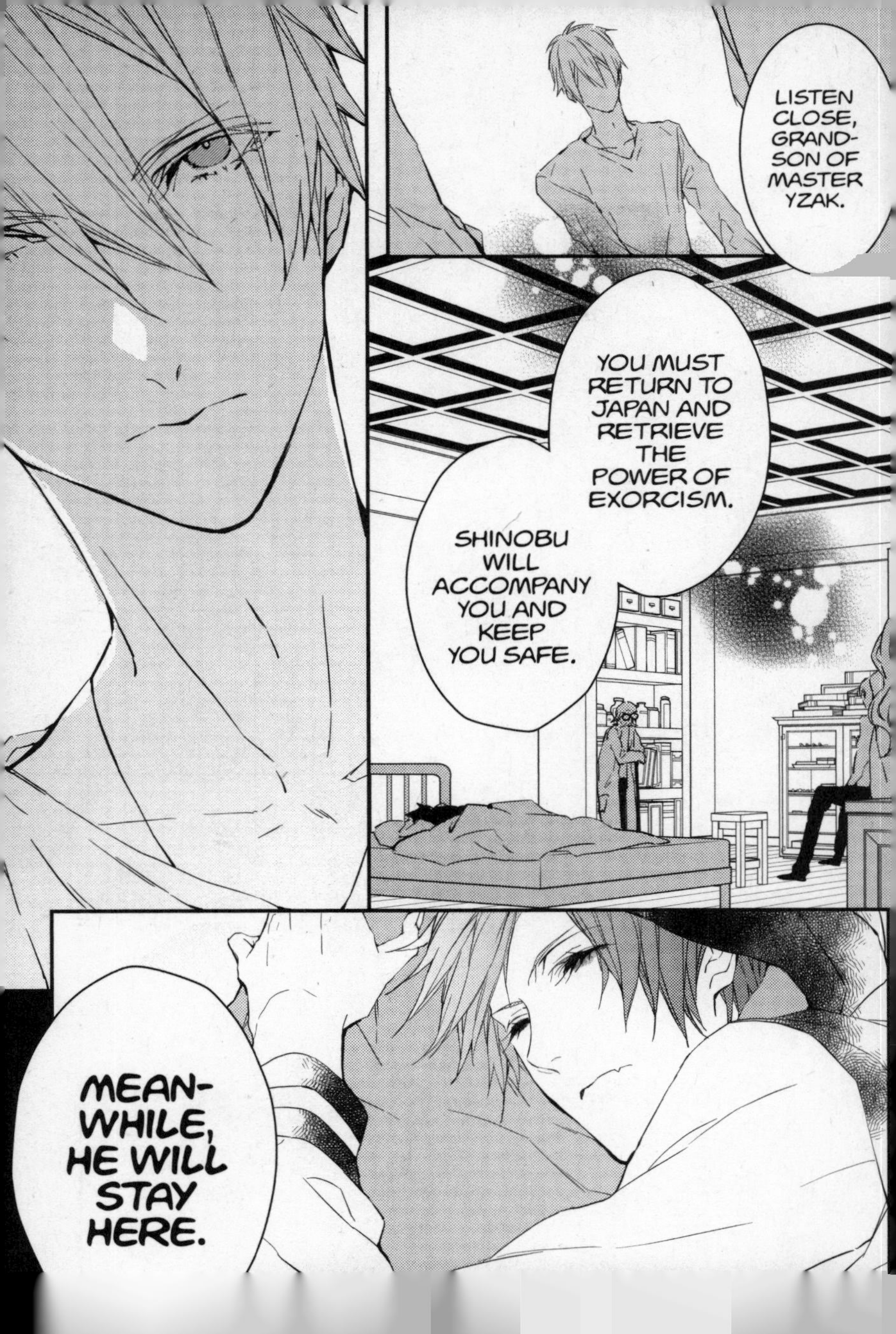
LISTEN CLOSE, GRAND-SON OF MASTER YZAK.
YOU MUST RETURN TO JAPAN AND RETRIEVE THE POWER OF EXORCISM.
SHINOBU WILL ACCOMPANY YOU AND KEEP YOU SAFE.
MEAN-WHILE, HE WILL STAY HERE.

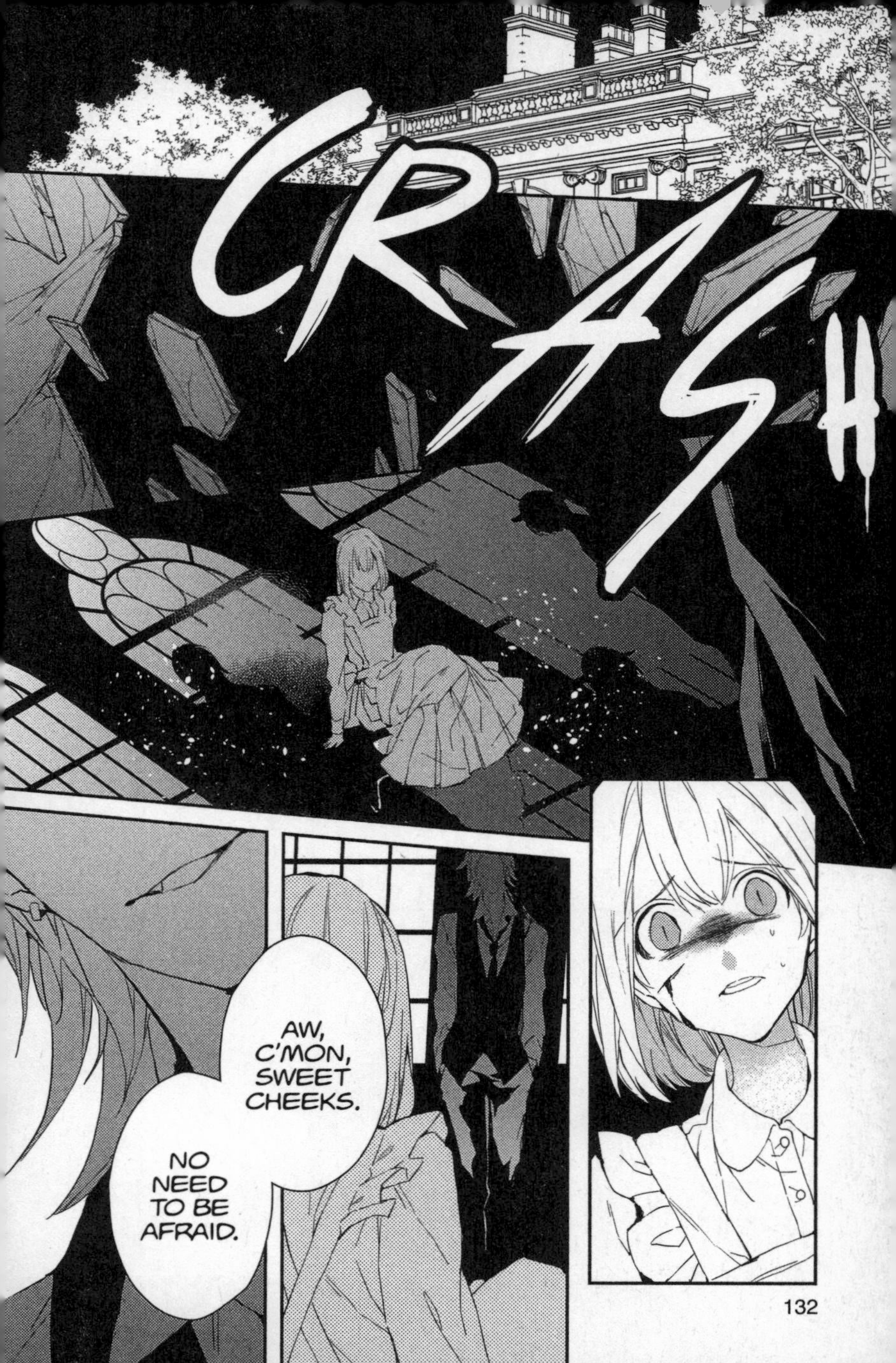
CRASH
AW, C'MON, SWEET CHEEKS.
NO NEED TO BE AFRAID.

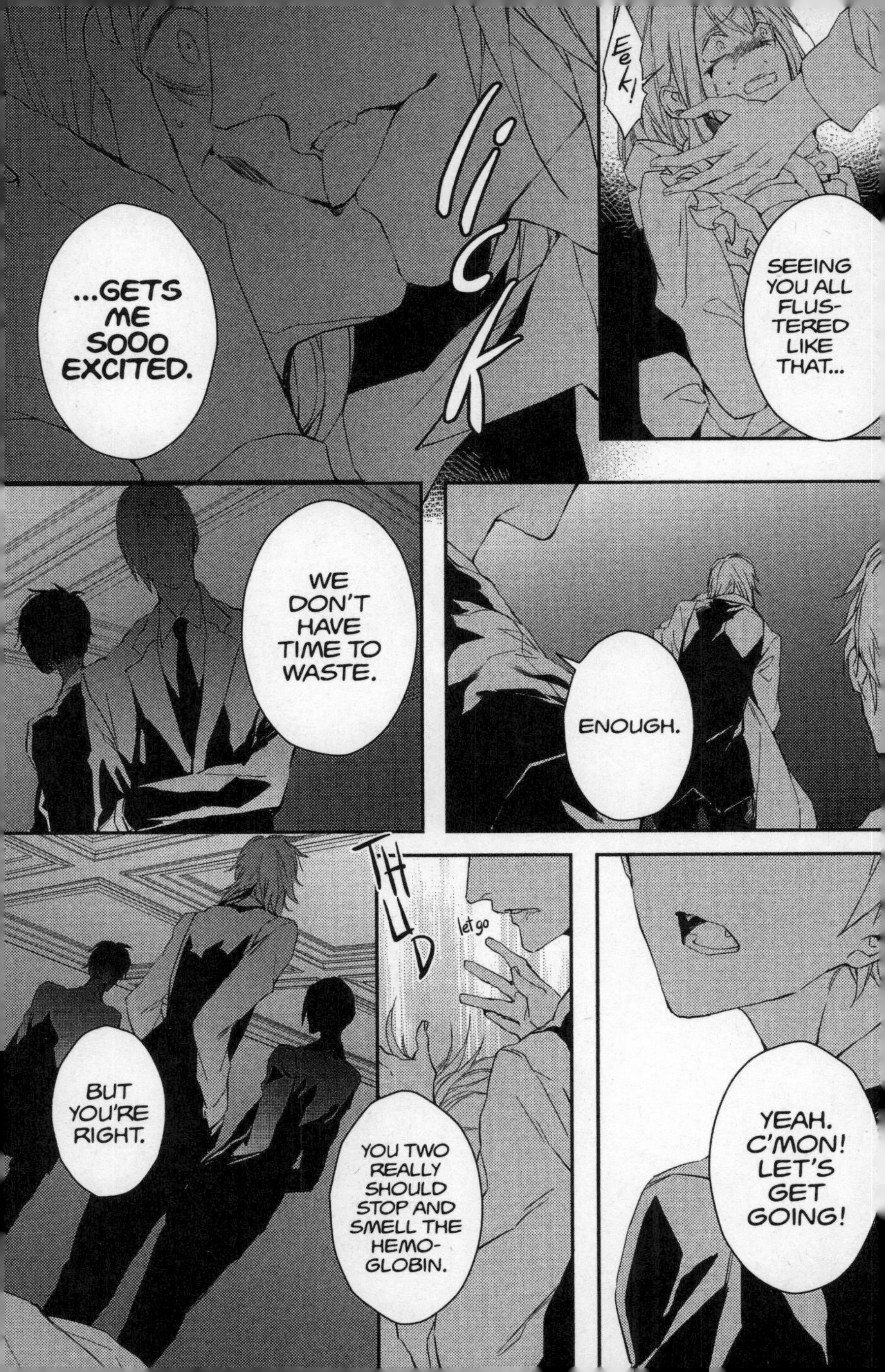
Eek!
SEEING YOU ALL FLUSTERED LIKE THAT...
liiick
...GETS ME SOOO EXCITED.
ENOUGH.
WE DON'T HAVE TIME TO WASTE.
YEAH. C'MON! LET'S GET GOING!
THUD
let go
YOU TWO REALLY SHOULD STOP AND SMELL THE HEMO-GLOBIN.
BUT YOU'RE RIGHT.

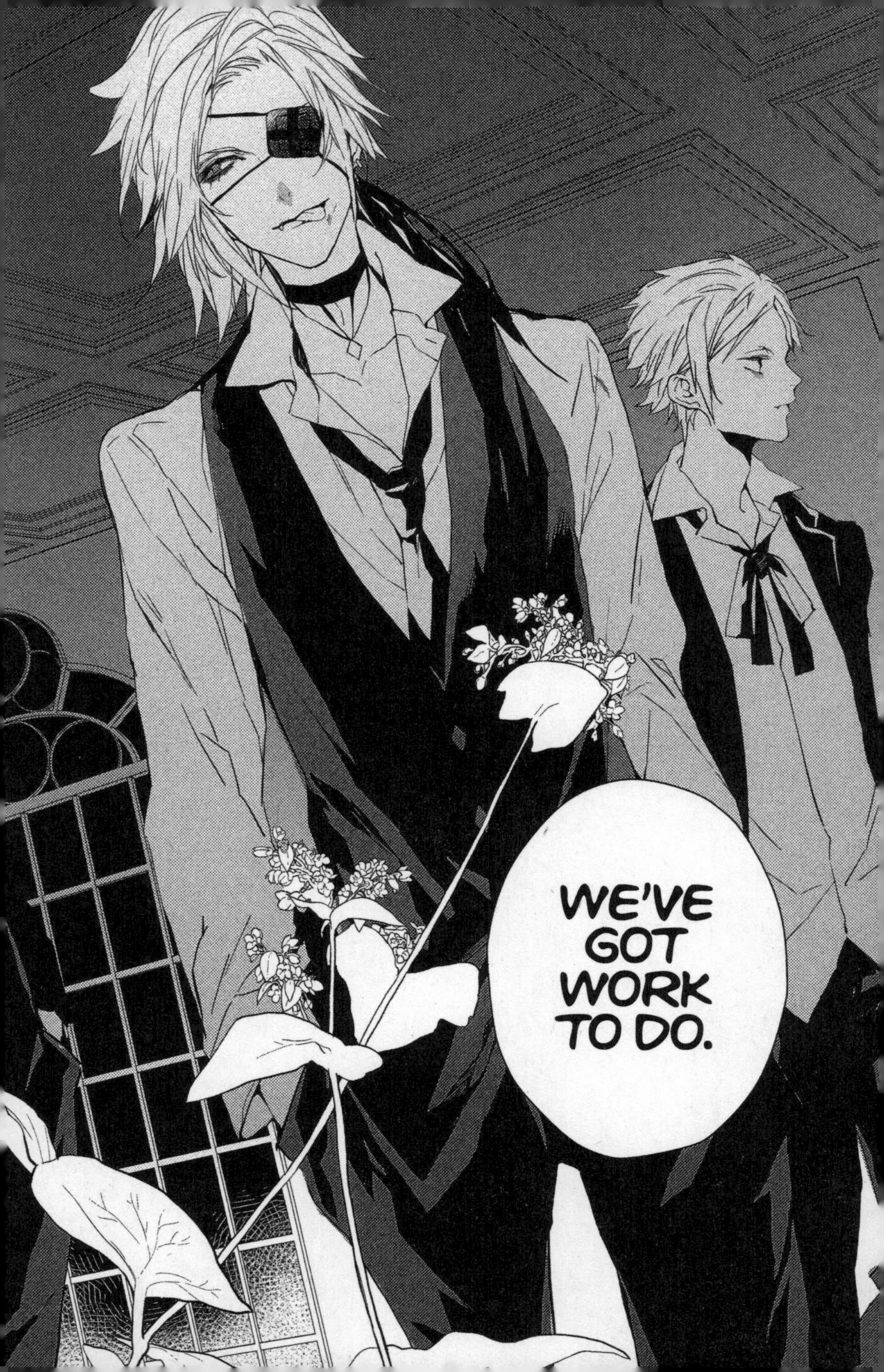
WE'VE GOT WORK TO DO.

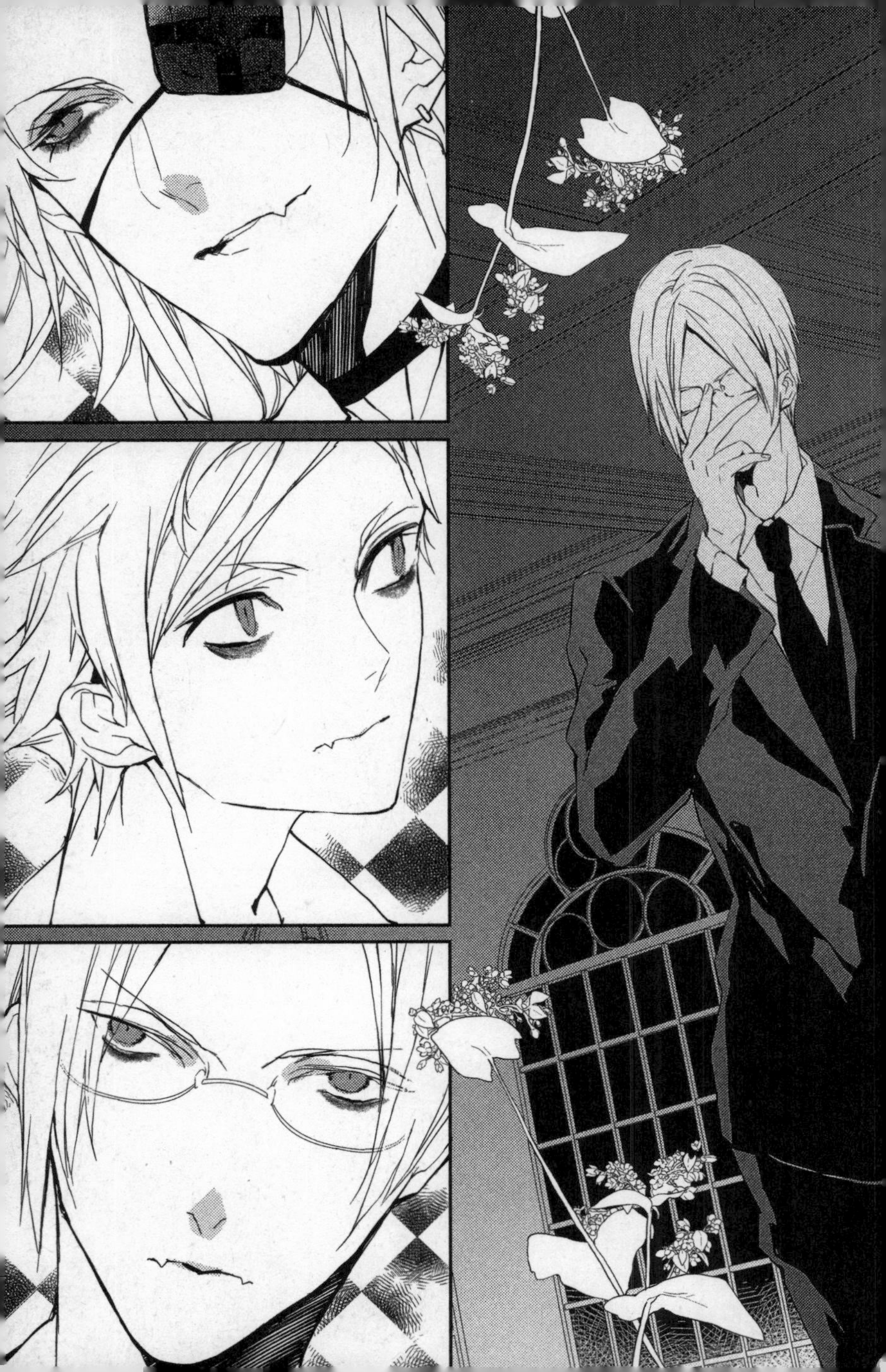

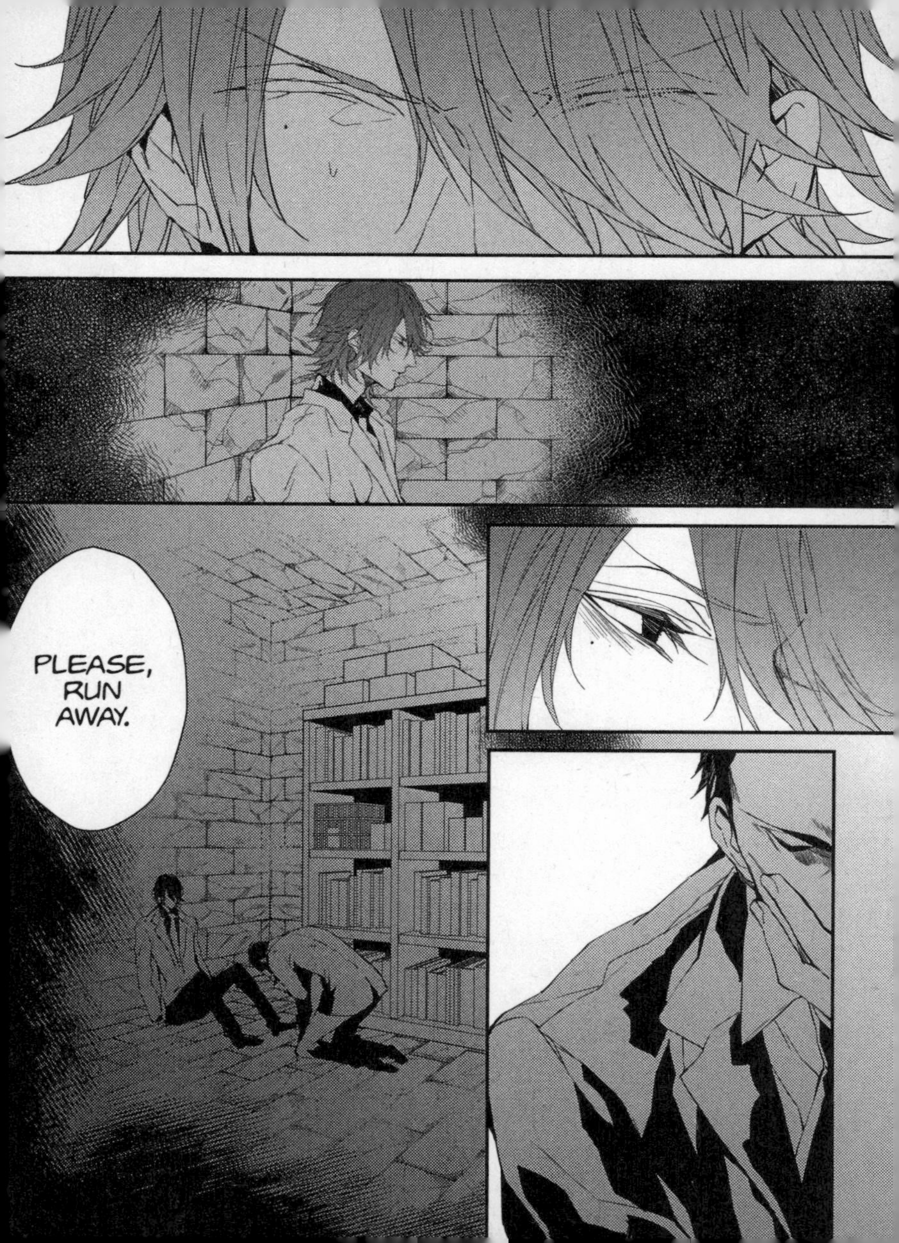
PLEASE, RUN AWAY.

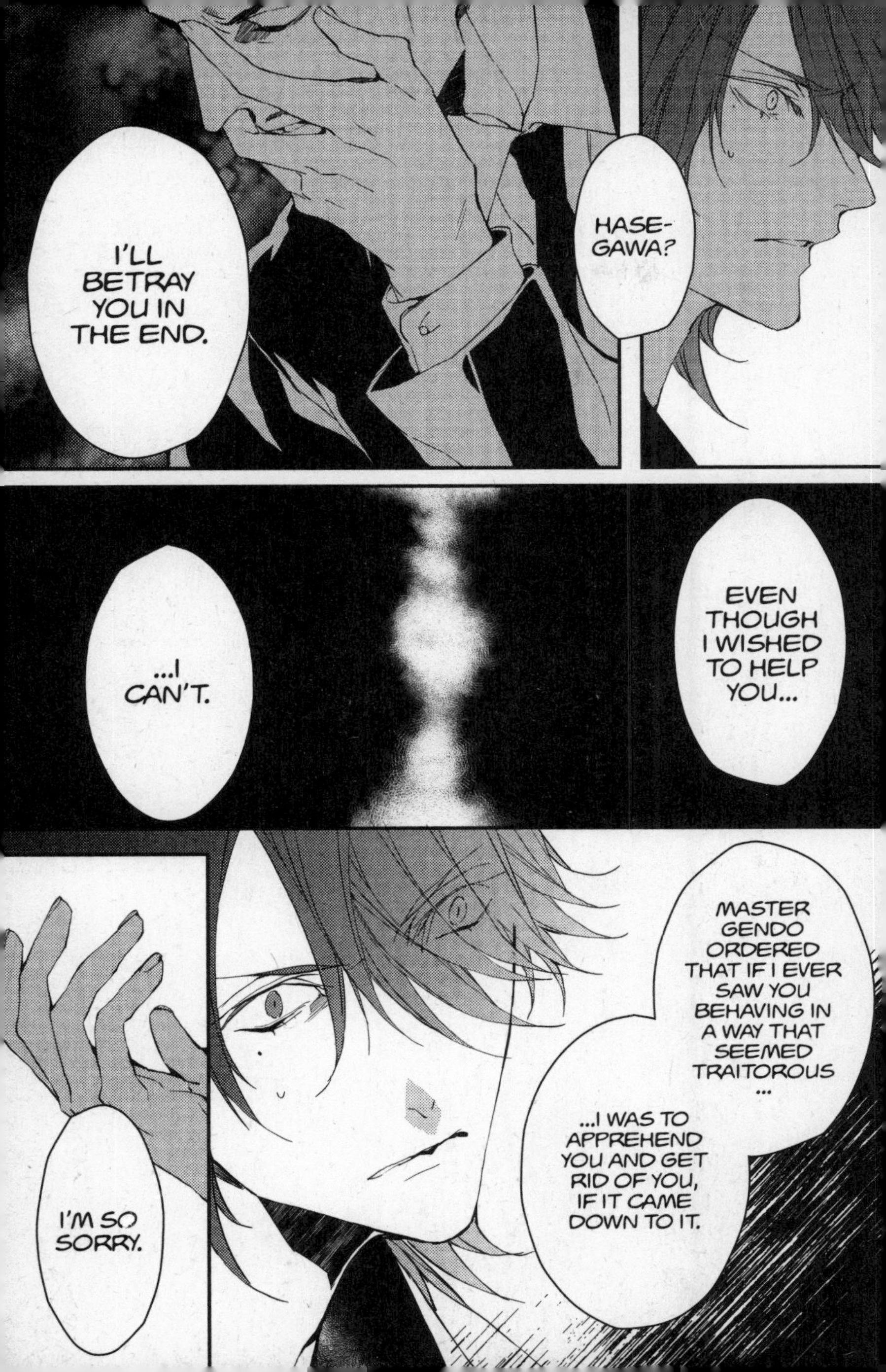
HASE-GAWA?
I'LL BETRAY YOU IN THE END.
EVEN THOUGH I WISHED TO HELP YOU...
...I CAN'T.
MASTER GENDO ORDERED THAT IF I EVER SAW YOU BEHAVING IN A WAY THAT SEEMED TRAITOROUS...
...I WAS TO APPREHEND YOU AND GET RID OF YOU, IF IT CAME DOWN TO IT.
I'M SO SORRY.

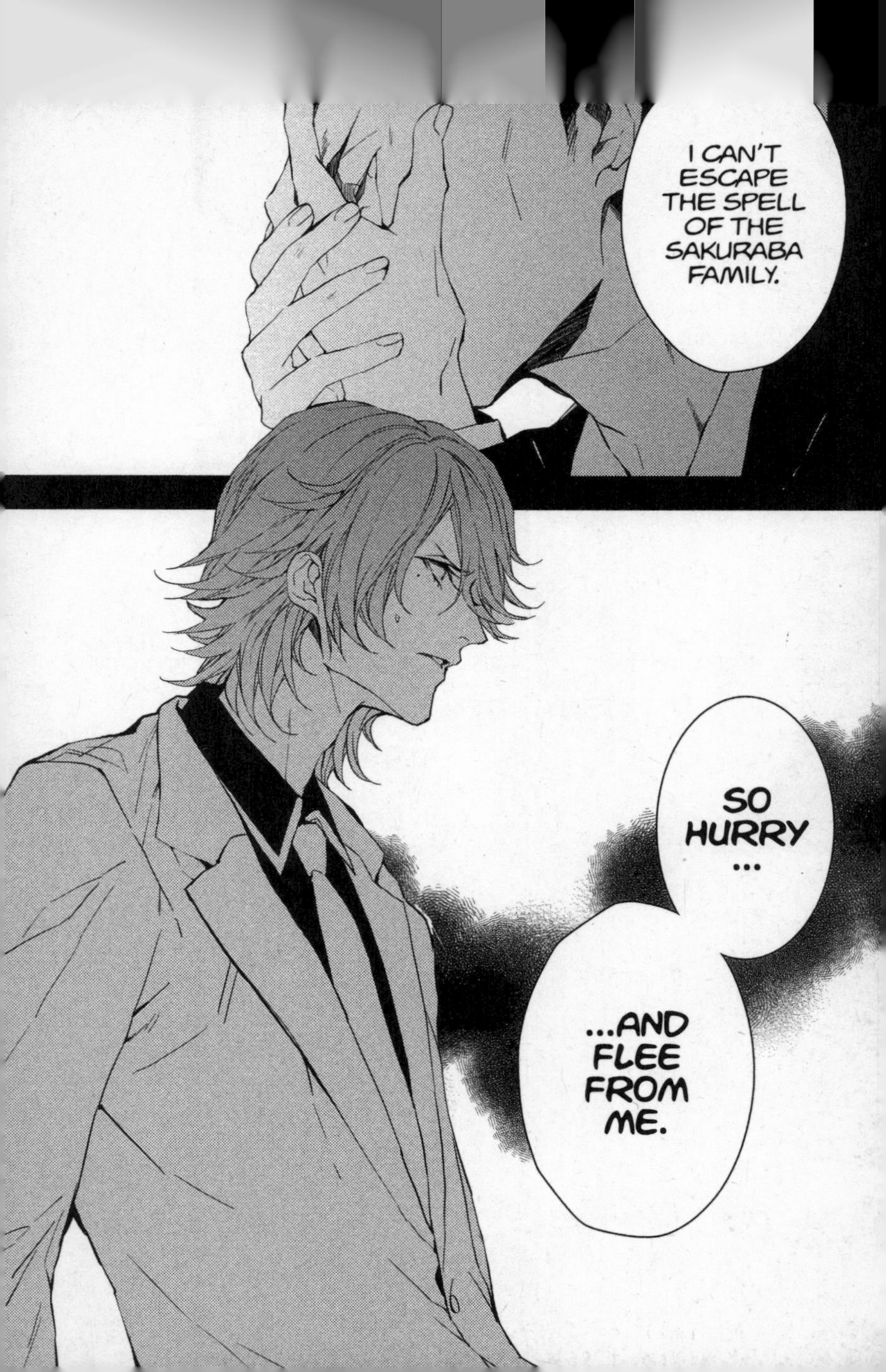
I CAN'T ESCAPE THE SPELL OF THE SAKURABA FAMILY.
SO HURRY...
...AND FLEE FROM ME.

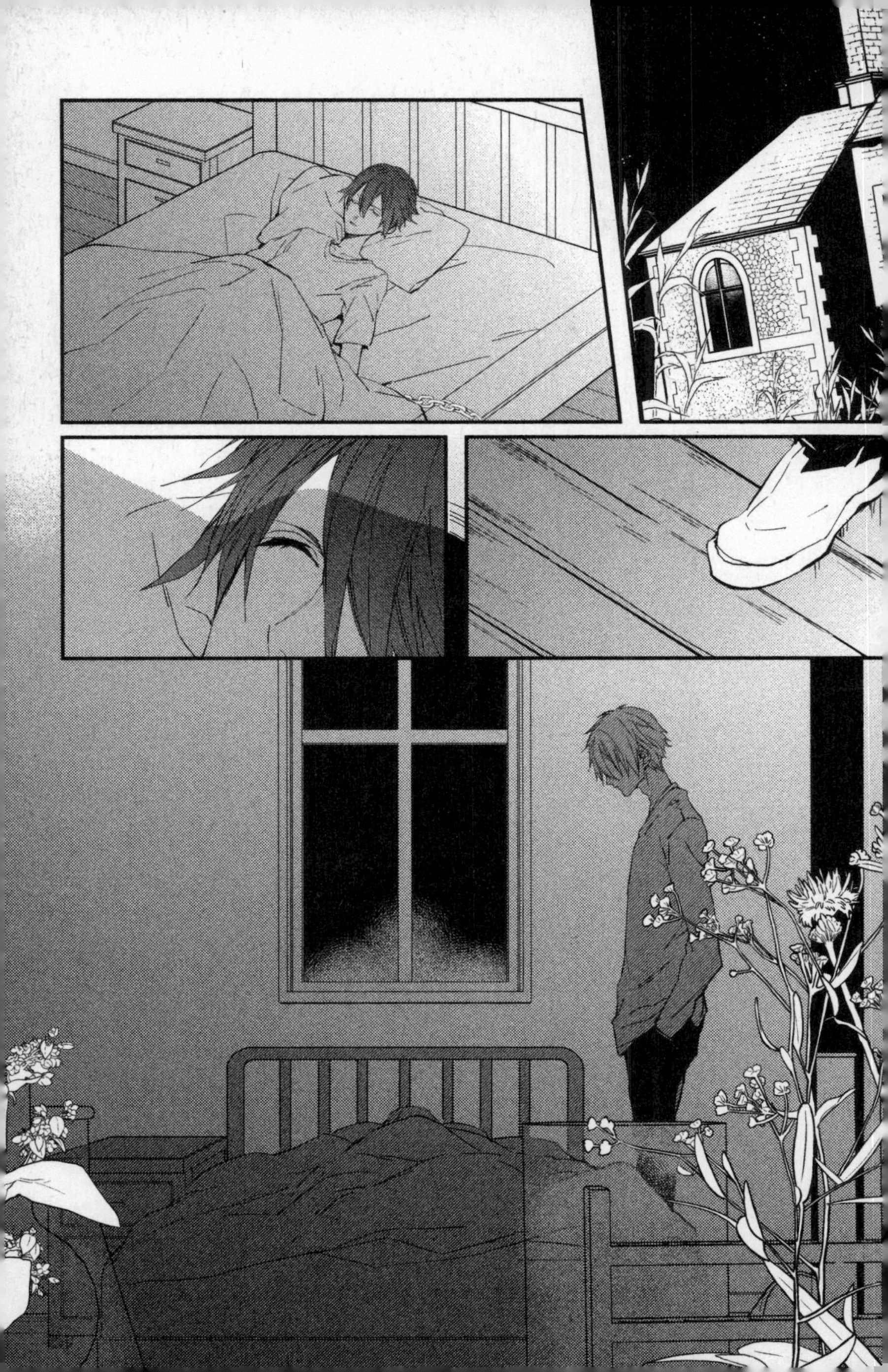

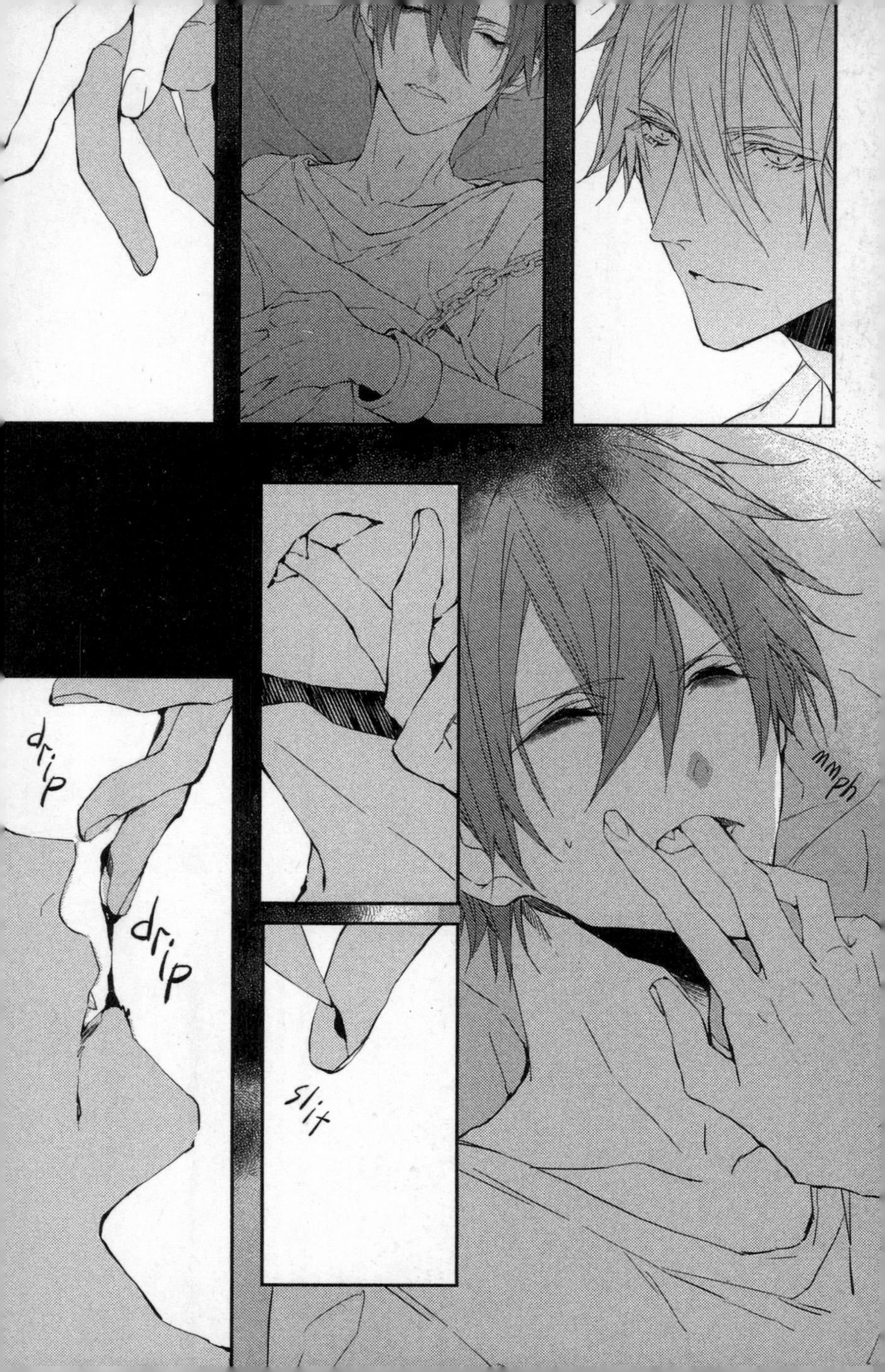
mmph
slit
drip
drip

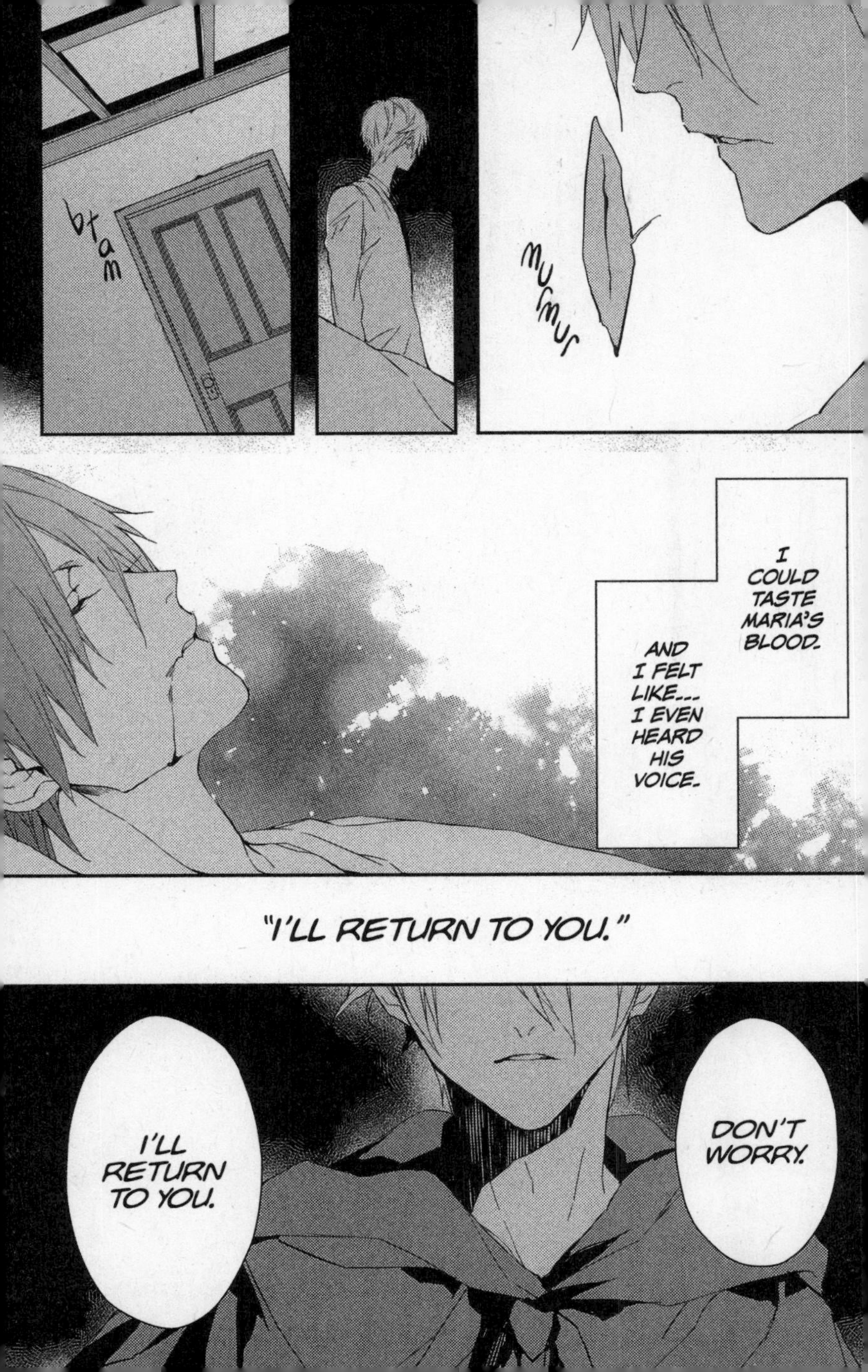
murmur
btam
I COULD TASTE MARIA'S BLOOD.
AND I FELT LIKE... I EVEN HEARD HIS VOICE.
"I'LL RETURN TO YOU."
DON'T WORRY.
I'LL RETURN TO YOU.

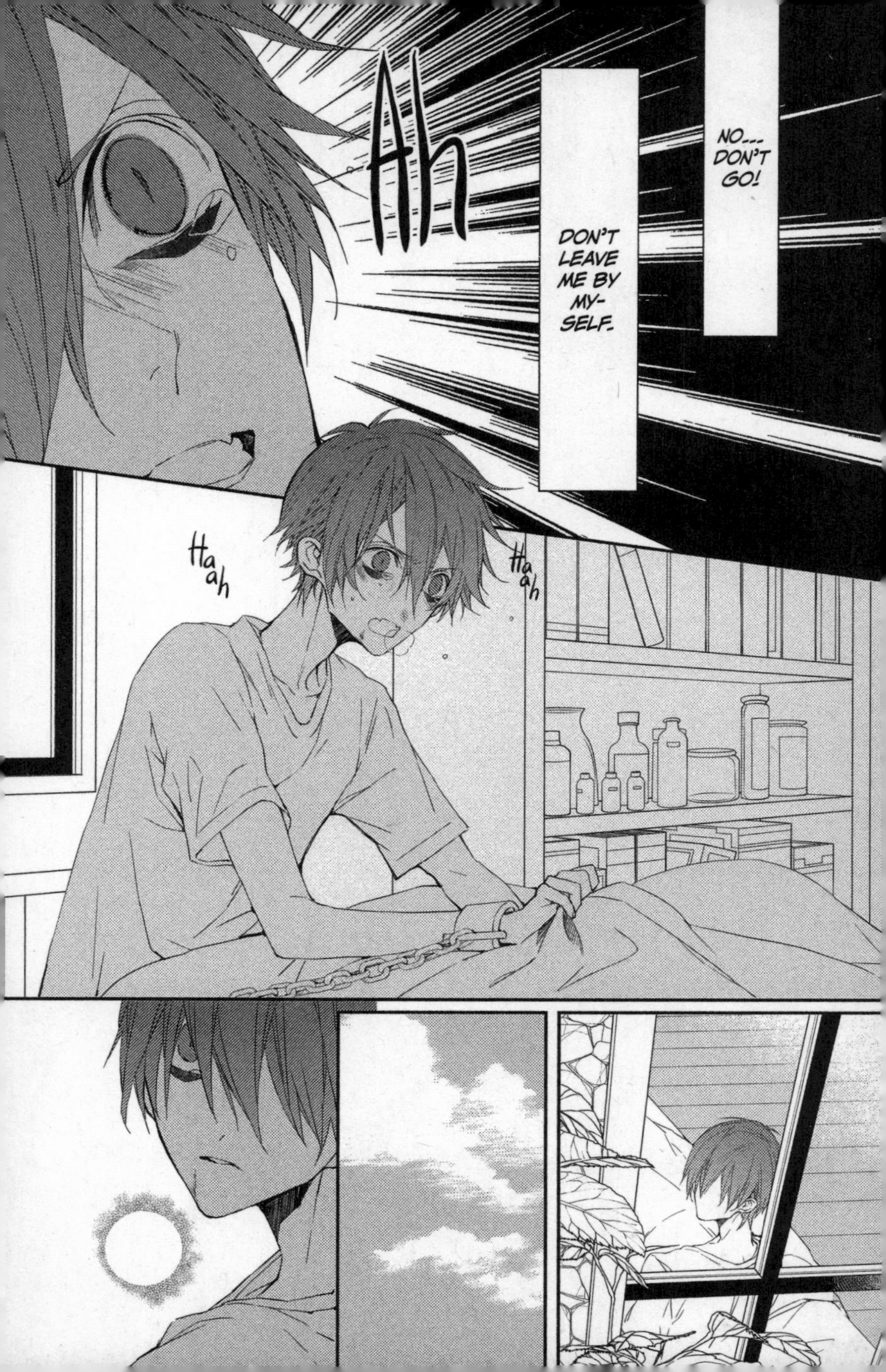
NO... DON'T GO!
DON'T LEAVE ME BY MY-SELF.
Ah
Haah
Haah

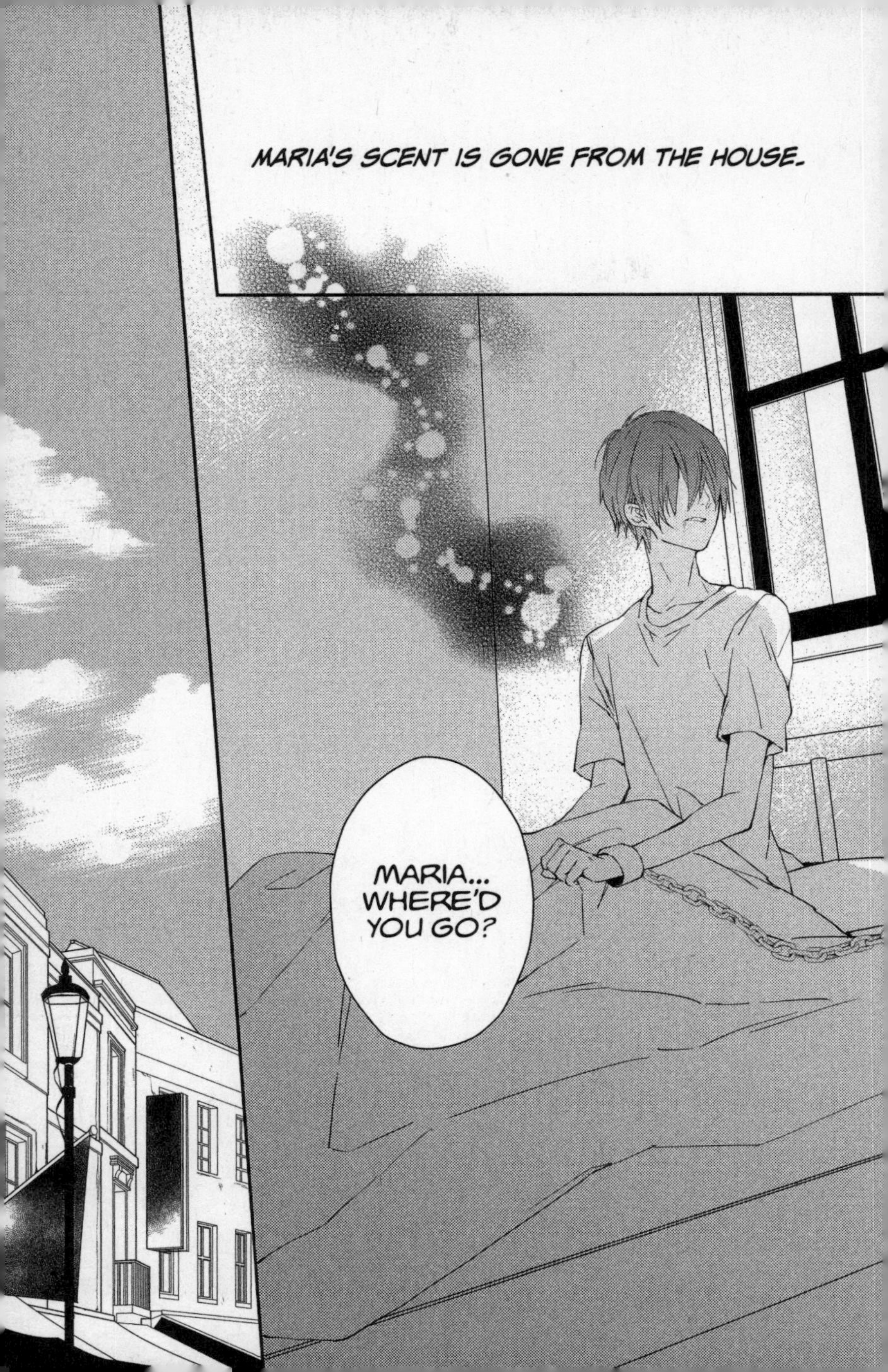
MARIA'S SCENT IS GONE FROM THE HOUSE.
MARIA... WHERE'D YOU GO?

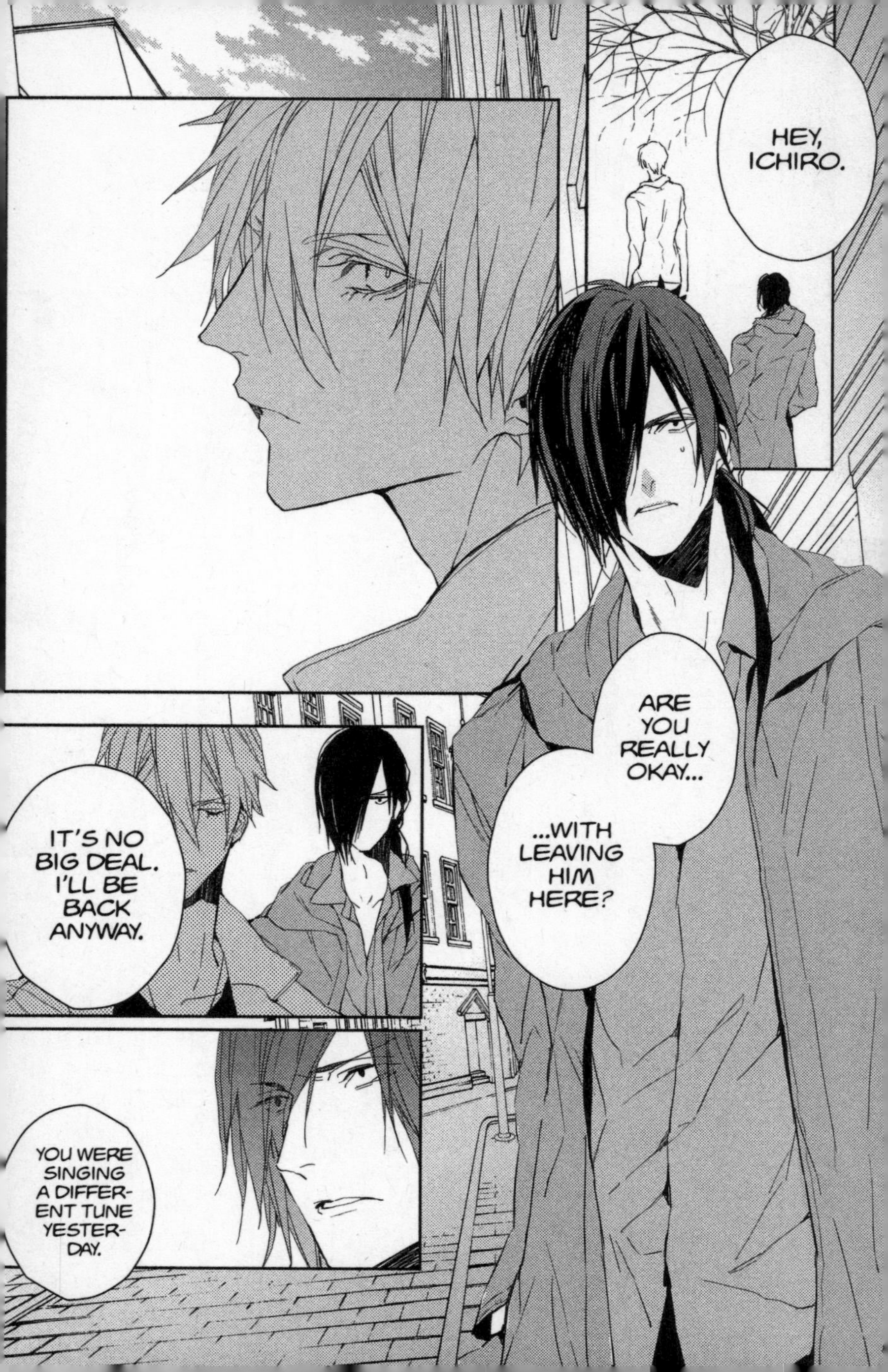
HEY, ICHIRO.
ARE YOU REALLY OKAY...
...WITH LEAVING HIM HERE?
IT'S NO BIG DEAL. I'LL BE BACK ANYWAY.
YOU WERE SINGING A DIFFERENT TUNE YESTERDAY.

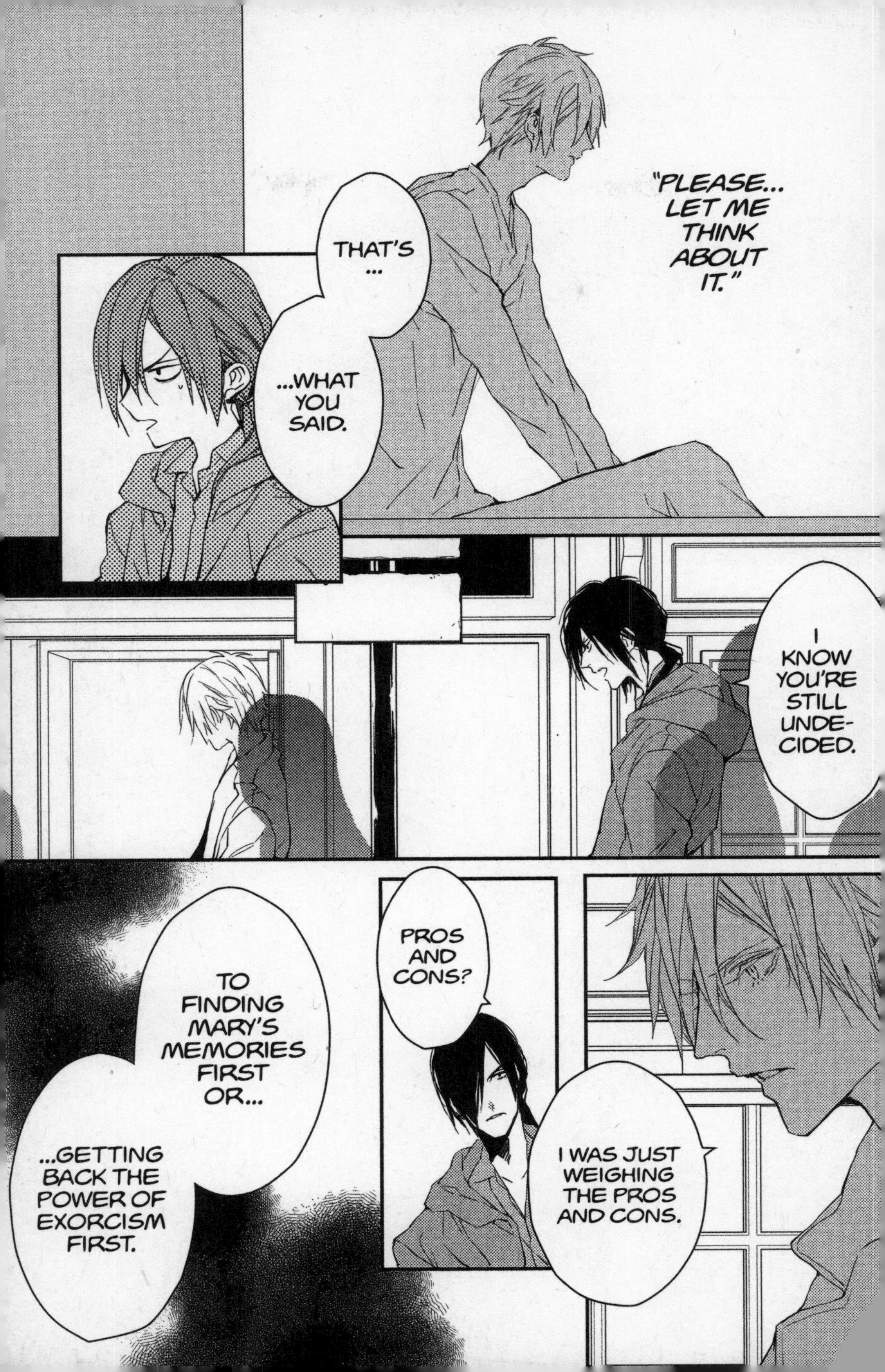
"PLEASE... LET ME THINK ABOUT IT."
THAT'S...
...WHAT YOU SAID.
I KNOW YOU'RE STILL UNDECIDED.
I WAS JUST WEIGHING THE PROS AND CONS.
PROS AND CONS?
TO FINDING MARY'S MEMORIES FIRST OR...
...GETTING BACK THE POWER OF EXORCISM FIRST.

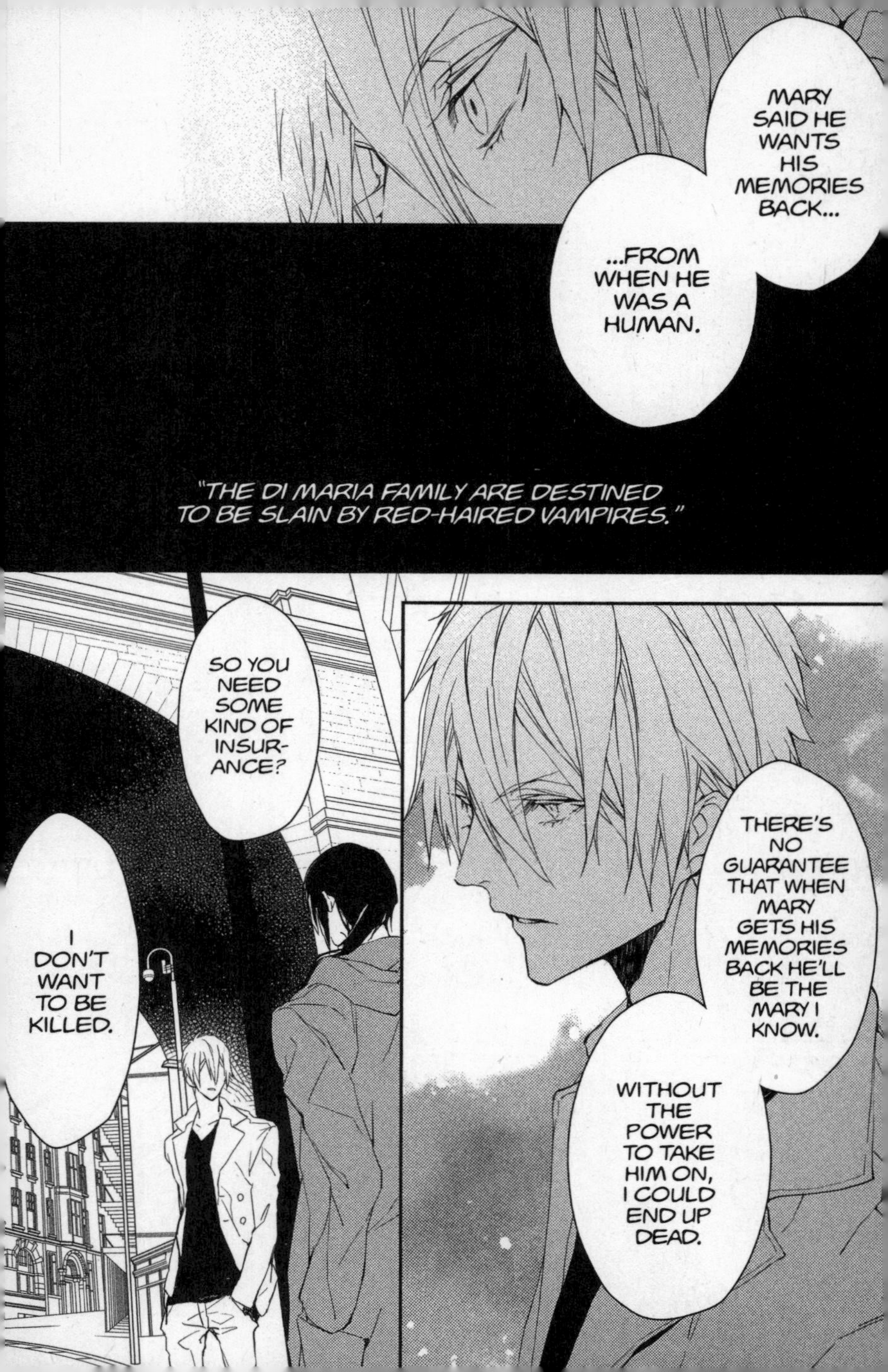
MARY SAID HE WANTS HIS MEMORIES BACK...
...FROM WHEN HE WAS A HUMAN.
"THE DI MARIA FAMILY ARE DESTINED TO BE SLAIN BY RED-HAIRED VAMPIRES."
THERE'S NO GUARANTEE THAT WHEN MARY GETS HIS MEMORIES BACK HE'LL BE THE MARY I KNOW.
WITHOUT THE POWER TO TAKE HIM ON, I COULD END UP DEAD.
SO YOU NEED SOME KIND OF INSUR-ANCE?
I DON'T WANT TO BE KILLED.

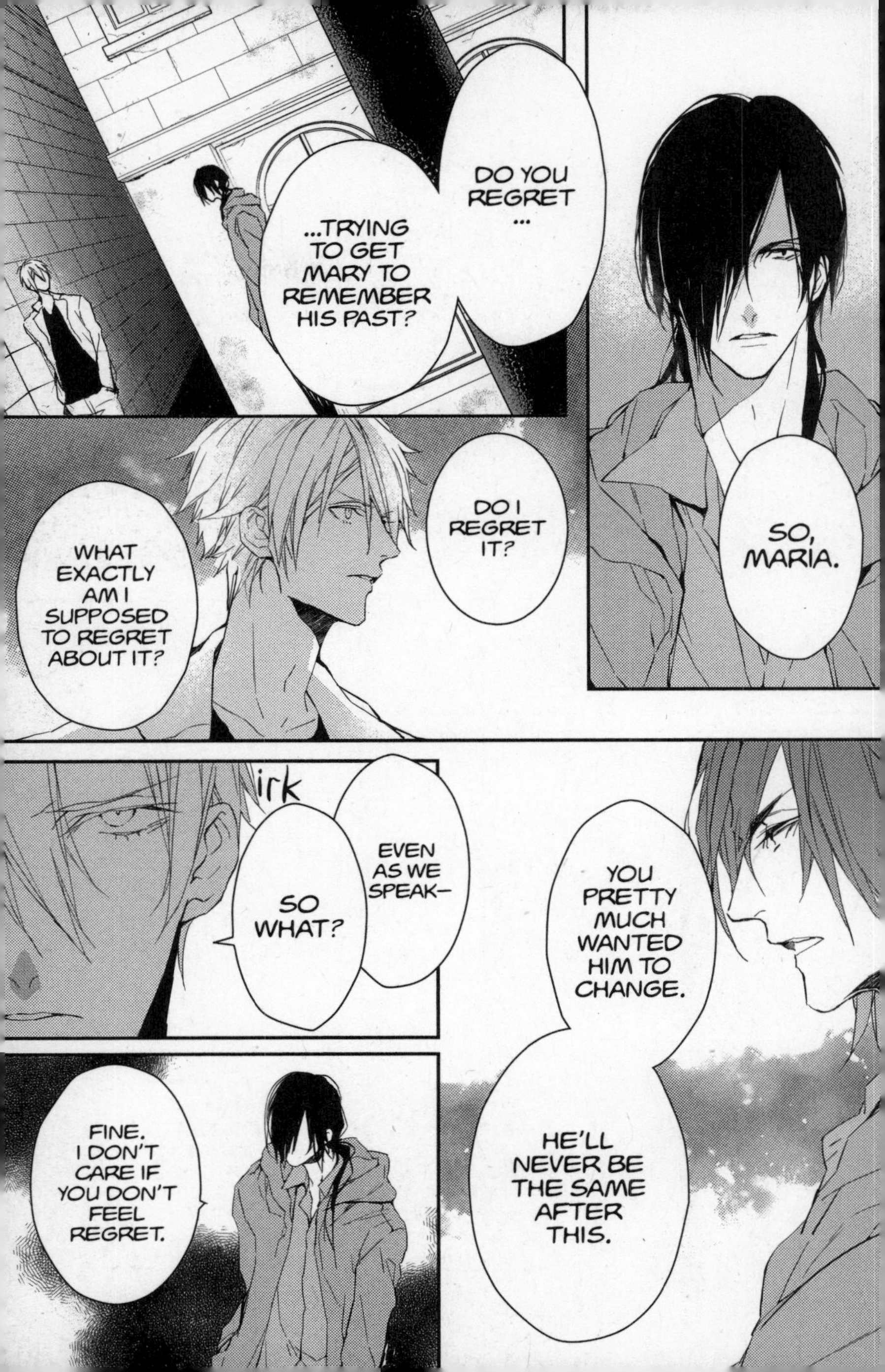
SO, MARIA.
DO YOU REGRET ...
...TRYING TO GET MARY TO REMEMBER HIS PAST?
DO I REGRET IT?
WHAT EXACTLY AM I SUPPOSED TO REGRET ABOUT IT?
YOU PRETTY MUCH WANTED HIM TO CHANGE.
HE'LL NEVER BE THE SAME AFTER THIS.
irk
EVEN AS WE SPEAK—
SO WHAT?
FINE. I DON'T CARE IF YOU DON'T FEEL REGRET.

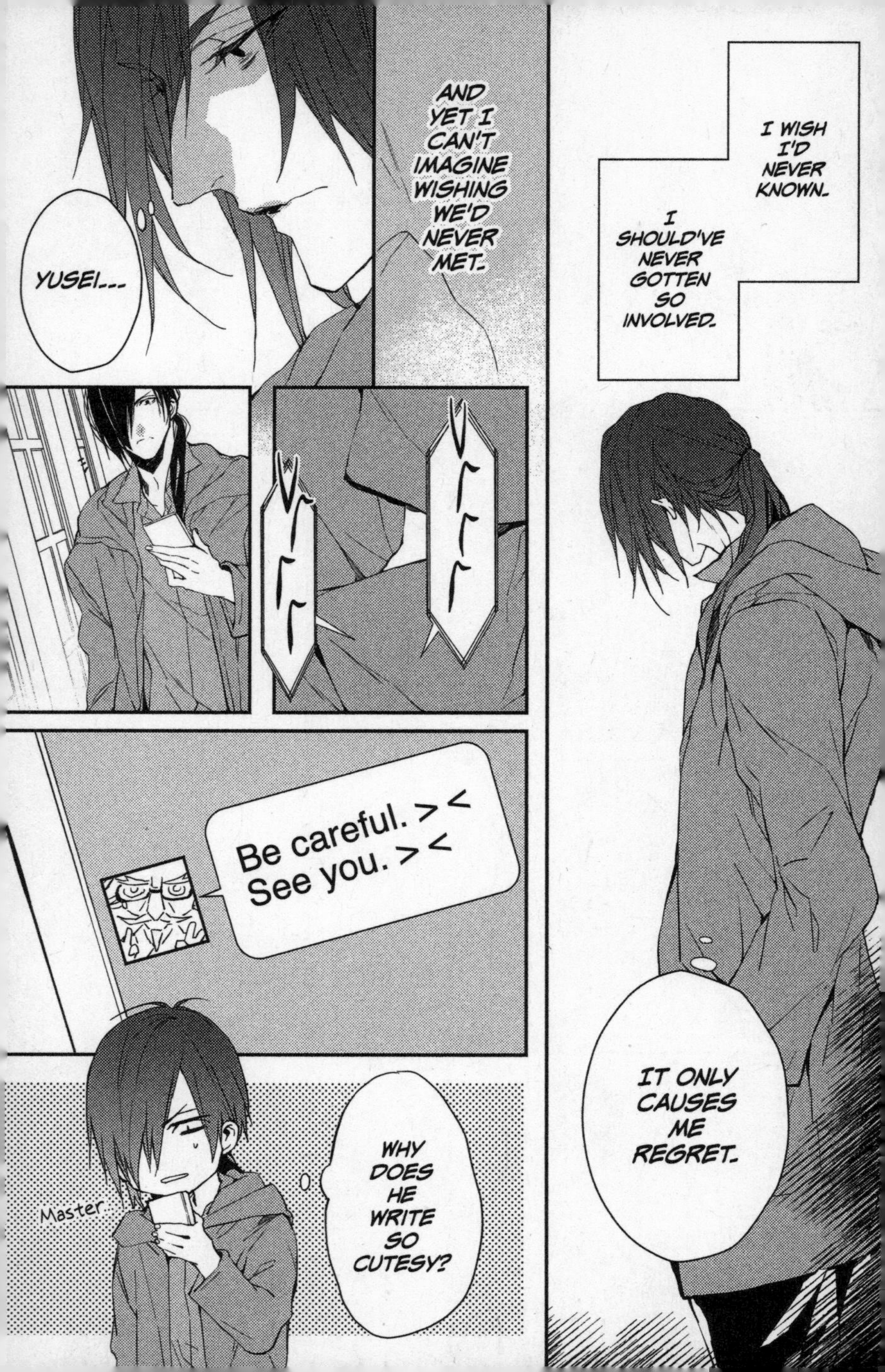
I WISH I'D NEVER KNOWN.
I SHOULD'VE NEVER GOTTEN SO INVOLVED.
IT ONLY CAUSES ME REGRET.
AND YET I CAN'T IMAGINE WISHING WE'D NEVER MET.
YUSEI...
Be careful. > <
See you. > <
WHY DOES HE WRITE SO CUTESY?
Master...

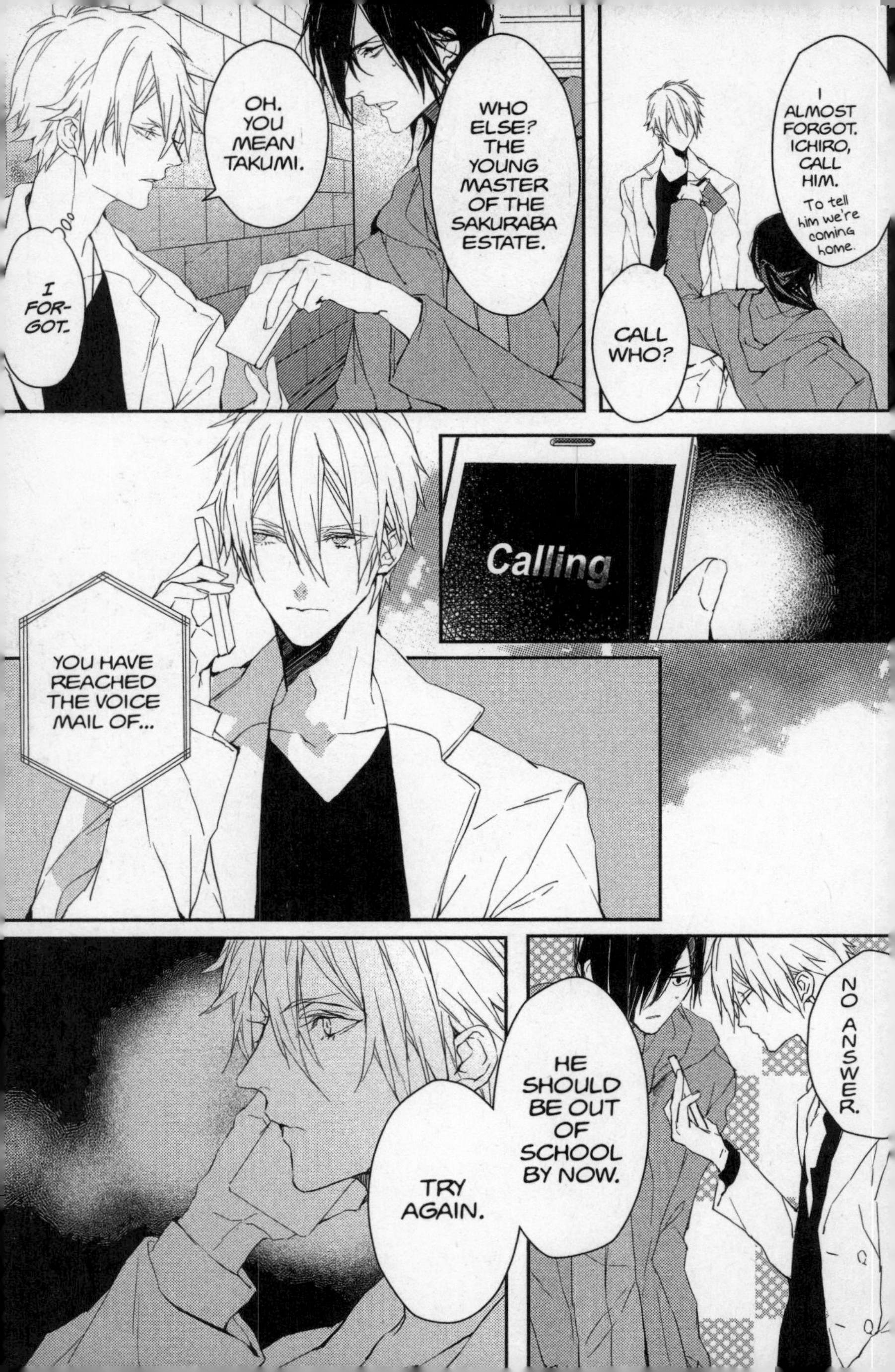
I ALMOST FORGOT. ICHIRO, CALL HIM.
To tell him we're coming home.
CALL WHO?
WHO ELSE? THE YOUNG MASTER OF THE SAKURABA ESTATE.
OH. YOU MEAN TAKUMI.
I FOR-GOT.
Calling
YOU HAVE REACHED THE VOICE MAIL OF...
NO ANSWER.
HE SHOULD BE OUT OF SCHOOL BY NOW.
TRY AGAIN.

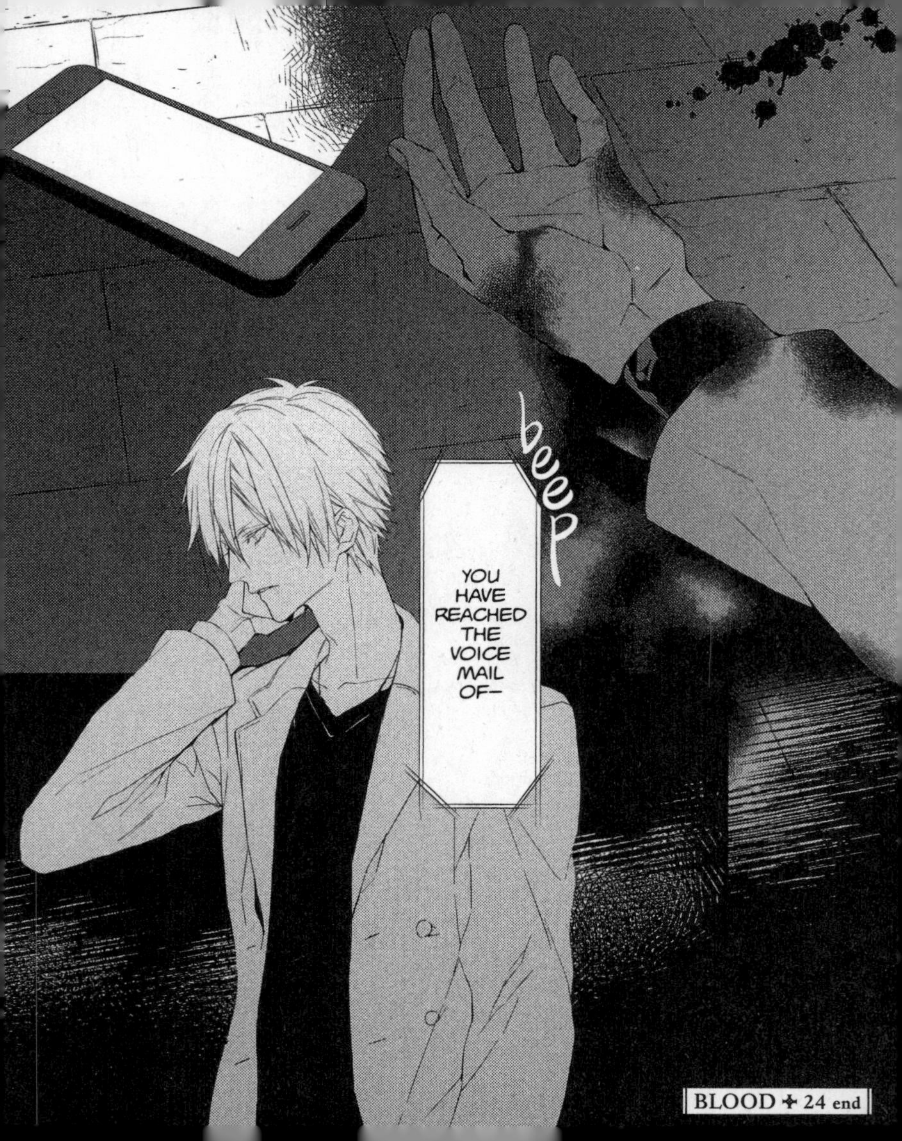
beep
YOU HAVE REACHED THE VOICE MAIL OF–

BLOOD ✚ 24 end

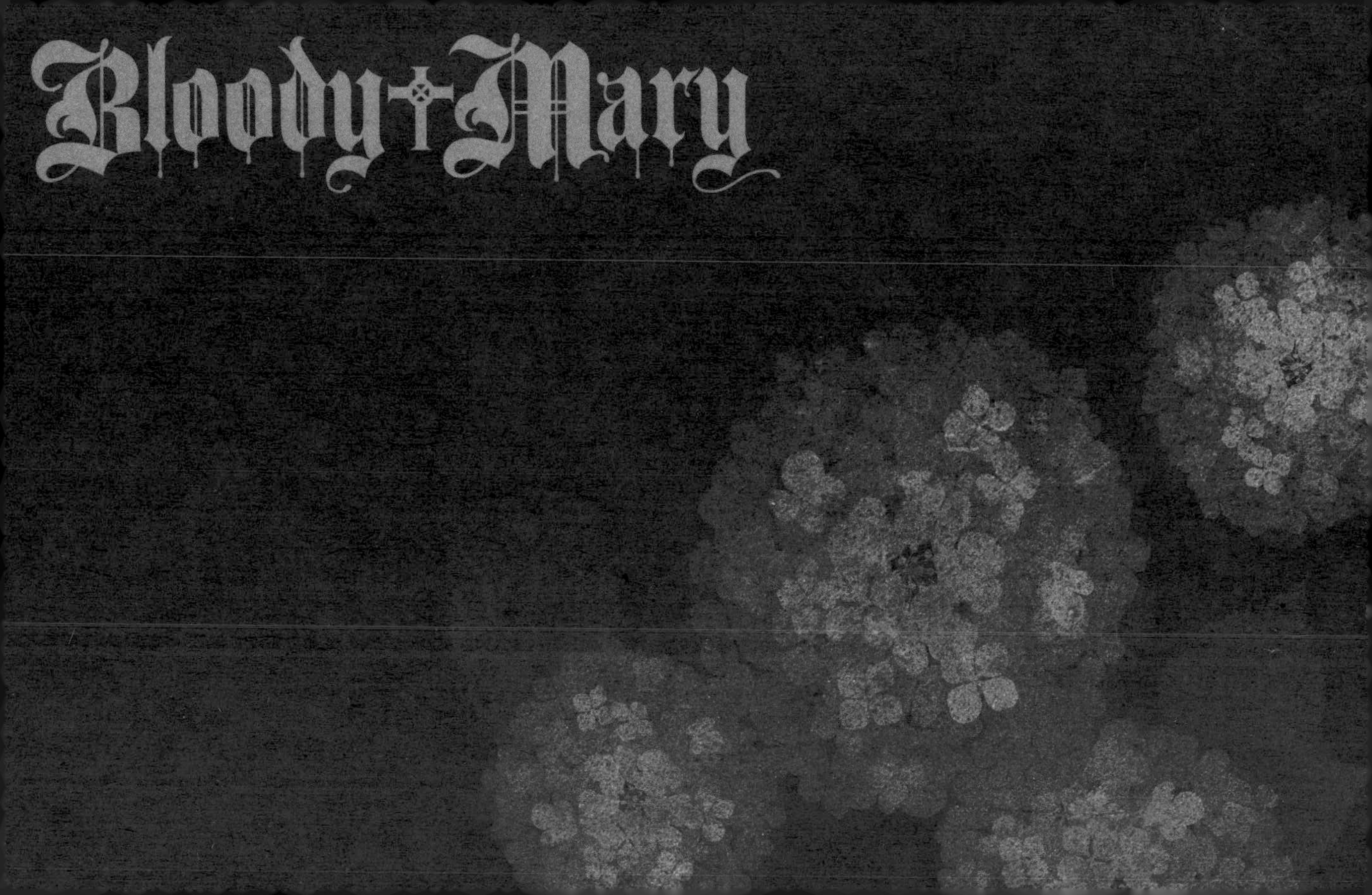
Bloody+Mary

Bloody+Mary

THEY GET ALONG BETTER THAN YOU'D THINK...

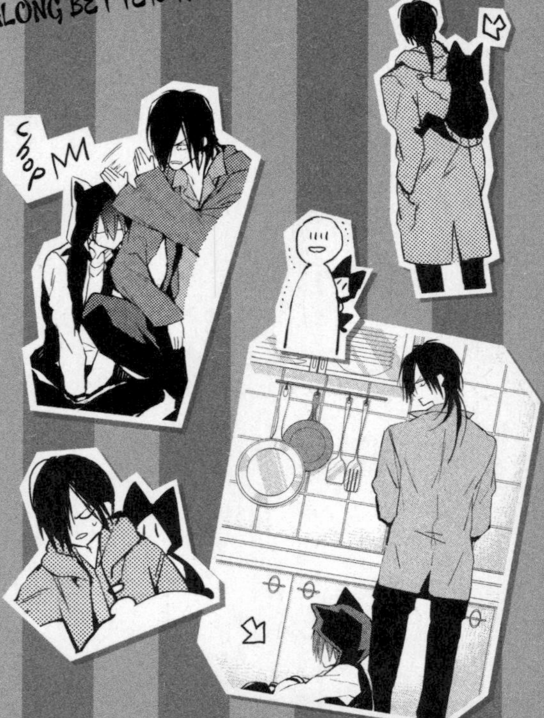
chop

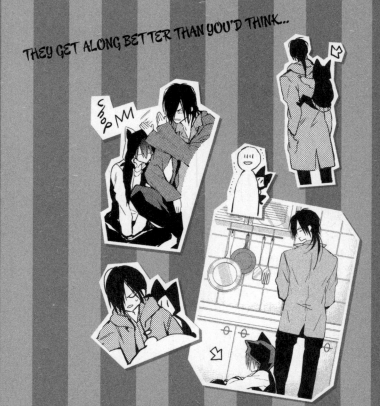

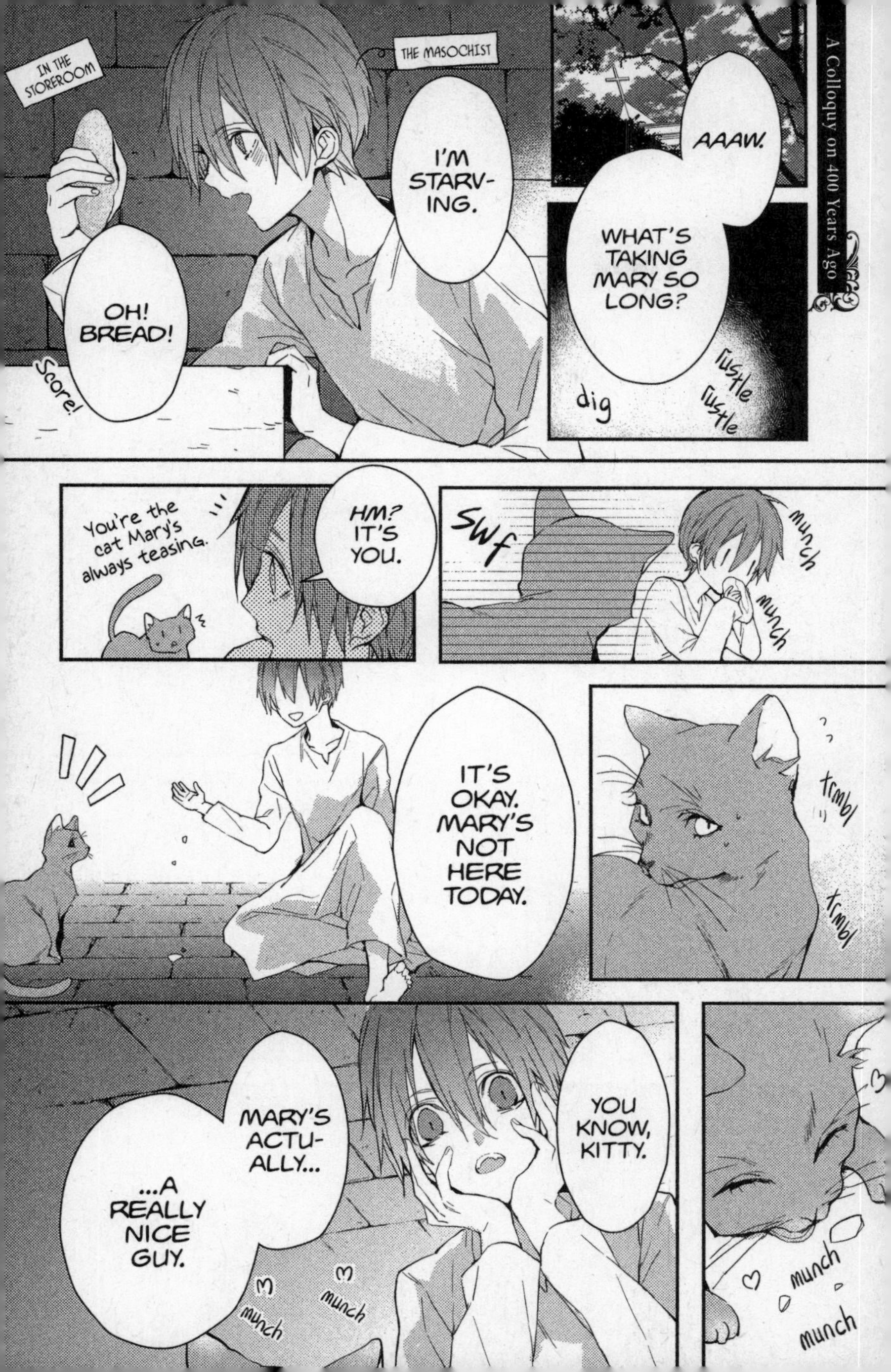
AAAW.
WHAT'S TAKING MARY SO LONG?
rustle rustle
dig
IN THE STOREROOM
THE MASOCHIST
I'M STARVING.
OH! BREAD!
Score!
SWf
munch munch
HM? IT'S YOU.
You're the cat Mary's always teasing.
trmbl trmbl
IT'S OKAY. MARY'S NOT HERE TODAY.
munch munch
YOU KNOW, KITTY.
MARY'S ACTUALLY...
...A REALLY NICE GUY.
munch munch

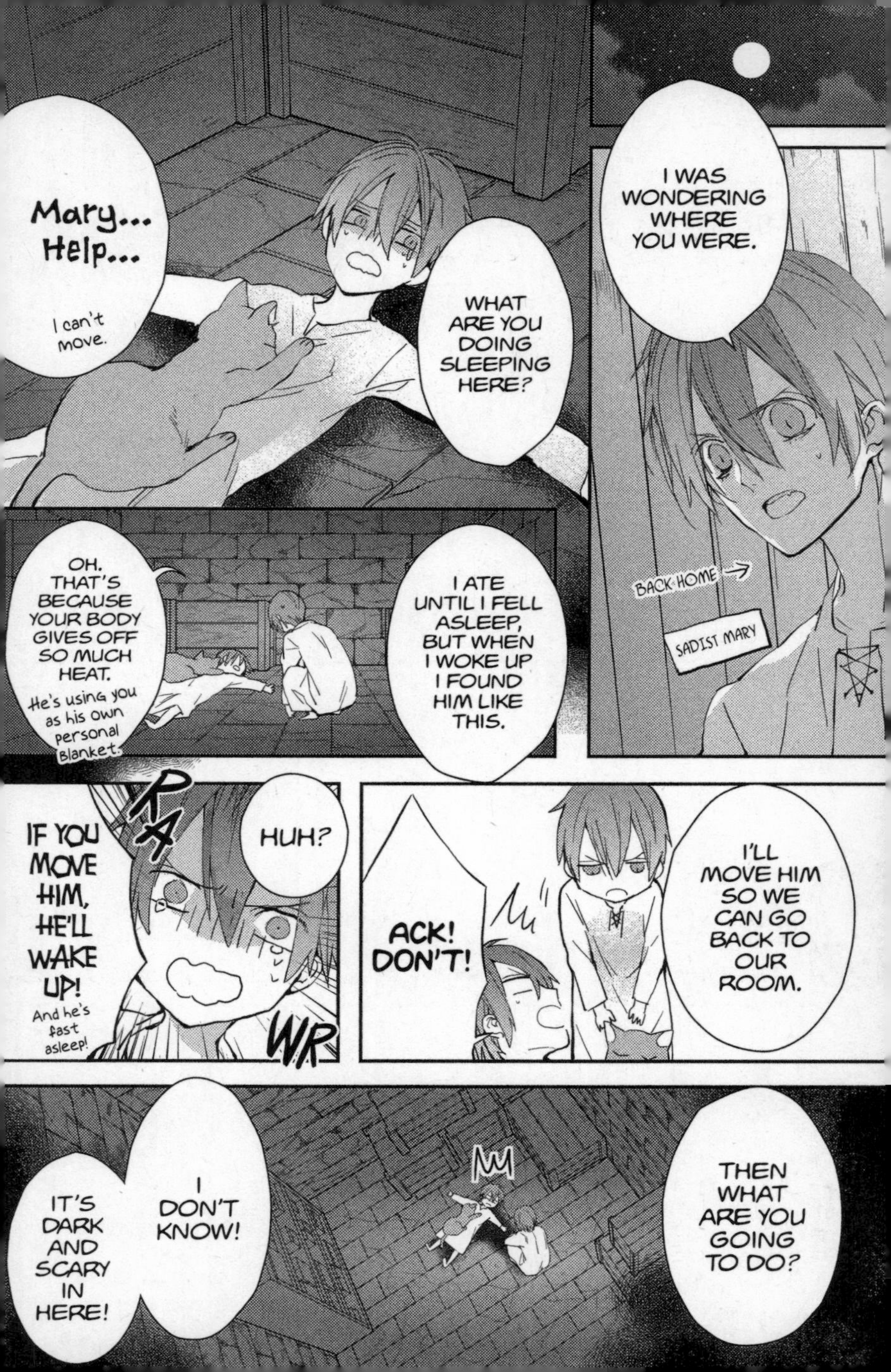
I WAS WONDERING WHERE YOU WERE.
BACK HOME →
SADIST MARY
WHAT ARE YOU DOING SLEEPING HERE?
Mary... Help...
I can't move.
I ATE UNTIL I FELL ASLEEP, BUT WHEN I WOKE UP I FOUND HIM LIKE THIS.
OH. THAT'S BECAUSE YOUR BODY GIVES OFF SO MUCH HEAT.
He's using you as his own personal Blanket.
I'LL MOVE HIM SO WE CAN GO BACK TO OUR ROOM.
ACK! DON'T!
HUH?
RA
IF YOU MOVE HIM, HE'LL WAKE UP!
And he's fast asleep!
WR
THEN WHAT ARE YOU GOING TO DO?
MU
I DON'T KNOW!
IT'S DARK AND SCARY IN HERE!

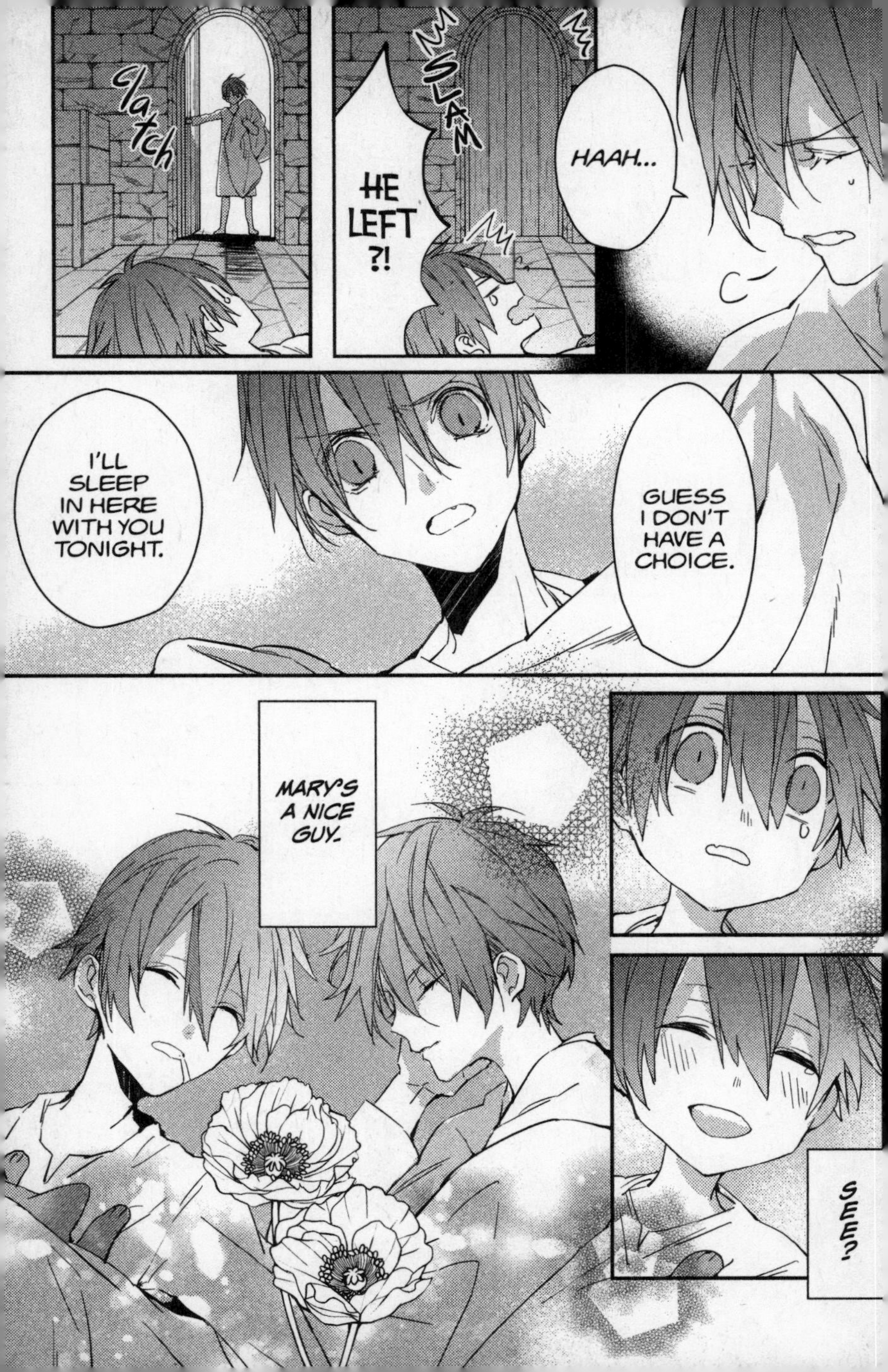

HAAH...
MM
SLAM
HE LEFT ?!
MM
clatch
GUESS I DON'T HAVE A CHOICE.
I'LL SLEEP IN HERE WITH YOU TONIGHT.
SEE?
MARY'S A NICE GUY.

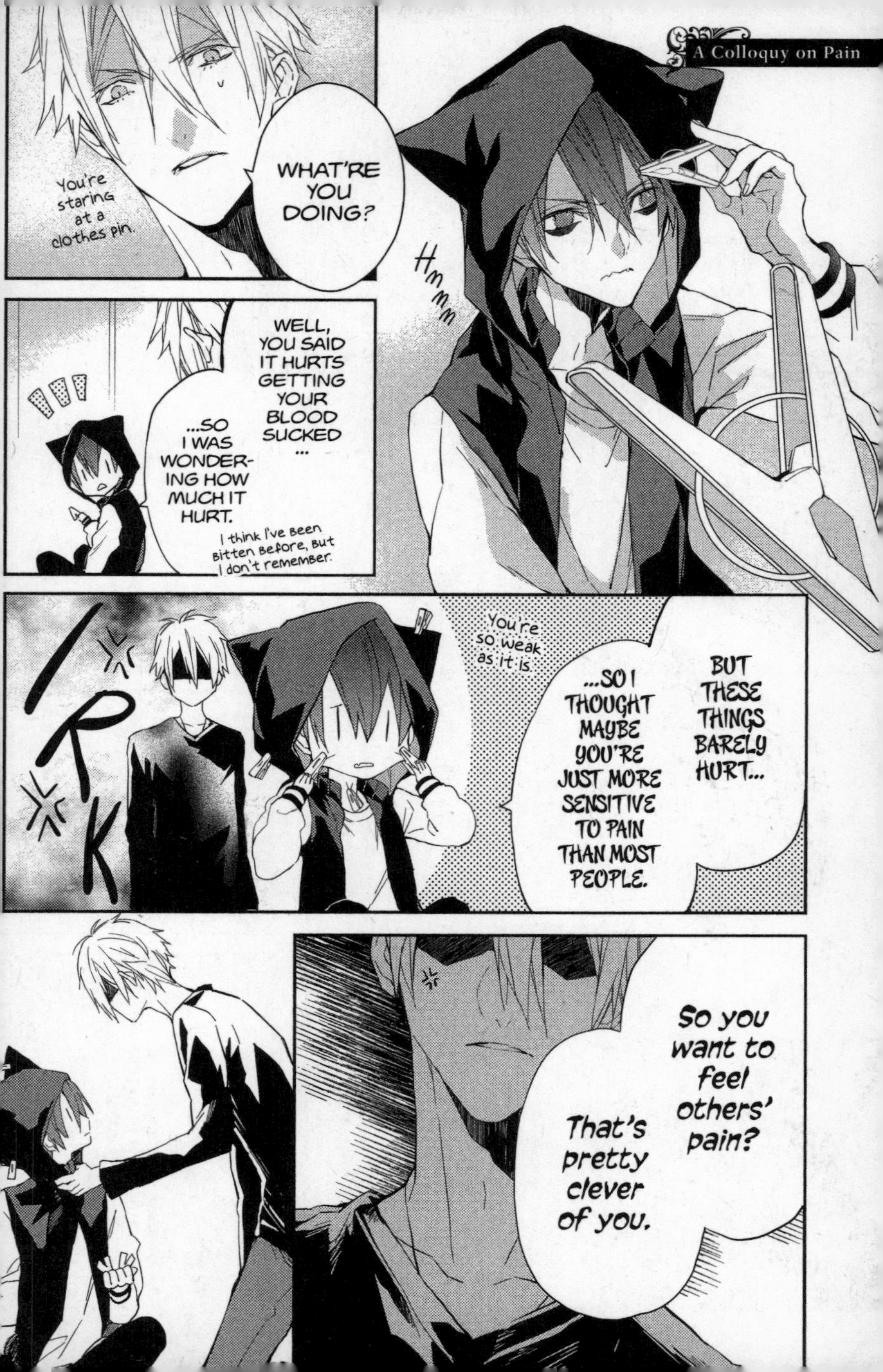
Hmmm
WHAT'RE YOU DOING?
You're staring at a clothes pin.
WELL, YOU SAID IT HURTS GETTING YOUR BLOOD SUCKED...
...SO I WAS WONDERING HOW MUCH IT HURT.
I think I've been bitten before, but I don't remember.
BUT THESE THINGS BARELY HURT...
...SO I THOUGHT MAYBE YOU'RE JUST MORE SENSITIVE TO PAIN THAN MOST PEOPLE.
You're so weak as it is.
RK
So you want to feel others' pain?
That's pretty clever of you.

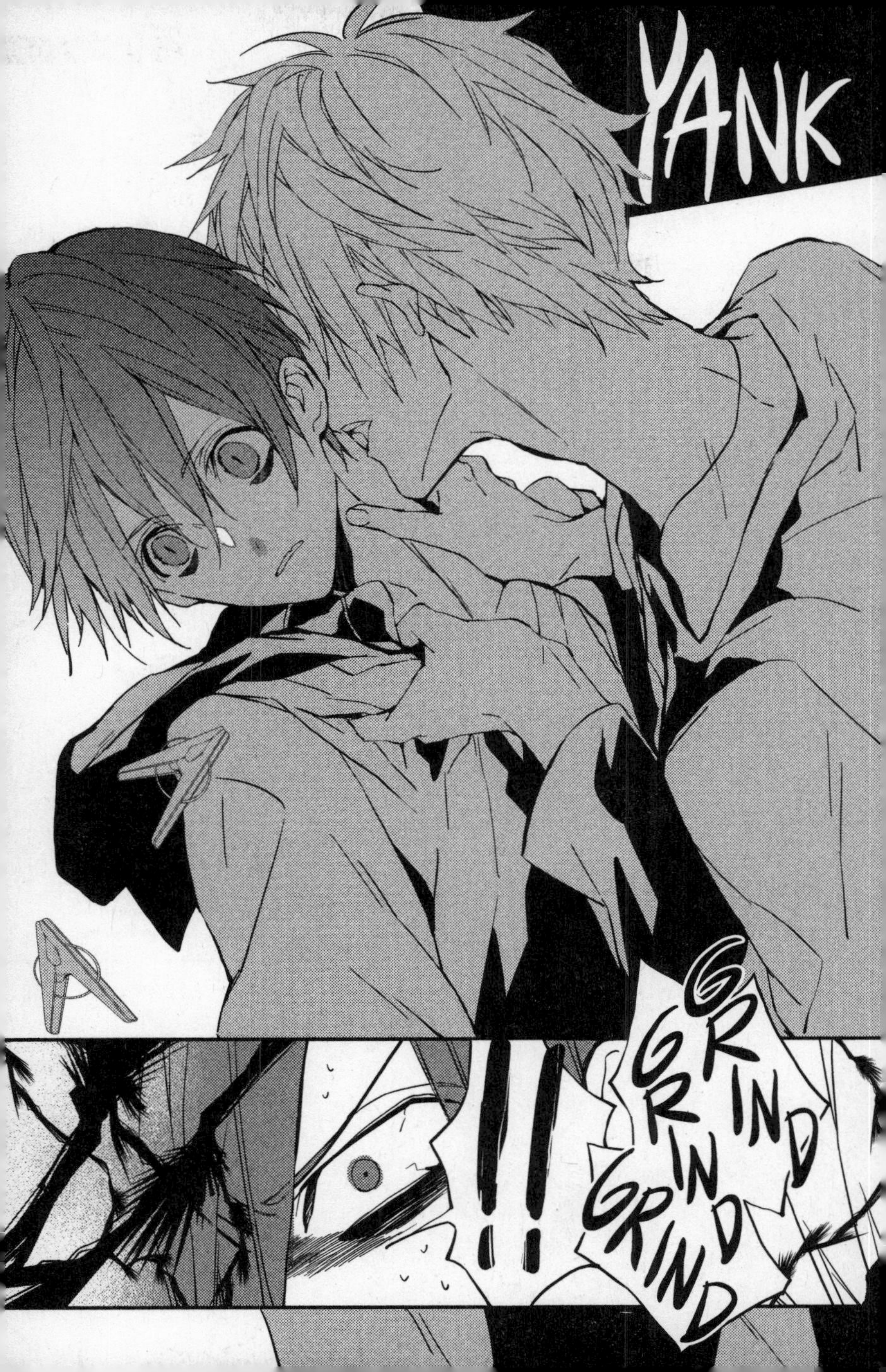
YANK
!!
GRIND GRIND GRIND

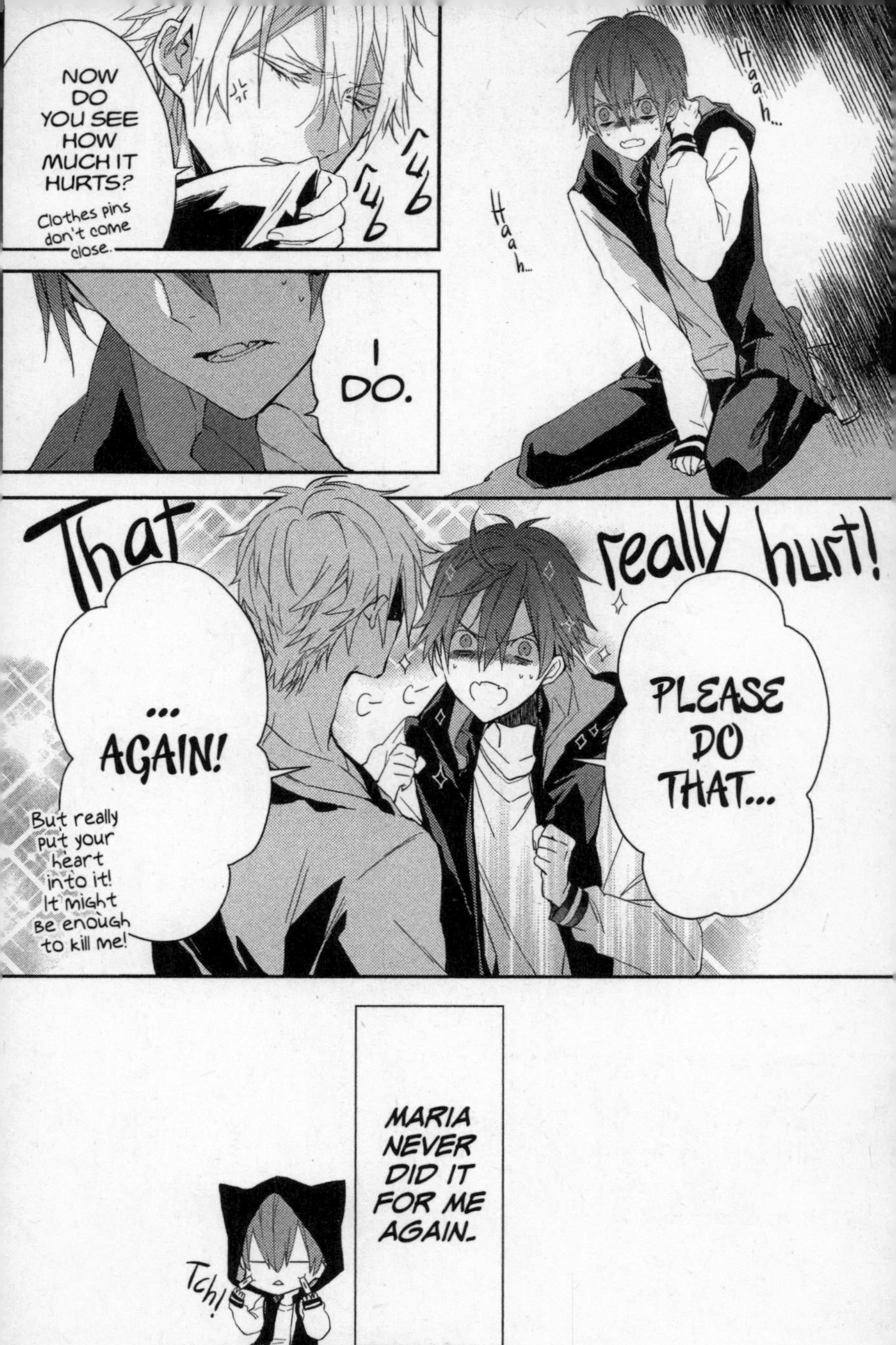
Haaah...
Haaah...
NOW DO YOU SEE HOW MUCH IT HURTS?
Clothes pins don't come close.
rub rub
I DO.
That really hurt!
PLEASE DO THAT...
...AGAIN!
But really put your heart into it! It might be enough to kill me!
MARIA NEVER DID IT FOR ME AGAIN.
Tch!

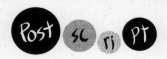

Post Script

★ Thanks to you all, we've made it to volume 6!
When the comic goes on sale in November 2015 [in Japan], it will be exactly two years since *Bloody Mary* first started serialization. Thank you so much for always so warmly encouraging me!!

★ Lately, I've stopped trying so hard to get my cat to stop biting my neck in order to wake me up in the mornings. But even light little nibbles hurt, which has made me realize that Maria probably endures a lot of pain when it happens to him. (And it continues in "A Colloquy on Pain").

Please join me again in the next volume!!

★ Initially, I'd considered having Yzak's kimono be folded the other way around—the way you do when dressing the dead—but I couldn't bring myself to do it and abandoned the idea.

SPECIAL THANKS

Mihoru / M-fuchi
H-gawa / T-mizu
Tko-sama / mdm-sama

Production Team/Support
Haruo / Sumida
M-ika / My sister

My editor / My designer
everyone who supported me

and
the readers

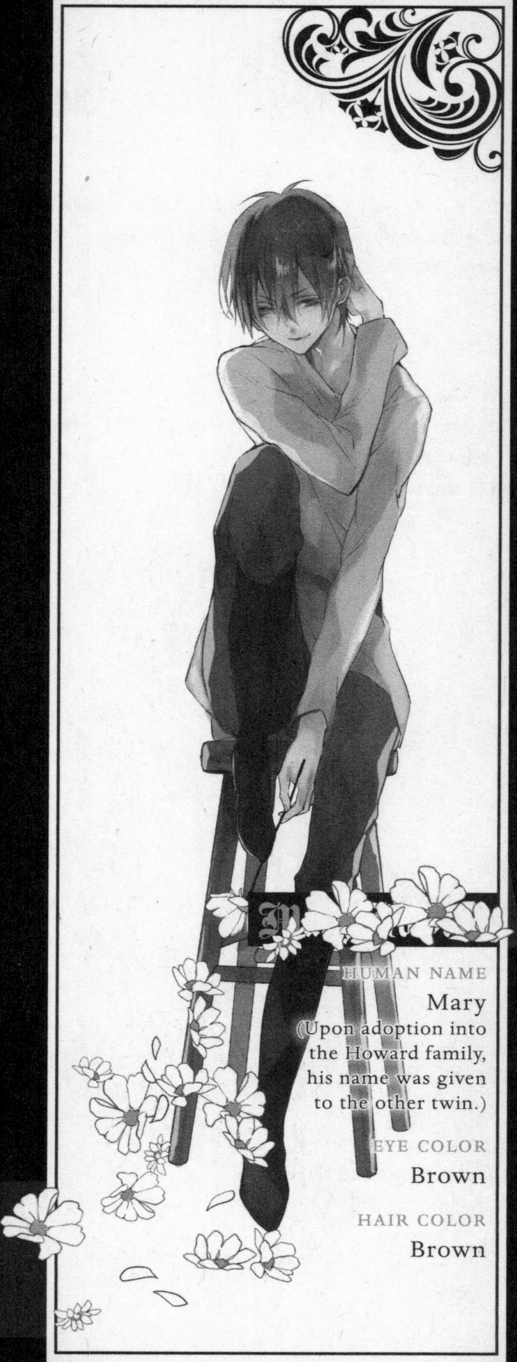
HUMAN NAME
Mary
(Upon adoption into the Howard family, his name was given to the other twin.)
EYE COLOR
Brown
HAIR COLOR
Brown

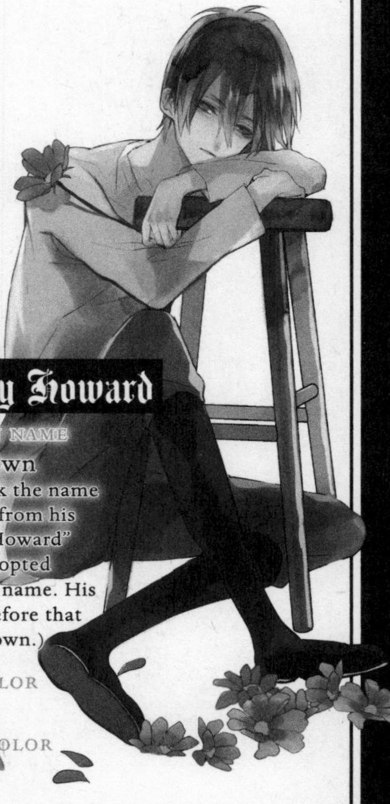

Mary Howard

HUMAN NAME

Unknown
(He took the name
"Mary" from his
twin. "Howard"
is his adopted
family's name. His
name before that
is unknown.)

EYE COLOR
Brown

HAIR COLOR
Brown

Bloody+Mary

YOU KNOW THE QUICKEST WAY TO TELL US APART?
HUH? THERE'S A DIFFERENCE BETWEEN US?

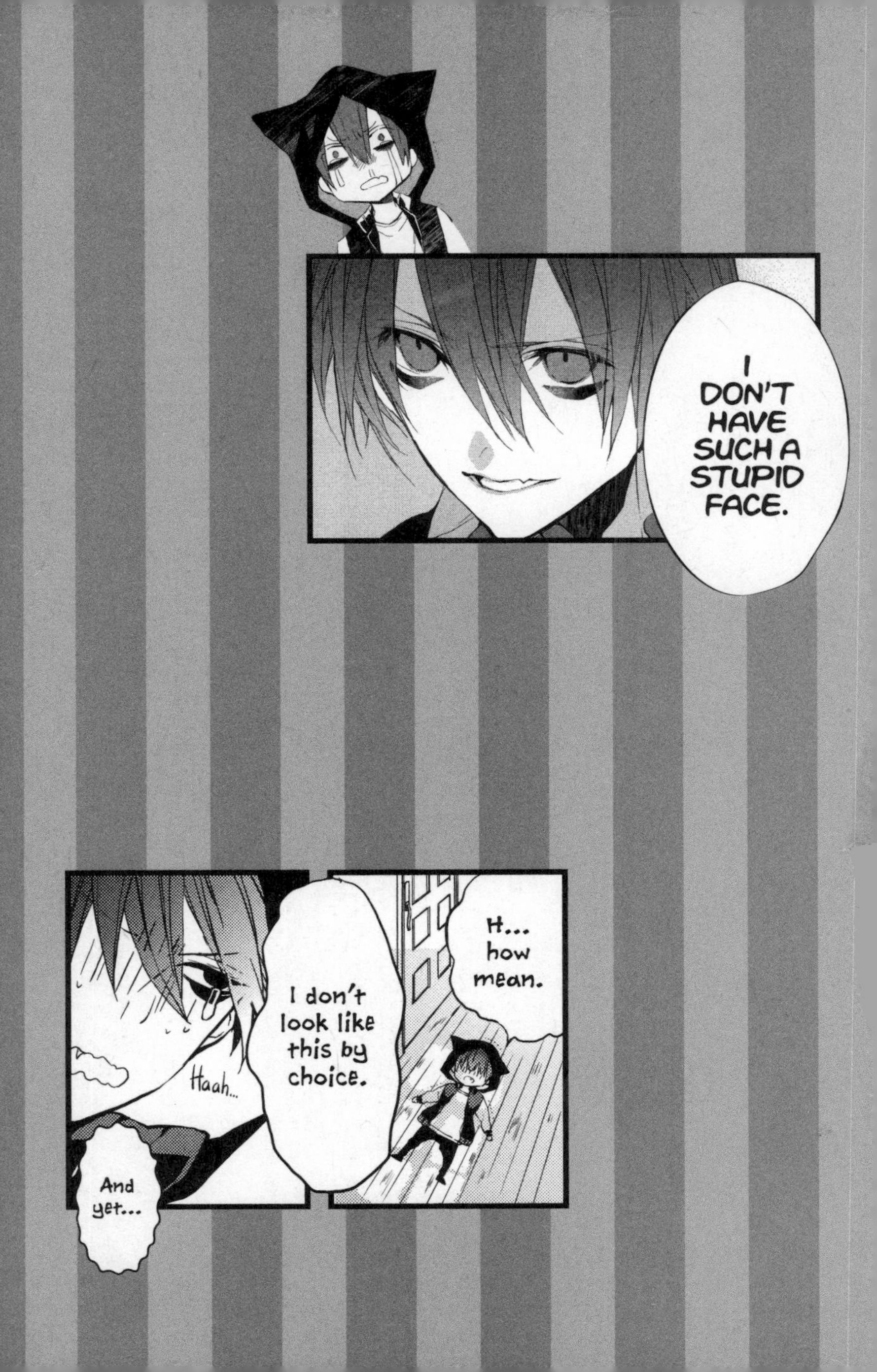
I DON'T HAVE SUCH A STUPID FACE.
H... how mean.
I don't look like this by choice.
Haah...
And yet...

akaza samamiya

Born November 7, Cancer, blood type B.
The cover of each volume has some kind
of plant-based motif. For this volume,
it's my favorite plant of all: hydrangeas.

𝕭𝖑𝖔𝖔𝖉𝖞 𝕸𝖆𝖗𝖞
Volume 6
Shojo Beat Edition

story and art by Akaza Samamiya

translation Katherine Schilling
touch-up art & lettering Sabrina Heep
design Shawn Carrico
editor Erica Yee

BLOODY MARY Volume 6
© Akaza SAMAMIYA 2015
First published in Japan in 2015 by KADOKAWA
CORPORATION, Tokyo.
English translation rights arranged with KADOKAWA
CORPORATION, Tokyo.

The stories, characters and incidents mentioned
in this publication are entirely fictional.

Printed in the U.S.A.

Published by VIZ Media, LLC
P.O. Box 77010
San Francisco, CA 94107

10 9 8 7 6 5 4 3 2 1
First printing, March 2017

www.viz.com   www.shojobeat.com

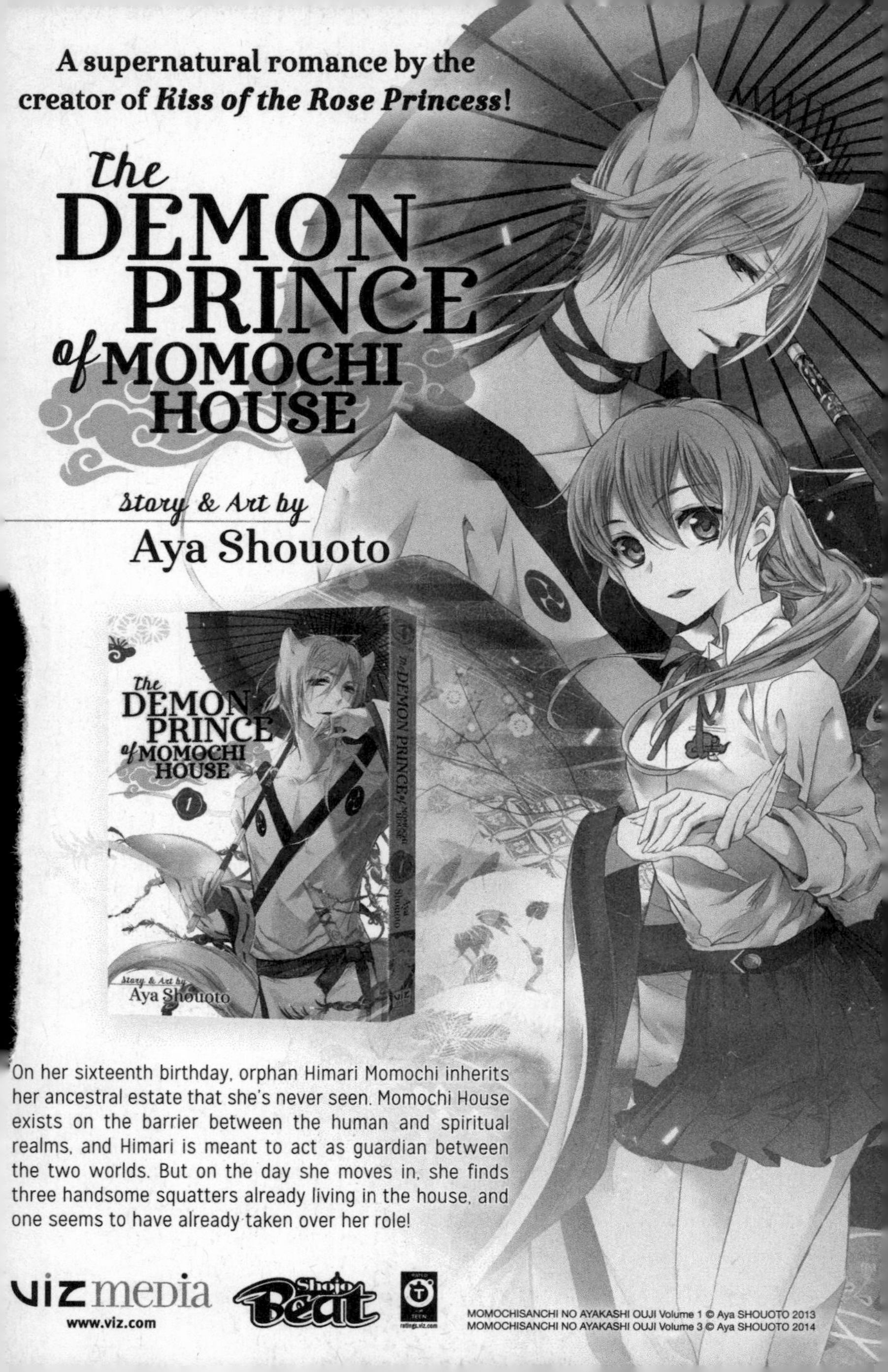
A supernatural romance by the creator of *Kiss of the Rose Princess*!
The DEMON PRINCE of MOMOCHI HOUSE
Story & Art by
Aya Shouoto
The DEMON PRINCE of MOMOCHI HOUSE
1
Story & Art by
Aya Shouoto
On her sixteenth birthday, orphan Himari Momochi inherits her ancestral estate that she's never seen. Momochi House exists on the barrier between the human and spiritual realms, and Himari is meant to act as guardian between the two worlds. But on the day she moves in, she finds three handsome squatters already living in the house, and one seems to have already taken over her role!
VIZ media
www.viz.com
Shojo Beat
TEEN
ratings.viz.com
MOMOCHISANCHI NO AYAKASHI OUJI Volume 1 © Aya SHOUOTO 2013
MOMOCHISANCHI NO AYAKASHI OUJI Volume 3 © Aya SHOUOTO 2014

Is this girl a devil in disguise...
or a misunderstood angel?

A Devil and Her Love Song

Story and Art by Miyoshi Tomori

Meet Maria Kawai—she's gorgeous and whip-smart, a girl who seems to have it all. But when she unleashes her sharp tongue, it's no wonder some consider her to be the very devil! Maria's difficult ways even get her kicked out of an elite school, but this particular fall may actually turn out to be her saving grace...

A Devil and Her Love Song
1
Miyoshi Tomori
A Devil and Her Love Song
2
Miyoshi Tomori
A Devil and Her Love Song
3
Miyoshi Tomori
A Devil and Her Love Song
4

Only **$9.99 US / $12.99 CAN** each!

Vol. 1 ISBN: 978-1-4215-4164-8
Vol. 2 ISBN: 978-1-4215-4165-5
Vol. 3 ISBN: 978-1-4215-4166-2
Vol. 4 ISBN: 978-1-4215-4167-9

Check your local manga retailer for availability!

RATED T FOR TEEN ratings.viz.com
Shojo Beat
VIZ MEDIA www.viz.com

pu nt 6

stop

YOU MAY BE READING THE

wrong way

IT'S TRUE: In keeping with the original Japanese comic format, this book reads from right to left—so action, sound effects and word balloons are completely reversed. This preserves the orientation of the original artwork—plus, it's fun! Check out the diagram shown here to get the hang of things, and then turn to the other side of the book to get started!

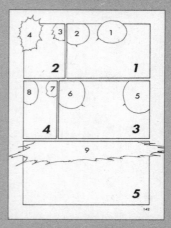